THE BUTTON THIEF

OF

EAST 14TH STREET

Scenes from a Life on the Lower East Side

1927–1957

FAY WEBERN

Author's note: All events really happened as described, within the limitations of memory. The names of public figures, Lavanburg administrators, storekeepers, dogs, and all members of my family are retained. In the interest of privacy, I have changed most other names. In a few cases I have combined events that occurred in two different families. Former Lavanburg tenants and their relations and descendants are welcome to write to me via my website to share further information.—Fay Webern

ISBN: 978-1-944697-11-2 (paperback)
ISBN: 978-1-944697-12-9 (ebook)
Library of Congress Control Number: 2016942472

Sagging Meniscus Press
http://saggingmeniscus.com/

Acknowledgements

Moon Love
Adapted from Tchaikovsky's Symphony No. 5, Second Movement
Words and Music by Mack David, Mack Davis and Andre Kostelanetz
Copyright © 1939 by Famous Music LLC
Copyright Renewed, Assigned to Universal-PolyGram International Publishing, Inc. and Sony/ATV Music Publishing LLC
All Rights on behalf of Sony/ATV Music Publishing LLC Administered by Sony/ATV Music Publishing LLC, 424 Church Street, Suite 1200, Nashville, TN 37219
International Copyright Secured All Rights Reserved
Reprinted by Permission of Hal Leonard Corporation

You Don't Know What Love Is
Words and Music by Don Raye and Gene DePaul.
Copyright © 1941 UNIVERSAL MUSIC CORP.
Copyright Renewed
All Rights Reserved Used by Permission
Reprinted by permission of Hal Leonard Corporation

(There'll Be Bluebirds Over) The White Cliffs Of Dover
Words by Nat Burton
Music by Walter Kent
Copyright © 1941 Shapiro, Bernstein & Co., Inc., New York and Walter Kent Music, California
Copyright Renewed
All Rights outside the United States Controlled by Shapiro, Bernstein & Co., Inc., New York
International Copyright Secured All Rights Reserved
Used by Permission
Reprinted by permission of Hal Leonard Corporation

Night and Day
Words and Music by Cole Porter
Copyright © 1932 (Renewed) WB MUSIC CORP.

All Rights Reserved
Used By Permission of ALFRED MUSIC

I Didn't Know What Time It Was
Lyrics by Lorenz Hart
Music by Richard Rodgers
© 1939 (Renewed) by WB MUSIC CORP. and WILLIAMSON MUSIC CO. All Rights Reserved
Used By Permission of ALFRED MUSIC

I Didn't Know What It Was
Music by Richard Rodgers and Words by Lorenz Hart
© 1939 (Renewed) by CHAPPELL & CO.
Rights for Extended Renewal Term in U.S. controlled by W.B. MUSIC CORP.
o/b/o The Estate of Lorenz Hart and The Family Trust U/W Richard Rodgers and The Family Trust U/W Dorothy F. Rodgers Administered by Williamson Music
All Rights Reserved. Used by Permission.

Let Yourself Go
by Irving Berlin
© Copyright 1935 Irving Berlin, Inc.
International Copyright Secured. All Rights Reserved.
Used by Permission.

Excerpt(s) from THE POWER BROKER: ROBERT MOSES AND THE FALL OF NEW YORK
by Robert A. Caro, copyright © 1974 by Robert A. Caro. Used by permission of Alfred A. Knopf, an imprint of the Knopf Doubleday Publishing Group, a division of Penguin Random House LLC. All rights reserved. Any third party use of this material, outside of this publication, is prohibited. Interested parties must apply directly to Penguin Random House LLC for permission.

Map source: Artfanaticus
Cover and map design: Royce M. Becker

To Tyler Gore, tragicomic author
who taught me to write in the first person

and

To my daughter MarthaLeah Chaiken,
always my first and best reader

Table of Contents

Illustrations

The

Button

Thief

of

East

14th

Street

I

A Bride in the Forest: How I Got My Name

The name I'm called, Fay, comes from "Feygela," little bird. My real name, the name my mother bestowed on me, is FeygaPinya. That double name belonged to newlyweds in Kovel near Kiev, in Tsarist Russia. They were cousins of my mother, one from each side of her family. They were modern Jewish socialists, idealists like Tolstoy, who supported the up-rising of 1905 with fiery speeches, but they meant no harm to anyone. When the uprising failed they fled into the vast forest. Someone snitched on them; it could have been in ex-change for saving a son from twenty-five years of service in the army. They were found in an old hut at the edge of a Gypsy camp. The soldiers raped and dismembered Feyga before her bridegroom's eyes. Pinya they dragged back to the town. They rounded up all the Jews and there at the town square, while ev-eryone had to stand and watch, they tied Pinya to the back of a horse, legs up and head on the paving stones, and a cavalry soldier raced the horse around and around the square until his head split open on the stones. Like a watermelon, Mama said. My mother was still a child when this happened. As the years went by, no one would name a newborn after them lest it bring the baby a bad fate and lest bosses in America would think they themselves were trouble-making socialists.

That meant the story of these brave young martyrs would not be carried into our family's history. My mother felt so bad about it that when I was born she gave both their names to me. I, FeygaPinya, registered on my birth certificate as Philip Fannie by some unknown person at the Postgraduate Clinic on 2nd Avenue and 15th Street in New York City, I am their

1

namesake, and for as long as I live, they remain always in my memory.

My first nursery rhyme was a revolutionary ditty from Russia. I used to sing it in Tompkins Square Park where Mama met up with her friends. They used to gather under the great old leafy sycamore tree, the first tree on the left as you enter from 7th Street and Avenue B. So many mothers sheltered their children in its shade that it was called the Nursing Tree. Mama would lift me from my perambulator and stand me up on a bench and tell me, "Sing Tsar Nikolay." It made a remarkable impression.

> *Tsar Nikolay Yob tfayu mat*
> *Zeyner mit veymen di hust khasena gehat*
> *A koreva, a blata, an oysgetrenta shmata*
> *Tsar Nikolay Yob tfayu mat!*

When I got old enough to become curious about the words, my mother told me they meant "King Nicholas, go punch your mother. Look who you married, a girl of filth, a worn-out rag." She explained that if the King's mother understood how it felt to be punched she might stop her son from hitting the Jews all the time.

But one day I sang "Tsar Nikolay" in the street to show off to my friends, and a Ukrainian woman grabbed hold of me and waggled her finger in my face and told me never to sing that song again, it was full of dirty words, including the dirtiest thing anyone could do to his mother, even worse than killing her. I ran home and screamed at my mother and stamped my feet. "You made me say dirty words! You made me say dirty words!" But she only laughed. "Every Jew in Russia sang that song," she said. "Besides, I taught it to you when you were a baby. How should I know you would remember?" Then, when I went back outside, a Ukrainian girl who had been watching told me the real translation:

King Nicholas, go fuck your mother
Look who you married
A whore, diseased, a worn-out rag
King Nicholas, go fuck your mother

I think that in my mother's heart she would like to have been the family rebel, a bride in the forest. Instead, she had an arranged marriage in America with a sewing machine operator in ladies apparel and had to make the best of it in the days when everyone struggled to make a living and keep a roof over their heads and raise their children to make something of themselves.

I wasn't supposed to be born. When my mother broke the news that she was in the family way, she already had three children and was living in a one-bedroom railroad flat on Avenue D and 8th Street with a bathtub in the kitchen, toilet in the hall, and a coal stove for cooking and heating. Maxie was eight, Ruthie was six, Sidney was seven months. My father was beside himself. Where was he going to get more money? Where would they find room for another child? How did she expect to take care of the house with a baby in each hand? But she would not agree to a scraping. She was afraid of infection.

Through an Italian socialist woman in his shop who was active in the birth control movement, he found out about something new, flushing pills. They were as illegal as a scraping, and just as expensive. But he had no choice. He bought them from a druggist down near the docks on the corner of Stanton and Goerck streets. Ma didn't take the pills; she asked around first and found out that women had died from them by hemorrhaging. When it was too late for my father to interfere anymore, she told him that the pills didn't seem to have worked. He made her go with him all the way to the drugstore to get his money back. My father, who normally would never get in a fight, was so upset that he grabbed the druggist by the lapels of his white jacket and shook him and called him a faker. Customers had to pull him away. My mother saw that she would have to take responsibility for the fourth child.

On Goerck Street between Houston and Stanton, on the way to the druggist, they had passed a big construction site. A sign on the fence announced:

> LAVANBURG HOMES
> Sanitary Housing at Low Rentals
> For Families of Small Income
> Inquiries Are Invited

It was signed Fred. L. Lavanburg Foundation. A drawing showed a large modern building with two courts and six entrances. Ma went back the next day, took down the address, and went for an application. At the Foundation office the Administrator, a young man named Abraham Goldfeld, explained that Mister Lavanburg was a philanthropist who had funded Lavanburg Homes as a model of urban housing for low-income working people. He believed that with everyone cooperating, such projects could become self-supporting and could uplift the surrounding neighborhoods as well. The Administrator reviewed the plan for my mother. Lavanburg Homes was to be six stories high to blend in with the neighboring buildings. It would be shaped like the letter E on its back: its two large courts would be open to the street and welcoming to the rest of the neighborhood. There were to be a hundred-twelve apartments with steam heat, plenty of sunlight and air, built-in closets, a tiled bathroom, a laboratory-style kitchen with a dumbwaiter for garbage collection, and a rack by the window for drying clothes; no outside washlines.

There were to be wide, well-lit stairways, a storage room for carriages, a basement social center with meeting rooms and

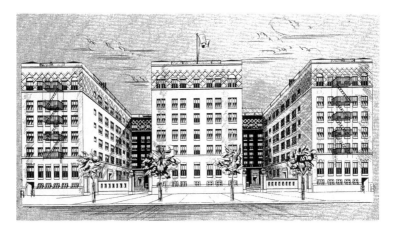

Lavanburg Homes. From *Practices and Experiences of the Lavanburg Homes, Third Edition* (Fred. L. Lavanburg Foundation, New York City, 1941). Used with permission.

game rooms, a playground on the roof in summer. He told my mother that if her family of six was accepted they would be assigned four rooms for eight dollars a week. This was only a dollar more than the old railroad flat on Avenue D, and was really the same rent because she was paying a dollar a week to keep Sidney's carriage in the spotless back room of a newspaper-delivery store. It was like a dream! To qualify, applicants had to live in substandard housing and had to show they could keep a clean home and pay rent on time. Also, no child must be over ten years old because the Foundation aimed to raise a new generation of model American children. She answered yes to all his questions and he said she qualified in every respect!

My mother could hardly wait to fill out the application. My father refused. He was a proud member of the International Ladies Garment Workers Union and a negotiator representing his shop. He did not want to declare his income. He did not want to live by the rules of a charitable institution. It was beneath his dignity to have his home inspected. The stand-off lasted months. Every argument between them ended the same, she wailing "You want to bury me," he muttering "There's no reasoning with her." The opening date for filing applications was July 1,1927. I was due two weeks later. On the evening of the first, when my father came home from work my mother climbed up on the window sill ready to jump down the air shaft. My father said "You're crazy" and signed the papers.

On the morning of July second my mother rushed to the Foundation office. They already had four hundred families to choose from. Applications were closed. My mother was only four-foot-seven and she carried big. At nine-months pregnant her belly stuck way out in front of her. This at a time when respectable ladies went into seclusion at the first noticeable bump. Through her Democratic Party District Captain, Mister Dembofsky, she found out where Mister Lavanburg lived. She rang the bell at the gate to his building and asked to see him. A man dressed in a gray suit said Mister Lavanburg was indisposed and would she care to leave a message. She grabbed the fence rails and eased herself onto the ground and said, "I will stay here until I get in to explain to Mister Lavanburg. I have to live in Lavanburg Homes. I qualify in every respect. I am about to have a baby. If I can't raise this baby in a clean and decent home, I will have it right here on the sidewalk and leave it with you." Passersby stopped to watch. A policeman came over. But no one dared touch her, much less try to move her away. So there she sat until a secretary in hat and gloves came out with a note from Mister Lavanburg. She got into a car with a chauffeur, the note, and my mother. They went back to the Foundation office. The secretary said to the Administrator, Mister Goldfeld, "Mister Lavanburg would like you to meet Mrs. Bessie Kessler. He thinks she's just the sort of dedicated tenant the Foundation is seeking."

I was not quite six months old when Lavanburg Homes officially opened on December 28, 1927. Mayor Jimmy Walker was there, and Party bosses and urban planners and utopian philosophers and settlement house leaders, and all the new Lavanburg families and all the nearby neighbors, celebrating the first low-rent self-supporting housing project in America. Every speaker pronounced the street name Gork, for G-o-e-r-c-k. The crowd giggled every time, for the whole neighborhood called it Gah-rick. At the end a band played while the Mayor cut a red ribbon. Mister Lavanburg, sadly, had really been sick the day my mother sat down in front of his gate, and he did not live to see his building finished. He was a bachelor and left no close relatives. The first boy born in Lavanburg Homes, Freddy Levine, was named after him. Some people said Freddy would get a college scholarship for bearing the name, but it wasn't true.

In the last week of January the streets were alive with tenants rushing to move in, one floor each day so as not to create a moving jam. All but six families came from within walking distance. Thirty-six families were headed by workers in apparel or accessories, nine were headed by sales clerks. There were seven peddlers, seven city laborers. The rest were public transportation workers, truck drivers, taxi drivers, housepainters, plumbers, waiters, bakers, office clerks, postal clerks, two barbers, a butcher, a watch-case maker, a bookbinder, a printmaker, a shoemaker, an auto mechanic, an artist, a photographer, an electrician, a sheet-metal worker, a piano teacher, a Hebrew teacher, a stenographer, a street cleaner, a window cleaner, a rag sorter.

There were three hundred fifty children, more to come. Half as many children lived across the street, and more children came every day from nearby streets to this one short block. Two apartments went to the management office and private quarters of Mister Goldfeld and his German Shepherd dog, and two apartments were rented at a reduced rate to graduate students in social work, three young women in one four-room apartment and two young men in the other. They had been assigned by the University Settlement House on Ludlow Street to settle down among us just like the social workers did in the London settlement houses inspired by Arnold Toynbee: living as neighbors, studying our needs, and helping out in the Social Center.

On my family's moving day, my mother was so excited and distracted that when Ruthie went to school in the morning she forgot to give her our new address. Maxie and Ruthie went to Public School 15, on East 4th Street near Avenue D. It was an old school with toilet sheds in the backyard. When class let out at three o'clock, Ruthie realized she didn't know where to go. She stood outside on the school steps in the freezing cold until Ma realized she was missing. Ma sent Maxie back to get her.

As the door to our new home opened, Ruthie was struck by the warmth of the steam heat, by the smooth white walls, by the sparkling new kitchen, by everything smelling so clean. She ran through all the rooms, looked out all the windows, opened all the built-in closets.

Back in the kitchen, Ruthie came upon a narrow drawer in one of the cabinets opposite the sink. It was at waist height and had a crystal knob. She pulled it open. It was lined in purple velvet. My mother came over and stared at the open drawer. She stroked the purple velvet with her fingertips. She told Ruthie it was meant for silverware. She said through tears, "That Mister Lavanburg. That sweet soul. May he rest in peace."

In the spring, new and used upright pianos began to arrive. One of my very first memories is of being held up in Ruthie's arms in the courtyard in the midst of a crowd of cheering children, watching as two pianos crawled up the brick walls on pulleys and were eased inside through naked window frames. I remember the very day—the sun was so bright you had to squint to look up—when we stood in the back alley watching a piano being hauled through the dining room window of our own apartment. By the time we ran around to the front and up the stairs, the beloved piano that Mama bought for Ruthie on the installment plan was already in place, adorned with a huge Russian shawl patterned with huge red-and-pink roses, a present from our Avenue C grandmother.

Not all worked out as planned. The modern efficiency kitchens, only eleven feet long by seven feet wide, were designed for homemakers to carry meals out to the dining room, but everyone ate in the kitchen as always, squeezing in as best we could at the utility table by the window under the clothes-drying rack. The oven had to be turned off at mealtimes as it was right up against one end of the table, and the table had to be covered with newspapers when wet clothes were dripping from the rack. The apartment walls were built solid enough so you didn't hear your next-door neighbors' business, but the dumbwaiter shafts conveyed domestic quarrels up and down the line with exquisite clarity and were put to use as listening posts. Nor was Lavanburg Homes to be quite the promised sanitary haven, for the dumbwaiters were only one of several convenient routes by which mice and cockroaches found their way into and among the new apartments. Bedbugs, lice, and those huge horrible waterbugs also invaded the apartments, just as they did the rest of the Lower East Side.

Patrons of the American settlement house movement often toured Lavanburg's. They commended the cleanliness of the hallways and courts. Mister Goldfeld's "deputy commissioners," a volunteer patrol of bullies among the oldest boys, saw to that—but they must have been disappointed to find the new generation of children as dirty and ragamuffin as the rest of the East Side kids. They never came on weekends when we were clean and all dressed up; they only saw us after school when we got into old clothes so we could play in the street.

One time Mister Goldfeld escorted some ladies out of the court while the boys were lined up along the curb seeing who could pee the farthest. The ladies pretended not to notice. Mister Goldfeld rushed to the curb to stop the boys. Just then the seltzer man's horse, Danny, claiming the territory the boys had invaded, started a great splosh of pee on the cobblestones right in front of him. Mister Goldfeld barely jumped back in time. He got the giggles, and soon the ladies and everyone else were laughing their heads off, except the boys, who were struggling to button up their pants.

But it was really the coal dust that made us look bad. Two Edison Company electric plants, one down below Grand Street and the other over on East 15th, spewed out clouds of black smoke all day long. Our Lower East Side streets nestled in the bottom curve of Manhattan Island and weren't exposed to the wind currents that swept the uptown streets clean from Hudson River to East River. Our clouds of soot whirled about willy-nilly. Coal dust and grit got all over us, our hands and faces and clothes. Mister Goldfeld used to call us his angels with dirty faces. It became the title of a movie that had nothing to do with us. On windy days we would get cinders in our eyes. From our earliest years we knew how to pull our upper lid over our lower lid and let the lower lashes wipe the cinder away. But if one of us got a speck that wouldn't come out, the whole gang would cross the street to Doctor Gelman's drugstore on the Italian side of Goerck.

Doctor Gelman was a kindly man with steel-rimmed glasses and thinning blond hair. We had no fear of him even though he wore a starched white jacket. He would roll a bit of cotton onto a fine stick, and then he would stand you on a chair and ask your name before he started.

He would flip your upper lid inside out with the side of the cotton stick, and when he got the cinder out he would give you the stick so everybody could look at it and see how big the speck was. If you asked him, he would flip both your eyelids for you so that the pink part came half-way down your eyes and you could stagger out of the drugstore like the Frankenstein monster with your hands drooped in front of your wrists. Even if you didn't have a cinder you could go in and ask Doctor Gelman, "Make me into Frankenstein?" and he would do it for you. Doctor Gelman wasn't a real doctor but everyone called him that out of respect. He seemed to especially like me. When I came in to have a speck taken out, he would roll out his piano stool from behind the counter and give me a twirl on it, and he'd give me and my friends chunks of rock candy for free. One time I was watching the coal go down the chute to our basement furnace room when the wind came up and I got cinders in both eyes. My father was standing by the ash cans when this happened, and he brought me in to the drugstore. When Doctor Gelman finished, he ruffled my hair and said to my father, "Look at these pretty curls, like Shirley Temple. Aren't you glad your Missus didn't flush her away?"

Upstairs in the house, with two cotton sticks in one hand and a piece of rock candy in the other hand, I said to my mother, "Doctor Gelman said you almost flushed me down the toilet." And that's how my mother told me the whole story of the flushing pills, up to the part where my father almost beat Doctor Gelman up and she saw the sign for Lavanburg Homes and got us in with her sit-down strike. When she was finished I asked, "Is that why you named me after the unlucky bride and groom who got killed, because Papa didn't want me to be born anyhow?"

11

"Oh, your child's head has it all twisted around," she said. "First of all, as soon as Papa saw you he changed his mind, because you were such a nice beautiful baby. Second of all, because you were almost not born, that means you were lucky to be born. You were born lucky. So that's how I got the nerve to give specially to you the names of Feyga and Pinya, because you already showed you had a good fate. And don't forget, even before you came into the world you brought luck and a good fate to the whole family. If not for you we would still be buried in that miserable grave on Avenue D and we would never have come to live in Lavanburg Homes, may God protect it."

The young Kesslers. Front: Fay, Sidney. Back: Cousin Ruth, Maxie, Ruthie.

II

A Wonder! A Cock-a-roach!

My mother took care of my brother Sidney. My sister Ruthie took care of me. Sidney was already four years old, I was three, and we still couldn't be in the same room for five minutes without him starting up. He grabbed things out of my hand. He shoved me and made me fall. He rushed at me yelling "Don't touch it." That he learned from our big brother Maxie.

Maxie spoke to us only to say "Don't touch it you'll break it" or "Shut up" or "Get out of here." Maxie was twelve, the oldest, and studious. My mother reminded us that he was an "A" student and not to bother him. She had hopes for him to become a professional.

Ruthie was ten, also an "A" student but not studious. She was very pretty and very nice, and Mama had hopes for her to become a secretary and marry a businessman or a professional.

Mama was pleased that the children she bore came out as two couples, boy-girl, boy-girl. That Maxie used to torment Ruthie and that Sidney now tormented me, she considered only natural, not only because they were boys but because Maxie had still been a baby, only twenty-three months old, when Ruthie came to take away all the attention from him, and Sidney had been even more of a baby, only fourteen months old, when I came.

My mother bragged to everybody that Ruthie was a born little mother. At night I slept curled up in Ruthie's arms. Sidney slept with Maxie in the big bedroom. They slept on opposite edges of the bed and tugged at the quilt all night, each pulling it off the other. Night after night I heard them break out in fights. My mother and father slept in a folding bed in the dining room. They wheeled it out from behind the girls'

15

bedroom door at night and put it back in the morning. When my mother and father had fights they stopped talking to each other. One would say, "Feyga, tell your father so and so," or "Ruthie, tell your mother such and such." They made us repeat every word even though the other one could hear it plain as day. When the boys had fights Maxie just shoved Sidney aside and went on giving orders.

It was my responsibility to stay out of Sidney's way and not give him a reason to beat me up. It wasn't only because he was a boy and because I had taken away his babyhood by being born. It was also because he had red hair. Mama called him *De Royter*, The Red One. She said it with pride. She said red-haired boys were born with a fiery temper, it couldn't be helped. "Leave him alone," she would say when he hit me. "You be the good one. Go to Ruthie."

During Ruthie's school days, while Sidney was still too young to go to school, my mother made me stay in my bedroom after breakfast, behind the closed door, to keep him away from me until Ruthie could come take care of me at three o'clock. The first thing I did when the door closed in the morning was go up to the bedroom window. I had to stand on the shoe-shine bench to see out. Maxie had made the bench in Shop class. All the boys made a shoe-shine box, a shoe-shine bench, and a study table. They were painted a deep glossy red. The table was in Maxie's room; the shoe-shine box was under his bed. He didn't need the bench. Ruthie had made an embroidery sampler in Sewing class. It was hanging by thumbtacks on the kitchen wall next to the window, above my father's head when he sat at the table. It said:

A Man Works from Sun to Sun
A Woman's Work Is Never Done

It showed, in many kinds of stitches, a round orange sun with yellow rays, flowers amidst many blades of grass, and a country cottage.

Opposite my bedroom window, the top part of an ancient gray house stuck out from behind the high brick wall of our back alley. It was only worth looking at when the windows were left open and the husband and wife inside were yelling at each other. One time I saw the woman bop her husband on the head with a shoe. Past the next old house on the right was an empty lot, and if I stood up high on the shoe-shine bench and pressed my left cheek against the windowpane, I could see a part of the street corner and watch people going to work, watch mothers pushing their baby carriages, and watch horse-and-wagons, cars, and trucks rolling by. I watched the street until I couldn't stay like that any more, then I sat on the shoe-shine bench with my back to the window and listened.

I heard the horses clip-clopping on the cobblestones. I could tell the milkman's wagon by its tinkle of bottles and rattle of milkboxes. I heard the rumble of the big black coal truck, the squeals and groans of its body being tilted up in front and the thunderous clatter of its coal rushing down the chute and into the cellars. I especially listened for the peddlers' cries because when I went out in the court to play house with my friends we always repeated the cries to each other and we all had to know what the others were pretending to sell.

"HAH-ees-COH, HAH-ees-COH" meant the ice-and-coal man who made deliveries to the old apartments across the street, a big cube of ice strapped to his back and a big bucket of coal in each hand.

"SHOP-ya-knife-SIZZ-IZZ, SHOP-ya-knife-SIZZ-IZZ" was the scissors grinder who struck sparks on his whirling stone wheel and also fixed pots and pans with hot melted metal right there from the back shelf of his wagon.

17

"WAW-dee-MEL-EEEN, TWO-cents TWUNny-a-ho." That was the watermelon man who was there when school started in September and left before the winter cold. He called from the back of his motor truck where whole melons were piled up behind the two-cent slices.

The sweet-potato man on my corner, who had a chimney on top of his pushcart and a stove inside, called out "heys-ARbis heys-ARbis, sweepa-TEYYY-DUS." "Heys arbis" are hot chickpeas. In summer he called "HotCORM-BUDDuh, hotCORM-BUDDuh." He dropped a shucked corn into a pot of boiling water, fished it out with tongs, and rolled it in a plate of melted butter and then into another plate of salt crystals and handed it to you while it was so hot you had to blow on your fingers.

I heard "Grapes? Grapes? Grapes? Grapes?" It was the Gypsy lady, sauntering along in the middle of the street with a basketful of dark blue grapes, holding up a perfect bunch by forefinger and thumb. "Grapes? Grapes?" For no reason, I imitated her call hopping on one foot then the other.

One sound, my favorite, came from the other side of my bedroom door: my father's roller canary in the dining room. As soon as the sun rose up from the East River and hit his cage he started singing his heart out, and he kept it up all morning. When my father was home he whistled the canary's song back to him, to make him sing more. I tried to whistle but I only sounded like steam hissing from the radiator.

A while after the sun hit the birdcage, it arrived at my own east window and traveled across the pink walls with its golden light, bringing along the shadow of the windowpanes, which slowly shrank from long-and-slanted to short-and-straight-up as it moved around the room. Then I napped, got called into the kitchen for lunch, came back to my bedroom, and took my sister's doll out of the green wicker doll carriage that stood between the shoeshine bench and the dresser. My sister said the doll was six years older than me. It had no name. A rich cousin of my mother's had given it to Ruthie but she was already nine and had no time for it. I sat the doll up on the bed and showed her the Thumbkin song that Ruthie had taught me. It starts with your closed fists facing each other, then a finger pops out of each fist when you call it:

> *Where is Thumbkin? Where is Thumbkin?*
> *Here I am. Here I am.*
> *How are you this morning?*
> *Very well, thank you.*
> *Run away*   One thumb goes back into its fist
> *Run away*   Then the other thumb.

The next finger is Pointer, then Middleman, Ringman, then Pinky. I entertained my doll by making believe the fingers were men who held imaginary conversations with each other. They quarreled, and bopped each other on the head, and kissed and made up. And so the time went by peacefully.

When Ruthie and Maxie came home from school, Sidney and I joined them in the kitchen for milk, bread-and-butter, and apple. Then Maxie went to his bedroom to study at his red table with the door shut, and Sidney went outside to play. After three o'clock the little children could go out by themselves and play in the court because then there were plenty of big children around to see that they didn't wander into the street. I didn't want to go outside until Ruthie finished practicing piano. She had to practice for a half hour every day as soon as she finished her three-o'clock snack, and she let me sit beside her on the piano bench. I watched her fingers. I knew them all by name from the Thumbkin song, so it was easy for me to follow them as they danced along the keys, especially because she repeated each exercise and each new piece many times. When she finished, I would sit at the piano and pretend I was taking her lesson. One day, after her piano teacher left, I played the whole lesson, rolling the left-hand chords from thumb to pinky whenever I couldn't stretch my small fingers across the keys. Ruthie called my mother to the dining room. She said, "Watch Feyga," and made me play *Believe Me, if All Those Endearing Young Charms.* My mother got so excited. She called out, "*A zah vunder, a zah vunder!*" Such a wonder, such a wonder! She said she would show my father the minute he got home from work.

We went into the kitchen. Ruthie and my mother got supper ready while I played under the kitchen table with a deck of cards. Sidney came home and saw me there. He ran over and yelled, "A cock-a-roach, a cock-a-roach! Under the table!" He kicked at me and stomped on the cards. "I *am not* a cock-a-roach," I cried. "I am a *vunder!*" My mother laughed till her belly shook. The minute my father came home from work she repeated the story to him. More laughter. She forgot to make him listen to me play the piano. My mother repeated the story endless times after that. Always to more laughter. Always her belly shook. Cock-a-roach became my nickname.

III

Pa, Home from Work

My father always got a jump-up-and-down welcome from Sidney and me when he came home from work. He announced himself by ringing the doorbell in a series of short taps: *dir-dit-dit dir-dit-dit dit-dit*. Under his arm was a stack of newspapers he had gathered from the subway: the Daily News, the Daily Mirror, the Sun, Post, Times, some Jewish papers. Sidney and I both wanted the Mirror because it had the comics—we called them the jokes—on two facing pages so you could read them all at once. In the Daily News the jokes were scattered and you had to keep turning pages to find one at a time. The other papers didn't have any jokes. Papa made us play a choosing game for first one to get the Mirror. He put a knot in one corner of his big white handkerchief and showed only the tips of the four corners in his fist. Whoever plucked out the knot got the Mirror first.

Mama yelled from the kitchen, "I told you, don't bring the papers home from the subway, it brings in cock-a-roaches." My father answered, "They're clean papers, folded up, from the seats not the trash cans. You shouldn't be a hypocrite; you use the papers more than anybody." It was true. As soon as my mother washed the floors she covered them with newspapers so they could be clean for weekends and for company. We grew up shuffling about in a mess of crumpled papers. When someone rang the bell, there would be a frantic scurrying to pick up all the papers and stuff them in the dumbwaiter before Ma went to the front door. She also used Pa's newspapers to clean out the stove, to spread on the table to catch the drips from the clothes-drying rack, to wash the windows on Fridays, and to put under the Friday chicken when she pulled out its guts and salted it to draw out the blood. Pa took one sheet a day for his canary.

We stayed in the dining room until supper was ready. Sidney and I spread our newspapers on the floor and read the jokes on our bellies and elbows, feet in the air. Maxie and Ruthie read at the big mahogany dining table. My father went straight to the far end of the dining room, by the window on the right, to take care of his canary. He whistled softly between his teeth and it hopped over and cheeped to him while he put seeds and fresh water in the feeder cups and changed its sheet of newspaper. Then he poked the soils of his snake plant and rubber plant and gave them water too. Then he moved to the left window and fiddled with his fish tank. It was full of guppies and had snails hiding in the water-grass on the bottom, and it had a man in a diving suit who was about to explore an undersea castle. Papa caught the guppy babies in his net and put them in a glass bowl where they were safe or they would be eaten by the grownups. Then he sprinkled fish food over the tank while the grownup guppies streamed up with gaping mouths to snap at the flakes. Sidney always caught me watching and tried to snatch my newspaper, saying I wasn't reading and didn't know how to read anyway, and then Ruthie would have to go over and stop him.

When my mother called "supper's ready" Papa was the first to dash in. His chair was in the corner between the kitchen window and the stove, under Ruthie's embroidery sampler. I jumped up and followed so I could sit next to him. Ruthie would come right away too. She put out the seltzer, helped Ma serve, and sat next to me. Sidney stayed in the dining room until he finished the jokes, then he took the place opposite Pa. There was only room for four at the table. Maxie would wait until Pa was finished and then take his place. Ma ate the leftovers standing at the sink except when we had meat or chicken they went into the stock pot for soup.

Pa propped up the Jewish newspaper *The Forward* between the seltzer bottle and cutlery jar and read it while he shoveled food in his mouth. He stuffed both cheeks like a squirrel, chewed, gulped, and looked at his watch while Mama listed her complaints. She complained that other husbands hand over their pay envelopes. He said she spends too much and that if he gave her the whole week's pay she wouldn't put aside any money for the slack season. She listed all the things we needed. She always mentioned that I was still wearing Sidney's outgrown shoes and it was a disgrace before the neighbors that she couldn't buy me girls' shoes. Finally he would say, "I don't have time, later, I have to go to a meeting."

My father was a charter member of four organizations: the Modern Young Friends of Kovel which was his home town in Russia, the Kovel Friendship and Benefits Society of the Workmen's Circle which promoted the Yiddish language and culture, the Father's Club of Lavanburg Homes where we lived, and he was a shop delegate in his Garment Workers union. In all these organizations he was the Recording Secretary because he was known for writing Yiddish with a fine swift hand and excellent expressions. He had to be on time to read the minutes of the previous meeting and take the new minutes. Mama said, "Do you also have to stay in the cafeterias till the middle of the night?" He insisted that he didn't do this for his own pleasure; he had to be friendly with everybody on the committees so he could pick up side jobs during the slack season, or if he should ever, God forbid, need a loan from the treasury.

If my father did ever talk at supper, it was to complain about the prices the union set for the latest line of garments in his shop. He was a sewing machine operator and was paid by the piece. Every time the operators worked on a new dress style, a new piecework rate had to be set according to the complexity of the design and the difficulty of stitching the material. Always the operators, the union officials, and the bosses quarreled, and always the operators got cheated.

As Pa was leaving, Sidney and I would rush up for a kiss goodbye. He kissed with three quick pecks on each cheek. He would say with a wink and a smile, "Ah, I almost forgot," and would bring out of his coat pocket a couple of tin wind-up toys, or two china figures for the shelf, or two balloons. He would put one in each of our outstretched hands and duck out the door before Mama could yell at him for wasting money on trifles. Then she would call Maxie to come and take Papa's place at the table.

IV

The Pony Man

"The pony man is here! The pony man! The pony man!" We all ran over from both ends of the block, more than twenty of us. The pony was so adorable in its collar of paper carnations and big gold jingle bells. Its eyes were slanted and tender and sad. The boys were more interested in the camera that was on a tripod, draped in black. The girls surrounded the pony and asked if we could pat it.

"Go ask your mothers, ten cents a picture on the pony. Tell her a picture that won't fade."

Only Phyllis went. Her family was rich. The rest of us patted the pony, who stood there without moving, as if it were a merry-go-round horse. Phyllis came running back with her mother. She had changed into a pleated plaid dress. We all had to step back for her, as if she were a princess.

The pony man took out a gray sealskin coat with a white rabbit collar. It was beautiful. Her mother said, "No, we don't need that." The pony man lifted Phyllis onto the pony and placed the reins in her hands. He told her to lift her hands up higher and smile. He stepped back to the camera and put the black cloth over his head. Phyllis looked nervous. Her mother put her hand on Phyllis's back and looked up at her with a smile. She was going to be in the picture too. I held my breath in fear, desire, and envy.

Bessie Weber (Ma) at the age of about 19, circa 1915

V

The Ice House on Mangin Street

Rosie Shuster and Ruthie were doing homework on the bed. I watched from my old crib, dangling my legs through the rails, and waited for them to be finished. Outside the window the fog was so thick you couldn't see anything. Foghorns were sounding all day, *Whooooooo, Whooooooo*, like the sound when you blow into a bottle.

When it was time to walk Rosie home, I asked if we could go past the docks to see the river in the fog and watch the tugboats tooting their horns. Yes we could! How I loved my sister.

The river was two blocks away. We lived on Goerck Street. Ruthie used to say "pronounce it Gor-rick please, not Gork." Then came Mangin, which rhymes with engine, then the docks on East Street. On our side of Mangin Street was Junior High School 97 for boys only, where my big brother Maxie went to school. I could see his class from our kitchen window and once I saw him in person standing up. On the other side of Mangin Street, taking up almost the whole block, was the Knickerbocker Ice House. It was big and dark and it had a loading platform all the way across the building. Icemen came from all over to load up their wagons, starting in the night and finishing in the early morning. I always heard in my sleep the clip-clop of horses and the clatter of wagons but I only saw the loading of the ice in summertime when we passed by at six in the morning to get on line at the Third Street pier for a free all-day boat ride and health examination on the city's Floating Hospital boat. It took a thousand passengers at a time, and you could only go one time. but Ma brought a big homemade honeycake to the Democratic Party district captain Mister Dembofsky and she got us tickets for three times.

Except for the summertime crowds streaming to the Hospital boat and except for the Junior High School boys going in and out of school, Mangin Street was deserted in the daytime. But as we passed by on this gloomy, foggy afternoon, we saw a line-up of strange men alongside the loading platform of the ice house. The end of the line was almost lost in the fog. Instead of heading straight for the river we turned in at Mangin Street and walked by the ice house to see what was going on. The men were shabby, tired-looking, with stubble on their faces, with beat-up old hats, crumpled old clothes, shuffling along the line in worn-out shoes. Where had they come from? They didn't look like the Jews or Italians of the neighborhood, who might be desperate but hardly ever looked stranded. Above them on the platform, clean-faced, clean-shaven Christian men were handing out a bowl of soup from a ladle to each person on the line. Farther along, other Christian men added a slice of bread, a spoon, and an apple. At the end of the ice house another Christian man stood on the sidewalk, below the platform, and collected the bowls and spoons. Watching in silence on the steps of the school were some of the Junior High School boys. The whole street was silent except for the shuffling of shoes, the drone of the man at the end of the line, "leave utensils here leave utensils here leave utensils here," and the sound of the foghorns, *Whooooooo, Whoooooo.*

When we turned the corner onto Houston Street and arrived at the docks, we saw through the mist a row of shanties that had never been there before. Ruthie said, "I feel like the whole city changed overnight while I was sleeping." The shanties were put together from wood planks, cardboard, and tar paper, and roofed over with sheets of tin. Then Rosie said, "I know! This is the Hooverville! And those men back on Mangin Street, they must be the hoboes! I heard all about it on our new radio."

VI
A Dispossess on Columbia Street

My mother and I were walking along Columbia Street on our way shopping. At the corner of Columbia and Rivington we came upon a lady and two boys sitting beside a kitchen table at the curb. Piled up all around them were furniture, cardboard boxes, and bundles of clothing and bedding tied with clothesline rope. A third boy was stretched out on a sofa, right across the sidewalk, reading a joke book. You had to walk around him up to the table to get by. The lady pretended not to notice as people stopped to put money in a jar on her table. Mama said to me, "It's a dispossess. They were thrown out of their house because they didn't have money to pay the rent."

I asked if I could put money in the jar.

"What are you crazy? We could use money ourselves."

"Could we be thrown out of our house?"

"Don't worry. God forbid. *Ptu ptu ptu.*" She pretend-spit three times to chase away the evil eye of envy. "Don't worry, by night she'll have plenty of money. At least she was smart enough to choose a good corner location. And it's Friday, pay day. Plenty of people will give her money. Maybe even the Communists will come and move her back in. It's possible."

I stared at the boys by the table. One of them stared back at me, and before I could look away he made a smirky face and held out his palm and tickled it with the middle finger of his other hand. I knew right away it must mean something like a dirty word. I thought, Serves you right.

VII
"Liar! Liar! Liar! Liar!"

The doctor said my brother Sidney had to have his tonsils out. Sidney was only five years old. My mother didn't know how to tell him. She got him a brand-new pencil box with two drawers in it and a pencil and a pencil sharpener inside the drawers and she told him she was taking him to school. But she took him to Beth Israel Hospital. The nurses dragged him away screaming.

When Ma got him home next morning he ran through the house trailing a thin sick sound from his throat, "Liar! Liar! Liar! Liar!" and pulling down china figures, dining room chairs, the piano bench, the piano cover, until he got to his bedroom and slammed the door shut. We heard him shoving and scraping the bureau. The vase and bowls on it clinked dangerously. He was barricading the door! Mama called from outside the door: "Here's Dixie-cup ice cream. You need it for your tonsils. It's melting."

Silence.

"Well, I'll have to give it to Feyga."

We heard him shoving and scraping the bureau back the other way. The door opened a crack. A hand reached out and groped in the air like a blind snake. Ma put the whole Dixie-cup in his hand, with the little wood spoon sticking up. I watched as the hand pulled in all of the ice cream. And the door closed.

VIII

The Great Depression Comes to Lavanburg Homes

Menshn trakht und Gut lakht.
People plan and God laughs.

—A Jewish proverb

A private Jewish-owned bank on Delancey and Allen streets went under in December 1930. It was known as the pants-pressers bank because thousands of garment workers kept their savings in it and the pants pressers were the last to get laid off when the slack season started. Then the bank would lend the savings to the garment factories to buy fabrics so they could start up again after the slack. The bank had grown prosperous on the interest they charged for the loans and it had erected a beautiful corner building with tall marble pillars. But after the stock market crash of October 1929 the garment factories lost a lot of orders and couldn't pay back what they owed. The bank lost its reserve of money. The thousands of garment workers lost their savings. Lots of other private banks had to close, too, when business went bad and customers weren't buying, but because the pants-pressers bank had given itself a grandiose official name, The Bank of the United States, many people in the rest of the country, and even in the world, thought the United States Treasury had failed, and they panicked. They ran to their banks to get their money out. That made everything worse. The country went from the Stock Market Crash to the Bank Panic to the Great Depression.

Many people blamed the Jewish bankers. But the Jews said it was the fault of J.P. Morgan and the other big money-bags who always helped each other out but wouldn't make an emergency loan to rescue a Lower East Side bank that was owned by Jews.

At our Lavanburg Homes half the tenants had lost their jobs by the time the Depression settled in. No work, no rent. But Lavanburg Homes was built by a utopian Jewish philanthropist, Fred. L. Lavanburg of the Straus department store family, who was on a mission to prove that with careful planning and everybody paying their rent on time, working-class people could make new, decent, modern apartment buildings self-supporting, and then they wouldn't have to live in slums or be subjected to private charity or government regulation. The Lavanburg Foundation wasn't allowed to make up for the lost rent out of its own funds because that would spoil the experiment. The board members of the Foundation decided to let the out-of-work tenants owe rent until times got better, and in the meantime they set up a desk in the office of the Administrator, Mister Abraham Goldfeld, to help the tenants apply for Home Relief and civil service jobs. The Foundation also let Mister Goldfeld use building-maintenance funds to give out part-time jobs to tenants. My father, Benjamin Kessler, who was a highly skilled garment operator, a union representative, and the Recording Secretary of four organizations because of his elegant handwriting and expressive vocabulary, was also out of work. Mister Goldfeld gave him a job as a part-time janitor. With his delicate hands and long sensitive fingers he stoked the coal furnace in the evening and banked it at night. And in his one good suit and his pointy-toed freshly shined shoes he climbed the six flights of stairs in all six buildings to sweep and mop the hallways and change burnt-out light bulbs.

Nobody addressed my father as Mister Kessler any more. They called him Benny. When he caught children playing ball on the stairs, he confiscated the balls and gave them to my brother Sidney and me. The children grabbed them back from us next day, sometimes with a punch or a shove to make sure we wouldn't snitch on them.

Little Elya Schwartz, the tiny shoemaker with owl-like eyes whose shop was across the street, also couldn't pay the rent. His former customers were walking around with cardboard in their shoes because they couldn't pay Little Elya to repair their worn-out soles. Mister Goldfeld took money from the Foundation's fund for "Leisure Time Activities" and made Little Elya the Leather Crafts teacher in our basement Social Center. Nobody called him Elya any more. They addressed him as Mister Schwartz. Lots of us children lined up with our family's shoes, and Mister Schwartz demonstrated how to repair them, letting the girls apply the glue and the boys pound in the nails.

The commercial photographer got a studio in the Social Center for a photography club, and the bookbinder got a shop for a bookbinding club. Other out-of-work parents became leaders of sports teams, reading clubs, a knitting club, a carpentry shop, or they helped supervise the two crowded game rooms. When the Center closed at the end of June we had a Rally Day of plays, dances, and exhibits followed by an outdoor party in the main court. Then we moved our activities to the roof for the summer, and the parents who were on the basement staff got part-time jobs on the roof or, if they couldn't operate without basement equipment, they became leaders of trips around the city's parks and museums.

Despite the efforts of management to help the tenants ride out the Depression, many families still didn't have enough money to cover all the necessities. Mothers were leaving their kitchens to look for work. With no one home to empty the shallow ice pans under our low-to-the-ground modern-design iceboxes, the pans overflowed and water soaked through the floors. Ceilings were damaged in the apartments below. Fights broke out. Mister Goldfeld persuaded the Lavanburg Foundation to buy refrigerators. That way the tenants could save money on ice and the Foundation could save money on repairs. To the Foundation's surprise, the tenants sent a delegation to the management office to protest the plan for refrigerators. They didn't want the three Italian icemen to lose all their hundred-ten customers and have to go out of business for their wives and children to starve. After some negotiations Mister Goldfeld hired the icemen to join the Maintenance and Repairs staff, and we got the new refrigerators. My big brother Maxie made horrible rum-and-raisin ice cream in the freezer unit. We all had to eat it so as not to hurt his feelings, except Papa said he never ate ice cream and Sidney ran out of the house before his share hit the kitchen table.

The icemen's horse, Frankie, who used to eat apple cores out of my hand, lost his job. My father told me Frankie lived in a warehouse on the Italian side of Goerck Street and was now one of the rental horses who were hitched to a wagon from the lot and hired out by the day. I went to see him by myself. I sneaked out a whole apple to give him. First I had to wait at the corner for a grown-up to take me across Stanton Street to the Italian side. Then I had to walk all the way to the other end of the block, where I saw the warehouse.

The staircase had been replaced by a ramp so they could lead the horses up to their stalls. The horses were sticking their heads out of the upstairs windows and looking down at the street just like people. On the fire escape of the building opposite the warehouse a green parrot was raising its crest at the horses and shuffling its legs from side to side and shrieking "*pastafaJOO-LA!!! pastafaJOO-LA!!!*" The blacksmith in the lot led me up the warehouse ramp to see my horse friend Frankie and give him my apple. The blacksmith told me the green parrot, whose name was Greenie, was saying "bean soup" in Italian.

IX
"J-O-E Spells Joey"

I sat on my stoop in front of my E building in Lavanburg Homes and watched my friends jumping rope in the middle of the court. I had my skirt pulled down and my feet tucked under. They sang:

> *Your mother my mother live across the way*
> *Two-fourteen East Broadway*
> *Every night they have a fight*
> *And this is what they say:*
> *Lady Lady turn around*
> *Lady Lady touch the ground*
> *Lady Lady show your shoe*
> *Lady Lady please skidoo.*

That was the trouble. You can't jump rope without showing your shoes. I had outgrown my shoes again, they split open in front, and I had on my brother Sidney's old lace-up shoes. My mother and sister said no one would notice the difference but they were lying just to make me go outside. Boys' shoes were thicker and laced up higher. Besides, most of my friends had on low shoes with buckles and not any laces.

They sang another song with feet in it:

> *Charlie Chaplin walks like this* (turn toes out)
> *Charlie Chaplin talks like this* (fake smile, finger on chin)
> *Charlie Chaplin throws a kiss* (kiss hand and fling it)
> *Charlie Chaplin misses like this* (skip rope under feet)

My sister Ruthie was sitting on the stoop of the F building, doing cross-stitch embroidery with the other older girls. A gang of eight- and nine-year-old girls was on the other side of the court, on the C building stoop, playing pick-up-sticks. My brother Sidney and his friends were running around and around the two court entrances, playing tag with a filthy janitor's mop. Other boys wrestled each other to the ground in what was supposed to be a game of Johnny-on-a-pony.

While I sat on my E stoop doing nothing, it started getting dark. I hoped Ruthie would come over and we could go back upstairs, but then the sun came out again.

It was my best-friend Celia's turn.

> *Cinderella, dressed in yella,*
> *Went uptown to buy an umbrella*
> *On the way she met a fella*
> *How many kisses did she receive?*

The rope turned faster and faster, whipping the pavement, until Celia missed. Twenty-two rope jumps counts for twenty-two kisses. That was a lot.

Lovey jumped next.

> *Fat and Skinny had a race*
> *Fat fell down and broke his face*
> *Skinny said I won the race*
> *How many kisses did he receive?*

Again the rope turned faster and faster. Lovey got fourteen kisses. Not so good, but better than I ever got. I liked being a rope turner, especially turning fast or doing double-dutch with two ropes at a time. I wasn't a good jumper even when I had my own shoes on. I was always among the last ones in all the jumping and running and hopping games. Ruthie said all I needed was confidence but I didn't know how to get it.

The new boy came out of the F building, squeezing his way past my sister and her friends. The boy had on a clean shirt and freshly ironed shorts. It didn't look like his mother would let him get dirty. He went out to the sidewalk and watched my brother and his gang running wild with the janitor's mop. Then he watched the other gang of boys wrestling on the ground from their Johnny-on-a-pony game. Then he came back and sat next to me. I pulled my skirt down more.

"What's your name?" he asked.

"Fay."

"Mine is Joey. I just moved in today."

"I know, I was watching. What apartment did you get?"

"We got F62 on the top floor."

"That's where the social workers used to live. How many rooms do you have?"

"Four."

"Me also. I'm on the second floor in this building, apartment E21."

"My front windows face the court," he said. "I can look down and see everybody playing. And from my bedroom window I see the East River."

"My windows face the back," I said, "but from my bedroom window I see the corner of the street by the lamppost and across the alley I see a house where a crazy lady lives and from my kitchen window in the back I see into P.S. 97 where my big brother goes to school on Mangin Street, that's the next street after ours. He's fourteen, and I have a sister who's twelve and another brother who's seven."

"I have a sister who's ten," Joey said, "and I'll be five years old on September twenty-third."

"I'll be five years old on July eighteenth. I'm older than you. That means you can't be my boyfriend."

"I can so. My mother is older than my father."

I got embarrassed. The father was always supposed to be older. I didn't know what else to say. He didn't say anything else either.

39

My rich friend Phyllis's turn:

I can't go to Macy's any more more more
There's a big fat policeman at the door door door
He'll squeeze you like a lemon
A khalyatshka zul im nemen ("A fit should take him")

Enela jumped in, squeezed Phyllis, and pushed her out.

I can't go to Macy's any more more more.

Phyllis stumbled over the rope. She said "It doesn't count. Enela pushed me too hard." Enela said she didn't. The game stopped while they stood around arguing. Then Celia said "Let's just play something else." Then they argued about what to play next.

I said to Joey, "Put up your hands and I'll show you a clapping game." I sang:

I am a pretty little Dutch girl, as pretty as I can be
And all the boys around my block are crazy over me.
My boyfriend's name is Jello. He comes from Monticello
With a pimple on his nose and two fat toes he is a jolly fellow.

I sang the song twice clapping against Joey's hands and then I made him clap with me:

I	(Clap your hands)
am	(Clap each other's hands)
a	(Clap your hands)
pretty	(Clap each other's right hand)
little	(Clap your hands)
Dutch	(Clap each other's left hand)
girl	(Clap your hands twice)
As	(Clap the back of each other's hands)

pretty	(Clap the front of each other's hands)
as	(Clap your hands)
I	(Clap each other's right hand)
can	(Clap your hands)
be	(Clap each other's left hand)

"Now we do the same claps over and over while I keep on singing till the end."

Joey got it all mixed up, and he laughed every time he made a mistake. After many tries and each time busting up laughing, he got it right, so I made us go faster and faster and then I was making mistakes and laughing also. We were having so much fun that we didn't notice the sun had gone away until it got very dark in the court and Missus Mandelker opened her window and yelled "Esther! Get the laundry from the roof quick!"

The dust started whirling and lightning flashed. A loud clap of thunder and a sudden downpour sent everybody running for the hallways. Joey and I jumped up and ran from the stoop to the first row of the inside steps. Girls and boys rushed in, pushing and shoving for places on the steps. Someone noticed Joey. "Hey, here's the boy who just moved in." They crowded in on him.

"What's your name?" "What's your apartment?" "I live in the F building too." "Me too." "How old are you?" I left my place and snuck away upstairs before anyone could notice my brother's shoes on my feet.

My mother came home right after me, dripping wet from the rain. I yelled, "I have to have shoes! I have to have shoes!" I stamped my feet and started to cry.

She said with a laugh, "Guess what? Here's shoes. What, you think I forgot?" And she took out of her leather shopping bag a pair of shiny brown shoes with big gold buckles on the sides. I tore off Sidney's shoes and put them on. They were too big.

"They have to be big because you're growing. Wait, I'll get cotton to stuff in the toes, and I'll make an extra hole in the straps."

"Later. I'm in the middle of something. Help me get them buckled." "What, I don't even get a kiss?" I kissed her fast, got the shoes buckled, and ran back downstairs.

It was still pouring rain and everybody was still sitting on the inside steps. I pushed and shoved my way to the front. Phyllis was sitting next to Joey. I said, "That's my place. I was sitting here."

"You gave it up."

"I did not. I just had to go upstairs a minute. Joey, didn't you save my place?"

Joey said "Yes, I did."

I pushed Phyllis over and squeezed in next to him. The boys blew wolf whistles. The girls clapped their hands and chanted, right in our grinning faces:

> *Feygie has a new boyfriend*
> *Feygie has a new boyfriend*
> *What's his name? I know his name:*
> *J-O-E spells Joey!*
> *First comes love*
> *Then comes marriage*
> *Then comes Feygie with a baby in the carriage.*

Then the girls switched over to Phyllis, who was sitting there silent and sullen:

> *Don't you worry*
> *Don't you care*
> *You should marry a millionaire*

42

"J-O-E Spells Joey"

He should die, you should cry?
You should marry another guy!

And Joey was my boyfriend for the next six years, until his father died and his family moved away.

Fay at five

X

A Nickel Here, a Nickel There

We were waiting to get on Home Relief. My father's garment factory stayed closed during the whole fall season of 1932 because of the Depression and it looked like a long while before it would open again, if ever. My mother made us potato-onion soup for breakfast and again for lunch, and for suppers we had pickled herring with day-old bread and vegetable-barley soup with bits of meat. We stopped going to the grocery store across the street for milk; my mother was ashamed to ask for more credit. Every day after school my sister Ruthie borrowed my older brother Maxie's school briefcase and took Sidney and me all the way to the children's free milk line that Eleanor Roosevelt started in Jackson Street Park by the bend in the river at Cherry Street. We each got on line twice, once with our hats on and once with our hats off, so Ruthie sneaked home six half-pint containers of milk in the briefcase, four for drinking and two for cooking. For the herring Ma went to her mother, who pickled them by the dozens in two large crocks and sold them right from her apartment on East 8th Street. From there my mother went to a bakery over on East 11th Street that sold day-old bread. For the potatoes and soup greens she went to Rivington Street late in the day and bargained with the pushcart peddlers for the stunted and bruised leftovers.

On Fridays she stopped in at the butcher on Avenue D between 4th and 5th, where for ten cents a pound she bought two pounds of cheap meat for the week's soups: lungs, heart, and lamb necks. Because she was an old customer he would throw in a bone with meat on it. On Sundays she went to the appetizing store next to the butcher and bought a pound of tub butter and a dozen cracked eggs, and she got a pile of leftover lox skin for free. This is how our family of six lived on less than a dollar a week while we waited and waited for the Home Relief to come.

One night when my father sat down to his supper of herring, stale bread, and vegetable-barley soup he said with a wry smile, "Ay, this is eating like in Russia again." My mother flushed.

"What do you expect when we have money like in Russia again? With the kopeks you bring in the house you expect me to serve you steak and lamb chops?" Her voice began to climb. "Where are the loans from the loan funds you gave your money to? Where are all your friends you gave favors who are supposed to throw you some work when you need it?" She stamped her foot. "Into the garbage, that's where!"

Ruthie said, "Please Mama, Papa, don't fight. I can't stand it." He put a she's-crazy expression on his face and got up from the table. Ma shouted after him: "Go! Go to the cafeterias with your good friends! There you won't have to eat like in Russia!" The door slammed. She let loose a stream of complaints in a wail that went through your bones like a police siren. Ruthie, Sidney, and I stared down at our soup, waiting for her fit to die down. Then Maxie came in from reading the newspapers in the dining room and sat down in my father's place. Ma wiped her eyes with her apron and served him his supper.

The Shopping Bag Factory

My father began dropping in at Mister Toperick's shopping bag factory on Broome Street, just to chat, go out for a cup of coffee, maybe discuss some issues from the last meeting of the Modern Young Friends of Kovel, their home town in Russia. Mister Toperick lived well. He had an apartment somewhere uptown, he dressed in good suits, went to the theater, and was something of a ladies man. He would have been handsome except for his thick glasses, which made his eyes look tiny and strange. His shopping bags were made of oilcloth, an imitation leather made out of linseed oil mixed with pigment and pressed onto a tough cotton canvas. Mister Toperick was the only one who made such a bag. He had thought it up himself when his father-in-law's luggage factory went out of business. He made a plain black rectangle, taller than wide, with sturdy handles stitched into the top. The material was a nuisance to sew; the needles would break if the stitching went too fast. It was lowly, monotonous work. My father was a highly skilled operator on a well known moderate-price line of ladies dresses. The factory had a receptionist, a showroom with two models, and a designer. But he had to put away his pride. He told Mister Toperick he wouldn't mind helping out in the shop sometimes if Mister Toperick found himself short-handed.

One evening my father came home with a parcel containing a present for my mother: a leather shopping bag from Mister Toperick's factory. While she examined it, surprised and pleased, he took his place at the supper table instead of first going off to fiddle with his fish tank and canary. Pa always started his meal with a shot-glass of whisky, which he downed in one gulp followed by a lump of bread. This time he lifted the whisky bottle and said, "Come, Pessa, get a glass and celebrate with me. I made that shopping bag myself. I got work from Toperick, not much but something. Off the books." And Toperick had a message for Ma. Would she be interested in selling his bags in the neighborhood while he took samples around to the leather-goods shops uptown. "So, what do you think? While you're shopping, maybe you could sell a few bags along the way?"

"Could be," she said. "It's a nice bag. Strong. Well, why not?" She wiped her hands on her apron, got a small wineglass from the narrow cabinet above the silverware drawer, and held it out to him. "*L'khayim*, to good health. What can I lose?" He filled her glass with a flourish.

I wasn't in school yet. Sidney went to first grade and came home at noon for lunch. Ruthie and Maxie took a lunch sandwich with them in the morning and didn't come home till three. Next day, after Sidney went back to school at twelve-thirty, my mother said to me, "Now we'll get dressed nice. We're going to Toperick's factory." She put on a two-piece navy twill dress and her gray felt Robin Hood hat with its snap brim and two sharp partridge feathers. She let me wear my new Cousin-Pearlie's powder-blue Spring coat over my red corduroy Saturday dress with the white lace collar. Ruthie had to be home by three o'clock to take charge of Sidney if we didn't get back in time.

Toperick's factory was in a part of the Lower East Side I had never seen before, Broome Street between Suffolk and Norfolk. We walked from home along Goerck Street to Delancey, then under the Williamsburg Bridge to the other side of Delancey, then one block more to Broome Street, then we turned right all the way up Broome past Clinton Street. There were no pushcarts in the gutter on Broome Street, no children hanging around on the stoops, no grandmothers watching from the windows with their elbows on a pillow. The streets here were narrow, the buildings were older, taller, darker, and were hung with signs in Yiddish. They seemed to be leaning toward each other, squeezing out the light. Most had a store on each side of a steep flight of iron stairs, with two more stores or factories on the upper landing. From there an inside staircase led to apartments and sweatshops on four upper floors.

Toperick's factory, on the left side of the landing, was over a store where they rolled tobacco into cigars. A carved wooden Indian stood outside, dressed in a tobacco-leaf skirt and clutching a long wooden knife to his naked chest. He was chained to the front post of the iron stairs. Ma told me cigar makers were very educated people because they chipped in money for someone to read to them while they worked, and they chose only the best books from all over the world. The store on the right side of the iron stairs had a red-and-white-striped barber pole out front. The stripes kept revolving downward and disappearing down the bottom. The loft windows above the barber shop were boarded up. I took my mother's hand going up the iron stairs because the steps had no risers and I was afraid of falling through the open space.

Mister Toperick's shop door was open. An odor like medicine and camphor balls drifted out. Inside, the odor was stronger and the air was dusty. A pale dusty light from the plate-glass front window reached in only a few feet to the edge of a low platform that was placed against the window. The platform was covered in frayed old carpeting. The rest of the floor was almost hidden under strips of oilcloth, unraveled threads, and lint. I stood in the doorway holding my mother's hand. Across the dim room I saw an operator bent over a sewing machine that had a built-in lamp above the part where a needle went up and down. Two machines alongside his were idle and dark. Down the middle of the narrow room a light bulb, dangling from the ceiling, cast light on a man bent over the cutting table. My mother called out, "Good day, Mister Toperick!" The sewing-machine operator turned his head. It was my father, with his shirt sleeves pulled up by garters. He nodded to us as he went on stitching the cloth, his foot keeping up its rhythm on the treadle. Mister Toperick hurried over from the cutting table and shook hands with my mother. She told me to wait on the platform step, and he led her to a desk way at the back end of the room, by a barred window you couldn't see through.

I lifted up the back of my dress and coat and sat on my slip by the corner of the platform near the door. I looked around for something to play with. I caught sight of a bright pink piece of velvet in a mound of lint and reached in to pick it up. It wriggled. I jumped back. It made tiny squeals. I had disturbed a nest of blind baby rats! I tiptoed over the mess on the floor to my father, terrified that the mother rat would jump out and bite me. He let me stand next to him and watch him sew until my mother came back. She had three shopping bags in each hand. She said we were going to Orchard Street to sell them.

The Weaving District

Outside, I pulled my mother across the street to watch two women sitting in a storefront window facing each other across a small table. They wore glasses and were dressed in plain housedresses, and they were hand-weaving in the feeble strip of sunlight that entered the store through the plate glass.

Displayed against the lower part of the window were two big plaid shirts, one marked BEFORE and the other marked AFTER. The BEFORE shirt had a big hole from a cigarette burn. In the AFTER shirt the weaving was so perfect that you couldn't see where the hole had been. On our way up Broome Street to Orchard Street we saw another store with two women weaving in the window. It also had displays of plaid shirts marked BEFORE and AFTER. It was just like the first store all over again. And then I saw another! My mother said we were in the weaving district.

Buying and Selling on Orchard Street

As we neared the corner I heard a great roar and thought something wonderful or terrible was happening, but when we turned into Orchard Street it was only the tumult of people buying and selling. Shoppers were moving slowly along the narrow sidewalks on both sides of the street, between an endless line of pushcarts in the gutter and storefront merchandise in racks and bins. Signs in English and Yiddish hung from all the buildings. Awnings jutted over the storefronts.

Ma chose to walk along the outside of the sidewalk. We walked past racks of dresses and pants, past bins of table linens, ties, socks, pocketbooks, belts, past rolls of fabric ranging from curtain netting to silks, velvets, and tapestry. We passed ancient grocery stores that filled the air with the heady aromas of halvah, cardamom, ginger, anise, and coffee. Stacked in three neat rows in front of the grocery stores were burlap sacks filled with beans, nuts, and grains of all kinds. All along the way, the pushcarts in the gutter were stacked with fruits and vegetables, cutlery and kitchenware, toys and novelties. Merchants standing in front of their stores and peddlers standing in front of their pushcarts called out their bargains in one language after another. The sidewalk between them sometimes got so crowded with shoppers that I could only see coat bottoms and feet. I had to clutch my mother's skirt to keep from losing her, and I had to watch that I didn't get stepped on or have parcels swung in my face.

Some of the women carried brown-paper shopping bags with cord handles. They wrapped a handkerchief around the handles to keep the cord from cutting into their palms. Other women cradled paper bags in their arms and dangled parcels from their fingers by the string. No one had a nice big leather bag like Toperick's. No one was better dressed than my mother and me. I was proud to be moving along with her on this exciting street, wearing my powder-blue coat and holding onto her skirt, even though I was hot and tired and sometimes tripped over my shoes.

My mother saw an opening to make her first sale. She planted herself at a bin next to a rich-looking lady who was trying to see the sizes in boys' caps with the ends of her fingers while her arms were full of packages. My mother opened one of Mister Toperick's shopping bags and said in Yiddish, "Look, only twelve cents for this fine strong leather bag. Go ahead, try it, you can fit all your bundles in here, look, plenty of room. I bring it straight from the factory, below wholesale. Uptown this bag sells for a quarter." The lady peeked out over her parcels and said, "Five cents." My mother laughed and moved on. The lady called after her, "Hold your horses. How much?" My mother turned back and made the sale at a dime. "God willing," she said, "it will last your whole long and healthy life."

In the four blocks of Orchard Street from Broome until we reached the end at Houston Street, my mother sold three of Mister Toperick's shopping bags, each time offering it for twelve cents, each time settling for a dime. She had thirty cents, half for herself and half she would have to give back to Mister Toperick. "How much can I buy with fifteen cents?" she said. "Well, let's get a few things now, and tomorrow we'll go sell on Rivington Street where it's not so much crowded."

"Tell Him Your Jewish Name."

Near the end of Orchard Street my mother stopped at a grocery where she was friends with the owner, a tall skinny man with thick black eyebrows, a bushy mustache, and mournful eyes. She called him by his first name, Avrom, and he called her Pulla, her Russian name. She asked for oat flakes, split peas, barley, and dried mushroom bits. At each request he snapped open a paper bag, flitted his long arms over the sacks like a magician, plunged a scoop into the sack, poured from the scoop into the bag, rolled the bag shut, and put it in Ma's leather bag. Each time he called out the price and said "Next?" She asked for a little olive oil. "Give me the best price." He stepped inside near the door and poured out oil from a large golden can into a jar. "Next?" She asked for laundry soap. He picked up a cleaver and hacked off a thick slice of brown soap from a foot-long block. He said, "What else?" She said, "Avrom, be a sport. Throw in a few peanuts for my little girl here. We walked all the way from Goerck Street by the river and she didn't eat since breakfast." He turned to me.

"*A sheyna meydl*," he said. A pretty girl. "What is your name?"

"Fay."

My mother said, "Tell him your Jewish name."

"My Jewish name is FeygaPinya."

He stared at me with his eyebrows way up. "What? The newlyweds of Kovel who were slaughtered by the soldiers?"

"That's right," my mother said. "Feyga and Pinya. They were both my cousins, from different sides of my family. A bitter fate. I was right there, I still see his head split open on the stones." Her eyes filled with tears. She always did that when she talked about my name.

"That took some nerve to give her their names," Avrom said with respect.

"Everybody told me it would bring in a bad fate," Ma said, "but it's the opposite, I should live so. Mine Feygela brings in luck since before she was born, in the darkest times, may they rest in peace." The tears flowed. I tugged at her skirt. "Okay, I'm finished," she said. She set down her leather bags and wiped her eyes.

Avrom bent all the way down until his eyes were even with mine. "Are you a good girl? Do you help your mother?"

I said "Yes."

My mother beamed. "The best. You should hear how she sings." I tugged at her skirt again.

"Hold out your hands," Avrom said. He smiled. "Nopey-dope, your hands are too small." He snapped open another paper bag and poured a full scoop of peanuts into it and gave it to me to hold. He stuck his scoop into a sack and pinched my cheeks with both hands. "You have a wonderful mother," he said, tugging at my cheeks until they hurt. "A very brave woman, you know that? Always remember." He let go of my cheeks and clutched my head. He pressed my forehead into the knot of his apron. "Feyga and Pinya," he said. "I cannot get over it."

We reached Houston Street at the end of Orchard. Mama asked if I was tired. I said no. I didn't want her to fuss over me. "You're hot," she said. "Your cheeks are red. Let's go in here on Ludlow Street. I'll take off your coat and you can rest on a stoop and eat some peanuts. I'll buy a penny seltzer."

The Ludlow Street Twine and Paper Company

Ludlow Street, behind Orchard, was the street of cartons, twine, paper goods, and novelties. It had warehouses, too, and cobblestone alleyways leading to stables at the back. I pulled my mother over to a Betty Boop doll in one of the windows, all of her made of celluloid. She wore a strapless red bathing suit and high heels and was surrounded by little American flags. "You don't want that doll," my mother said. "She looks like a chippy."

Next came a window showing twine and wrappings. It had two piles of small brown paper bags, like the kind you get in the candy store, but in these bags one pile was stamped with a red elephant and the other with a red "5¢" sign. I stopped to look.

"Those are for peanuts," my mother said.

"I *know*. I want to buy one to put my peanuts in. I want to eat my peanuts from an *elephant* bag."

"You have to buy by the gross, that means a dozen dozen. All these stores are wholesale. They only sell to people in the business."

I put my head down and tightened my lips to keep from crying.

"Wait," she said. "I have an idea. You sit down on this stoop here. I'll go in and make believe I'm interested in the business, so maybe I can get you a sample."

She set down the leather bag alongside me and draped my powder-blue coat over the top. She put the two unsold leather bags on the other side of me, folded one inside the other, and tucked in my bag of peanuts. She opened the collar of my corduroy dress. Then she resettled her hat and tipped the brim to one side. The two partridge feathers stood up nicely on the other side. "Wait here," she said, and marched into the store.

Ludlow Street was so quiet. Only a few men walked by. Across the street two workers were taking flattened cartons out of a horse-and-wagon and piling them up on the sidewalk. The horse waited while its driver read a newspaper up front. I watched the horse shift its feet and twitch its muscles. I almost fell asleep.

Ma came out with a batch of elephant bags and put them in my lap. "Wait here a minute," she said. She got me the glass of seltzer and put down a handkerchief on the stoop so she could sit beside me in her good navy-blue skirt. She picked up an elephant bag and snapped it open with a flick of her wrist, just like Avrom did. She took a handful of peanuts and half-filled the bag. She folded one corner into a triangle, then the other, then folded the top down over the triangles and slid her fingernails across the top to give it a sharp edge. She handed the bag to me. "Here's your bag of peanuts. They showed me inside. Does it look right?" It did! It was folded just like a real bag of peanuts, and it had a red elephant on one side and a red "5¢" sign on the other side!

"Fresh Peanuts Here, Five Cents"

And that was the beginning of how my mother got into her own business of selling peanuts in Battery Park. The Ludlow Street Twine and Paper Company delivered a large carton of grosses of elephant bags. Avrom sent over a burlap sack of peanuts every Thursday. Around the dining room table after school Ma snapped the elephant bags open, Sidney and I half-filled them, Maxie and Ruthie folded them and put them into Mister Toperick's leather bags. We went to Battery Park every weekend all summer unless it rained. I stood next to my mother at the Statue of Liberty line and I sold "Fresh Peanuts Here, Five Cents," from my own wicker basket with a high round handle and I saw the great ships and ferries and blue skies and felt on my face the clean cool breezes filled with the scent of green grass, fresh fish, the salt sea. Maxie and Ruthie sold across the park at the Aquarium. Sidney wore his sailor suit and marched back and forth along the waterside prome-nade between the Statue of Liberty line and the Aquarium en-trance, waving two American flags from the Betty Boop store, one in each hand. Mama didn't have a license to peddle so Sidney was the spotter. We all kept an eye on his flags. If he spotted a policeman he crossed and uncrossed the flags while he marched over to the Aquarium and through its open iron gates and stone archway into the dark round interior. The rest of us quietly followed. We visited the barking seals and giant turtles and electric eels and ran up the balcony to the seahorses and anemones and the million fishes of all colors, all for free, until the police moved on and the coast was clear.

We made much more money than when Mama was selling Toperick's leather bags. And we had chicken every Friday and pot roast every Saturday and Papa's french fries with delicatessen and soda every Sunday, just like before the Depression. And Mama said that my name, "FeygaPinya," made Avrom give me a lot of peanuts and my clever head, "*dayn kliga kup*" she said, found us the peanut bags, and that those two things together put us in the peanut business, so again Feyga and Pinya watched over me and I brought good luck for the whole family.

THE BUTTON THIEF OF EAST 14TH STREET

XI

Lice

I didn't know that lice use a person's head for a nest. I didn't know that lice crawl up a strand of your hair and glue their eggs to it and the eggs hatch baby lice right there on your head. I thought lice were like mosquitoes or cock-a-roaches that land on you by chance, just ordinary bugs that you swat or squash. When I felt a louse crawling around on the back of my neck and picked it off, how should I have known it was my own louse, a louse that lived on me? This important lesson of insect life was brought home to me on my very first day of school, in my very first minutes of kindergarten.

We were lined up against the side wall of an enormous room, boys alongside girls in size places, most of us in all-new outfits. I was marveling at the little oak chairs placed all around two matching tables, at the many jars of crayons on the tables, at the big doll house you could walk into, at the row of giant windows, each with maybe a hundred glass panes. I was in rapture at finally being on the inside of P.S. 188, wearing the brand-new peach crepe dress my mother made for me, and in the same class as my four best friends Celia, Lovey, Enela, and Phyllis, and especially my best friend Celia, who was two places behind me on line.

The teacher clapped her hands twice and sang out, "May I please have your attention?" My first teacher, as pretty as the teachers in the movies.

She said, in that way American-born ladies have of talking to us in sing-song: "Good morning children. My name is Miss Harmon. Each time I say 'Good morning children' you must say 'Good morning Miss Harmon.' Let me hear you say it." We shouted back in the same sing-song, "Good morning

Miss Harmon." Our voices were imprecise, like feet shuffling, revealing that we were new to this way of greeting. Miss Harmon wore a polka-dot navy blue dress with a white collar and a narrow red bow at the throat. She was flat-chested and had finely penciled eyebrows and bobbed hair. I was ready to love her with all my heart.

Miss Harmon walked up to a low platform at the front of the room and sat on a chair facing us. "I will call you up one at a time for inspection. We must make sure none of us has anything that is catching." This she said coyly, as though we all knew it was only a rule, that none of us dear children could possibly have anything that was catching. She made a big show of covering her lap with a paper towel and holding up a pair of wood tongue depressors, one in each hand, like the kind boys used for making double-winged airplanes. "First in line come up please. Hurry please, there are so many of us this morning." I watched as a little round boy in knickers swaggered over, afraid of nothing. She asked him to kneel on the platform. "Open your mouth and say 'Ah.' Let me see your tonsils." She was inspecting tonsils! I felt them swelling up in the back of my throat. My brother Sidney had his tonsils cut out of him before they let him into school. I prayed—please God, I said to myself, please don't let me have swollen tonsils. I turned around to signal my distress to my friend Celia. Celia signaled a "not now I'm busy" reply. She didn't want to miss a moment of the inspections. I tried getting her attention again by opening my mouth and pointing to my throat. I heard "Come up please, quickly now." My turn had already come.

"Open your mouth please, and say 'Ah.'" A tongue depressor landed lightly on my tongue. Miss Harmon lifted her eyes to mine and smiled. There was nothing wrong with my tonsils. Thank you God, I said to myself.

"Well, we certainly have lots of hair this morning. An Alice in Wonderland, aren't we?" I had thick curly-blonde hair that my mother braided at night and combed out into cascading waves in the morning. But why did Miss Harmon call me an Alice in Wonderland? She seemed to be teasing. "Put your head on the towel, please." She parted my hair with the two tongue depressors starting from my left ear and moving toward my right ear while I stared cross-eyed at the white polka dots on her dress and pondered. Maybe I was an Alice in Wonderland because I was not paying attention, because she had to call me to the platform. Then I heard her sing-song voice, now slightly hardened, declare the fatal words: "You have lice." I held still and stopped breathing. The polka dots blurred. "Stand up please." She lifted me by the chin with her tongue depressor. She held me at arm's length with both tongue depressors while she explained to me the natural history of lice and their nits, that nasty name for the eggs. The class murmured and rustled behind me. "Don't worry, dear. I'll give you instructions to bring home to your mother and we'll soon be rid of them, all right dear?" She pointed to an oak chair at the back of the room where I was to sit. "We don't want our lice jumping into other people's hair, do we dear?" she said, and carefully placed the tongue depressors into the waste bin beside her.

I sat on the little oak chair, perfectly still, hoping to be forgotten, wishing I were invisible. I could feel a whole colony of lice creeping around on my scalp. I itched terribly. I folded my hands tight to keep from scratching. I prayed to God for the morning to end, to be released from the oak chair so I could run home.

The time passed slowly. I kept my hands folded and my eyes lowered. I settled into a sort of sleepy trance that helped me not to mind the itching. I discovered that I could raise my

eyelids just enough to watch the class without anyone noticing. I watched the kindergarten children play circle games
and musical chairs and watched them spend a free-time period running in and out of the doll house and building things
with blocks. The neatest girls, like Phyllis, wore cotton plaid
dresses. I saw my best friend Celia reach out for Phyllis's hand.
I watched as they each pulled over a chair in front and sat side
by side while Miss Harmon read a story from a picture book.
It was about three pigs and a wolf that blew their houses down.
When Miss Harmon gave the signal, the children all shouted
the wolf's part, "Then I'll huff and I'll puff and I'll b-l-o-w
your house down." Each time Miss Harmon finished a page
she turned the book around and showed the picture to the
children. Sometimes she would say, "Children at the rear, can
you see?" and lift her arms higher. I didn't raise my head.

After the story, the chairs were returned to the tables for
drawing time. Miss Harmon took a little table out of the dollhouse and placed it in front of my chair at the back of the
room. She set out a paper and some crayons and said I should
draw. Tears blurred my eyes. She didn't move.

I picked up a crayon and swept it back and forth across
the page, pretending to be drawing. She watched for a minute
and went away again. Finally a bell rang twelve o'clock. Class
was over.

I ran home along the edge of the sidewalk, trying to make
my way past the dense crowds of schoolchildren, the page of
instructions folded and refolded and hidden inside my dress
pocket, aware that behind me Celia and Phyllis had begun to
spread the vile words that were sure to catch up with me and
stick to me: "Feygie has lice."

At home, my mother said "I don't need nobody's instructions. What does she think, you're the first one to get lice? Everybody gets lice. Your sister Ruthie got lice when she started

in school. It comes from other children. Come take your dress off, I'll fix you up."

My mother brushed my new crepe dress over the bathtub with a whisk broom and hung it over the towel bar. She left on my cotton slip. She stripped off the bed linens—pillowcases, quilt cover, sheet, mattress cover—and threw them in the bathtub, then she turned on steaming hot water and stomped them down with a stick. She threw open the bedroom window and sprayed the bare pillows, quilt, the mattress, and bedsprings with a Flit gun filled with fly-killer and kerosene. Back in the bathroom she squinched my head under the sink-faucet and scrubbed my hair with brown laundry soap and rinsed with hot water until my scalp burned. She wrapped the family towel around my dripping hair and moved me away from the sink. She reached up to the top of the medicine chest and brought down two strange-looking combs. One was a lice comb, palm-sized, with needle-like teeth along both sides. The other was a nit comb, a block of steel with steel teeth so close together no light could get through. She draped a flannel rag around my shoulders and marched me to the kitchen.

I sat on my knees with my head nestled in her lap. Under her housedress her thighs were plump and soft and had a homey odor, like warm chicken fat. She dragged the lice comb through my wet hair, slowly. It pulled. She pinched off lice from the comb, from my scalp, from the flannel rag. I could hear her cracking them between her thumbnails. Time passed. I felt cold. My scalp felt sore. My shoulders were stiff. My knees hurt. She said, "Another minute. A few more minutes." After a while she switched to the nit comb. It pulled much worse.

"Ow it hurts!"

"I'm almost finished."

I raised my head. "Don't tell Sidney." My brother, who always teased me.

"I won't tell nobody, only Ruthie." My sister, whom I adored.

Ma turned on the radio to WEVD, the Jewish station, named for the Socialist Party leader Eugene V. Debs. A man talked on and on in rapid Yiddish. The only words I could understand were *Forverts*, the Jewish newspaper "Forward," *Manischewitz*, a brand of matzoh, *dertsu*, "furthermore," and *a groysn dank*, "many thanks." At every half hour the station always played the "Internationale" in English:

> *Arise ye prisoners of starvation*
> *Arise ye wretched of the earth*
> *For justice thunders condemnation*
> *A better world's in birth*

Ma was just twisting my hair into two tight braids when Ruthie came home from school at three o'clock and read the teacher's instructions.

"Did you rinse her hair in kerosene?"

"I sprayed kerosene on all the bedding. That's good enough."

"It says you're supposed to cut her hair short, no lower than the ears."

I said, "Ooh, can I have a Buster Brown haircut with bangs, like Phyllis Feldman?" My mother wouldn't hear of it. "Let them keep their instructions. Such a head of hair, so beautiful, *kanayna hura*." She pretend-spit to keep away the spirits of envy. "I'll fix you up better than short hair. Ruthie, get bobbypins from the dresser." She finished my braids and started to pin them over the top in a crown.

"No!" I said, "Stop! That's for old people. I want a Buster Brown."

Ruthie said, "A Buster Brown is only for straight hair. On you it would frizz up, it would just look wild. Mama's right. You're better off with your braids up on top."

I hated my hair, I hated it. I hated my mother. She always kept saying my hair was so beautiful when it wasn't, it was ugly, and she let it get all full of lice without even noticing. She was old and fat, and the dress she made me for school was too fancy, it should have been cotton plaid. She was always making mistakes from being foreign-born. As soon as she finished my braids I got up and ran to the bedroom mirror. I looked foreign-born too, like I just got off the boat. I wanted to chop off all my hair and run away from home.

Next morning Miss Harmon called two other names besides mine, both girls, to come up for what she called re-inspection. I hadn't noticed them yesterday. Their hair was short and oily and reeked of kerosene. When my turn came Miss Harmon wasn't pleased with my long hair pinned up in a crown of braids. She said she couldn't re-inspect it well. She sniffed the air above my head. "Are you sure you soaked your hair in kerosene?"

My heart jumped. I nodded. I was afraid she would call me a liar and put me back in the chair but she just sniffed some more and said, "See me before you leave, I will have a note for your mother. Meanwhile you may join the class."

I went over to my friends. Enela sniffed me and said, "Pyu, I smell kerosene" and made a face. Then the others sniffed and said pyu. I turned and ran into the doll house. I came out at free time and walked around the edge of the room pretending to look at the pictures on the walls. All morning no one came over to me or chose me for a partner. The two other girls with lice were sitting together on little chairs at one of the tables, doing nothing. I stayed away from them.

After school my friends came up to me one after the other, held their noses and tapped me and ran away laughing. I knew I was supposed to play "it" and try to catch them, but I didn't. I walked home alone.

Ruthie read the second note to Mama. "Her teacher wants you to cut her hair short and soak it in kerosene." My mother took me to Doctor Steinmetz. He wrote all over a paper that had his name printed on top. He read out loud: "I have examined Fay Kessler today. She has no lice. Her mother understands how to keep her hair free of lice. There is no need to cut it." My mother nodded and smiled. He signed his full name in big letters at the bottom and rolled a wood-handled blotter over the ink. He winked at me and handed the note to my mother. She reached into her shopping bag and handed him a glistening honeycake topped with sliced almonds.

I brought the doctor's note to Miss Harmon. She looked shocked. "This was not necessary. Because you have no lice today does not mean you cannot become re-infected. There are obviously lice in your home environment. Well, we'll see what we can do." She had stopped calling me "dear."

Miss Harmon sent another note. My mother did not reply. My hair remained tightly braided and pinned up in a crown. I remained free of lice but I didn't try to join my friends. I was mad at them. In the play period I stayed in the back room of the doll house where nobody went, or I walked around the fringes of the classroom.

My mother would undo my crown as soon as I got home. She would comb my hair and make me nice thick braids tied at the bottom with red ribbons. I stayed in the house anyway. I read Sidney's jokebooks or played with the lady doll on the boys' bedspread or fiddled at the piano. Ma wanted me outside. She wouldn't leave me alone. When she forced me to go out and play, I went up on the roof instead and stared down at the boats on the river. Once I saw my boyfriend Joey coming up on the roof with a boy who lived on the top floor. Did Joey know about my lice? I clambered onto the fire escape and sat on the lower steps where he wouldn't see me.

Then one afternoon in the second week of school my best friend Celia rushed into my house all excited. "Phyllis got a Dydee doll and she's giving everybody a turn. Come on!" She took my hand and ran with me to Phyllis's house. Other girls were still coming when we got there. A silent crowd was bent over Phyllis's bed as if it were an operating table. There it was, the Dydee doll. Lovey's sister Goldie was giving it a bottle of water through a hole in its mouth. When the water was all gone she felt the diaper. It was wet. Goldie undid the diaper pins, lifted the doll's bottom, and removed the diaper. We pressed closer to get a look. It had wet through a tiny hole in the left behind. We watched as Goldie fastened on a dry diaper. Phyllis called out, "Who's next?" Wet diapers hung from the bedstead. Phyllis's mother cut out more diapers from a flannel sheet. We stayed all afternoon. I and everyone else entirely forgot about my lice. My self-exile was over.

Back in kindergarten I stopped hiding in the doll house and stopped wandering around the edge of the room. I played with my friends and got chosen in the games and even got a boy to come with me in the doll house and be the father. But I never went up to Miss Harmon. Other children brought their pictures for her to see, or sometimes they just hung around her. They would say, "How old are you Miss Harmon?" or "Do you have a boyfriend?" and she would joke with them. I was jealous. I would say to myself, please God, make Miss Harmon like me.

One day when we were all sitting on the little oak chairs at drawing time, Miss Harmon passed around big sheets of paper and told us to draw the street we live on. I drew tall buildings with windows up to the top and stores at the bottom. I put people on the street, wearing hats. I made a blue sky at the top. Miss Harmon came over and said, "That's very nice, now finish the sky. You have only a thin ribbon of blue at the top, but, you see, the sky comes all the way down to here." She pointed to the line where I made the street. I couldn't do that. People were there. The sky would crush them if it came down to the street. She asked me again. "Do you understand me? Here, take your blue crayon and fill up all this space here." I couldn't explain it to her. She repeated herself. She asked me if I heard her. She sounded mean. I put my crayon down and lowered my head. She walked away. Next day an observer joined the class and I felt her eyes following me. I went back inside the doll house.

School ended the last Friday in June. I didn't have to wake up early any more. I didn't have to tie my braids up like a foreign-born any more. I was free! I spent all summer on the roof in Lavanburg Day Camp and played cards and checkers with my boyfriend Joey and forgot all about kindergarten and Miss Harmon. But waiting in a file in someone's office in P.S. 188 was a report that Miss Harmon had placed on record, observations of my behavior and a recommendation that I be assigned to the ungraded class, the class for the retarded.

It didn't take long for the ungraded teacher to realize I wasn't retarded and get me transferred to the first grade. But I was put in the slowest class, 1A-4. There we sat in rows of chair-and-desk sets fixed to the floor and we studied new words every day and read sentences from a first-grade reader. One day, when it turned out that I was the only one who could pronounce the words "trudge" and "fox's den" correctly, I became best in class and teacher's pet. But I had no friends. My four friends were in 1A-1, the smartest first-grade class. They did their homework together after school and I was left out. Even after I was promoted to the smartest class next term and joined my friends, and even after that, I still felt left out. I felt there was something wrong with me, something lurking in some hidden part of me waiting to be found out and condemned, something like having lice or like seeming foreign-born or like being mistaken for an ungraded.

XII

The Election Night Fire of 1932

In late September of 1932 gangs of boys began piling up wood in their back yards and in vacant lots. They dragged empty crates from the dockside warehouses. They tore down old back-yard sheds. They pulled boards off the windows of stores that had gone out of business. By October the gangs raided each other's piles, and lumber fights broke out all over the Lower East Side.

On Election Night in November the gangs hauled out their loads of wood, dumped them in the middle of their streets, and following tradition, set the wood on fire. On Go-erck Street our block was lit up from one end to the other with mound after mound of burning wood slats. A shouting shoving mob lined the sidewalk on both sides of the street. Orange flames shot up. Their reflections danced wildly across the fronts of the buildings and across the faces of the people watching from open windows. The night sky itself turned orange. Fire engines with their sirens blaring showed up at both ends of our block but surging crowds ran into the street and stopped them. There was fear of a riot.

My father grabbed my hand and pushed his way to my brother Sidney. The three of us ran up the six flights of stairs to our roof at Lavanburg Homes and found places along a row of people leaning over the ledge. My father held me around the waist and we looked way down on the fire from above. The mounds of burning wood turned out to be flaming letters of the alphabet! The letters spelled

R O O S E V E L T

Roosevelt! And he won the election.

XIII

The Pretzel Lady at Union Square

The pretzel lady sat in front of the entrance doors to S. Klein on the Square. She sat near the curb, facing the stream of customers coming out of the world's largest outlet store for discontinued garments, overstock, and samples. She was round, nearly bald, wrinkled as an old apple, and grotesquely wide. Propped up before her on two soda crates was an oversized laundry basket filled with pretzels. More pretzels were piled up on rods all around the rim of the basket.

The pretzels were not like the pretzel sticks sold in candy stores out of tall glass jars, the kind that babies teethed on. These pretzels were plump, soft, fresh-made. They were twisted into a round figure-eight shape. But like the candy store pretzel sticks, they were made from bagel dough and were studded with large salt crystals.

Winter and summer the pretzel lady wore a thick sweater, a ragged shawl, and a coarse wool skirt down to the ground. Over all this she wore a dirty-white canvas apron, its two large pockets sagging with coins.

Her pretzels went for a nickel each. She conducted all her business—collecting money, making change, handing out pretzels—in fingerless men's gloves. The tips of her fingers were black and shiny from handling the coins all day. There was always a crowd around her waiting for a soft pretzel.

Every so often a young man—maybe her grandson— would cruise by in a shiny new car to deliver more pretzels and pick up more coins.

My mother would stop to watch the pretzel lady every time we came out of S. Klein's department store. She said the pretzel lady must have tons of money. She called her a *Var-*

shava ganef, a Warsaw thief, a term of admiration meaning a clever pickpocket or trickster, a *luftmensh*, someone who could pluck a living out of the air. My mother watched the pretzel lady with envy and regret, thinking of how few days of the year she was able to sell peanuts at the Statue of Liberty line in Battery Park. If only she had found a location with a year-round crowd. If only she had thought of selling soft pretzels in front of a big department store. We would all be rich.

XIV
The Dropped Wallet

I was just stepping off the curb with my mother to cross Delancey Street when a man in front of us, rushing for the trolley,
dropped his wallet while getting change out of his pocket. I
picked it up and ran after him. "Mister, Mister, your wallet!"

I reached him just as he got onto the top step. He gave me
a big smile and thanks.

I was so proud of my good deed!

My mother caught up with me as the trolley door closed.
She pinched my arm hard. "What did you do?" she hissed.
"Are we millionaires, to give away money?" She watched with
hungry eyes as the trolley moved off.

"But Mama the wallet was *his*. He *dropped* it."

"How do you know it was his? You think he would tell
you if it wasn't his? A fat wallet, did you see how fat? Who
knows how much money we lost!" She grabbed my hair in her
fist and shook me. "You have no sense! An empty head!"

By the time we got across the street she was still screaming at me and repeating everything and yanking my hair. The
whole crowd around us was staring and smirking. I dug my
nails into her arm and tore myself away and went and hid my
face against a store window, crying in fury and embarrassment.
I said to myself, she'll be sorry. I'll steal a lot of money and get
thrown in jail and she'll have to come get me out.

XV
Smelly Feet

I heard soft footsteps, the knob of my bedroom door turning slowly. I jumped off the window sill a second before my mother came in the room. "What are you doing there in the middle of the night?" she asked. "I'm just going to the bathroom," I lied. I was really just looking at the stars and listening to the sounds of the night.

When I came back from the bathroom Ma was sleeping in our bed, on the other side of Ruthie, head to foot. Next night I told Ruthie, "Mama slept in our bed last night. They're mad at each other again."

"She always sleeps in our bed, didn't you know?"

"She doesn't! Only sometimes."

"Always. She sneaks in about one o'clock and leaves at five o'clock. That's why she's always nodding off in the daytime when she thinks nobody's looking. She sleeps with her feet at my head. She says she doesn't want me to breathe in her breath." She laughed. "So I have to breathe in her smelly feet."

I went to the window and stared down at the street. I wished I could run away to the Hebrew Orphan Home on Second Street and sleep alone in a narrow bed with fresh clean sheets.

"C'mon back to bed," Ruthie said, "I told you to stop worrying. Pa's not going anywhere, believe me. He can't afford to lose his job."

XVI
The Snow-Shoveling Fight

The Depression dragged on, and the bitter cold winters. With every snowstorm an army of the unemployed and the underpaid lined up on the curb alongside the base of the Williamsburg Bridge, waiting to be hired as shovelers by the Department of Sanitation, waiting to be taken out for a four-hour shift and paid twenty-five cents an hour daytime, double for nights. Every twenty feet or so you'd see oil barrels glowing with coal fires, potatoes roasting on improvised grates, men standing in clumps around the barrels, their hands in shredded work gloves held out over the fires, their shoes wrapped in burlap tied with rags, trying to keep from freezing.

On one such night I was fast asleep under our heavy quilt, nestled against my sister Ruthie's shoulder, when I was awakened by an insistent whispering hissing sound like the swish of a snake, mixed in with a loud sharp voice: "No! I said no! Leave me alone!" It was coming from the boys' bedroom. Pa was trying to get Maxie to go shovel snow with him.

Suddenly a shout: "Get outa here! I'm not going. I have a Regents exam tomorrow."

Ruthie was awake, too, listening. She shifted onto her stomach and held her chin in her hands. I heard Ma rushing into the boys' room.

"Leave him alone. He has to go to school tomorrow. He needs the exam for college."

Nine-year-old Sidney, in the same bed as Maxie, bawled, "Hey, shut up everybody. Look it's three o'clock, are you crazy?"

"For college?" Papa said. "He needs the exam for college? What college? Who says he's going to college?"

79

"*I* say," Maxie snapped. "Now get out of here."

"I'm talking two, four dollars for shoveling and you're talking college? You know what four dollars is? In just one night more than half the week's rent. For five years I work nights for the rent after all day in the shop. You think I'm doing this all my life while you go to college? You're sixteen, grown up, you take food, you take shelter, you have to help out!"

Maxie said with scorn, "I don't take a dime from you."

Everyone except Pa knew that Maxie had a job after school.

He was clean-up boy in a chemical factory. He gave Ma half his money and kept half for himself. "*Mayn Mexela*" Ma would sob every payday, "you saved us." If Papa had known, he would have given her that much less and we would be back where we started.

Pa must have put a hand on Maxie to force him out of bed, or something, because suddenly we heard terrible yelling and screaming, Ma shrieking, the sound of furniture bumping and banging, then silence.

Ruthie and I jumped out of bed and peeked out the door. Pa was on the floor of the foyer between the two bedrooms, leaning against the wall, holding his hand to his eye, blood running down his nose! I saw the boys' bedroom door slam shut, and a glimpse of Ma rushing to the bathroom. Ruthie put her arm around me and quietly closed our door and led me back inside. I pressed my face against her to keep from crying. To see Papa on the floor, bleeding! We went back to bed and covered up, each in a separate space. We couldn't even talk about it to each other.

Max wouldn't sit at the kitchen table with us ever again except at Passover seders, and then he only did the required readings from the Hagadah. He ate alone at his secretary desk in the dining room, his back to us. Ruthie and I had to carry his food in from the kitchen, dish by dish. When he finished high school he worked in the chemical factory full time and went to Brooklyn College at night. He and Pa didn't speak to each other for years, not until Maxie said goodbye when he was drafted into the Army and Papa cried while he wished him good luck and a safe return.

Mr. and Mrs. Kessler: The Forced Marriage

XVII

Frank Wing Hand Laundry

Frank Wing Hand Laundry was the best place to warm your fingers and toes while playing in the snow. The tiny store was full of steam. Drops of steam ran down the inside of the store window and watered a baby orange tree on the inside ledge. Our gang would crowd into the narrow aisle. Frank Wing would be ironing shirts on the other side of the counter. His side was caged off by thin wood dowels. Behind him were shelves full of ready-to-go packages. There was just a small opening in the cage for customers to push through their laundry one piece at a time while he wrote out the ticket.

The boys came in a swarm, and as soon as they warmed up they pulled their eyelids into slits and chanted "Chinky-chink Fu Manchu, Chinky-chink Fu Manchu" until they got Frank Wing to pick up his broom and chase them out.

Frank Wing was learning English. He relied on us kids to read notices and name things for him, so he always let the boys come back in. But they took advantage and taught him dirty words. Each time he learned new words he would repeat them to the girls, and each time the girls would have to say, "No, no, don't say that one! That one's a dirty word!"

When I brought in my father's shirts I liked to watch Frank Wing count the prices on the beads of his abacus and write out my ticket in Chinese letters with the tip of his brush. I would linger to watch him hiss up the steam with his tiny iron as he pressed the shirts. His hands were delicate, his motions quick and light. When he swooped up a shirt by its arms and whirled it over to the folding table, he looked like Fred Astaire lifting Ginger Rogers up out of one dip and over into another in their ballroom dances. Behind him, on the apple-green wall above the shelves, were calendars from the Chinatown Businessmen's Association with pictures of brightly rouged Chinese girls surrounded by blossoms. He never took the old calendars down, and now there were six.

If not for Frank Wing Hand Laundry, my father would not have come back home after he ran away.

My father and mother were always fighting over money. There was never enough to run the house. She would say "You need to give me more." He would say "You need to spend less."

One day Uncle Hymie the furrier, while visiting my mother on his tea-rounds, let it slip that my father was paying the rent for his sister Minnie, who got shock treatment for a nervous breakdown and was still too confused to go look for a new job. When my father got home that night, he was hardly through the door before my mother started in.

"You give our money to Minnie! You pay her rent! I know everything!" He ducked down to take off his galoshes.

"What's the matter with you?" he said, eyes to the floor. "I just lent her a few dollars till she gets on her feet."

"Liar! Thief!" she yelled. She followed him to the dining room. "I slave into the night, your daughters do piecework like greenhorns, so your Minnie can rest up her delicate mind?"

Ruthie and I were cutting lace at the dining table. I scrunched down in my chair.

He said, "Listen to me, will you listen to me?" but she kept up such a commotion that he said "Aah, what's the use" and packed his valise and picked up his galoshes and walked out.

When he didn't come home that night or the next night, Ma tried to cover up. She told us he had gone to Canada to help Uncle Hymie at the fur pelts auction. On the third day she secretly went to Mrs. Lindenbaum, the lacework subcontractor, to tell her what happened and plead for more bundles to support the children.

Mrs. Lindenbaum was the most admired woman on the block. She was the first to have started her own business and the first to have bleached her hair blonde. She even smoked in public. She felt a responsibility to the women who worked for her, especially those with runaway husbands. She gave my mother some extra trimming work and promised to increase her bundles.

My father made a mistake, though. He sneaked back to Frank Wing's to get his shirts. Mrs. Lindenbaum was at her window watching for deliveries and she spotted him going into the store. She rushed over to our house to get my mother.

My father didn't have the ticket, and I don't even know if Frank Wing recognized him, I don't think he ever brought in his own shirts. All the laundered shirts were on the shelves, in neat brown paper packages tied with string. No names, just stamped numbers on pink or blue slips of paper. Frank Wing said he couldn't find the shirts without the ticket. My father got into a big argument with him, demanding that Frank Wing open up all the thick packages because he sent him a lot of shirts. Meanwhile, my mother and Mrs. Lindenbaum came running out in the freezing cold in their housedresses. I was across the street with a pile of kids all lined up for a slide down to the corner on our cardboard sleds. I saw them coming: Ma dark and squat with run-down shoes, Mrs. Lindenbaum tall and bony with bouncy blonde curls and pink house-slippers, both women panting and flailing their arms as they tried to keep from slipping on the ice and snow.

They grabbed me and my brother Sidney and started dragging us up the street. Sidney yelled, "What? What's the matter? What did I do?" They looked so wild that the sledding stopped and everybody, children and grownups, followed us to see what was happening.

At the door of the Hand Laundry, with my father still inside arguing with Frank Wing, my mother turned to face the crowd. She called out in mixed Yiddish-English, "Look at him in there. A father you see? A deserter! He's deserting his children! Just look at these beautiful children! He wants to leave them to starve!" I could have died of shame.

The mothers in the crowd shoved their way to the front. One after another they yelled through the door:

"*Aza shanda!*" Such a shame! "*Farshvundener!*" Deserter! "*Geyt shoyn, geyt aheym!*" Go on, go home! Then they chanted in unison, "*Geyt aheym! Geyt aheym! Geyt aheym!*"

My father came out with a fake smile on his face. "What's the matter with you?" he called out to the crowd. "It's all a misunderstanding. My wife and I had a little argument. Nobody's going anywhere. I just went to see my sick mother, and my wife had a misunderstanding." The women kept up the chant. "*Geyt aheym! Geyt aheym! Geyt aheym!*" He stepped off the stoop and came over to take my hand, still trying to smile and look innocent.

Frank Wing, terrified by the uproar outside and by the strange words being hurled through his door, thought a mob was gathering to raid his shelves for my father's shirts. He rushed out with his broom. "Can't give shirts. Can't give shirts. No ticket. No ticket." He saw my father holding my hand. "*She* got ticket!" He pointed at me. "Where ticket?" I stared back at him in total blank confusion.

Ma, Mrs. Lindenbaum, Sidney, me, my father, and the dozen women surrounding him made our way home through the crowd of kids. All of them followed us, everyone asking everyone else, What happened? What happened? One kid said my father was hiding in the store from my mother because he lost her money, another said no, Frank Wing lost his shirts and put the blame on me for losing his ticket, and so on and so

86

on. By the time we got to our building, the kids had combined their snatches and hunches into a story that my father spent all the family's money on his dying mother and then he couldn't get out a white shirt for her funeral because I lost his ticket. My whole gang was lined up on the entrance steps to my building. All my girlfriends were staring at me mournfully. All the boys were yelling with glee, "Boy, are you in trouble. You better find that ticket. You're gonna get some beating."

Mrs. Lindenbaum came upstairs with us. Sidney sneaked back outside. While I was still taking off my galoshes my mother collapsed onto a kitchen chair, moaning. "An *aguna*. He wants to make me an *aguna*." An abandoned wife, the worst disgrace.

Mrs. Lindenbaum blocked my father's escape to the dining room. "*Think*!" She beat a fist in the air. "Think what you *do*! Do you want to *bury* yourself? They will report you to the National *Desertion* Bureau! They will put your picture in the Jewish Daily *Forward*! You could lose your *job*! You could end up on the *Bowery*!"

My father turned red. His eyes and neck veins bulged. He gasped. "I'm choking, I can't take it. I'm choking." He pushed her aside and ran to the bathroom, the only safe room in the house.

Mrs. Lindenbaum turned to my mother. "You'll be all right now," she said with satisfaction. "He'll stay."

I didn't believe her.

Late that night I crept out of bed and curled up on the windowsill. The windowpanes were icy against my side, but I didn't mind. I wanted to sit in the cold moonlight and feel my sorrow. I was going to lose my father. He was a henpecked husband. My mother was nagging him to death. I was going to lose the best french-fried potatoes in the world.

He used to own a delicatessen store on Allen Street before he was married. It went bankrupt but he kept the wavy potato slicer and made us a mountain of french-fries every Sunday: crispy light-brown outside, soft and white inside. I was going to lose the cute wind-up toys he brought home, the newspapers from the subway trash cans with all the comic strips. No more excursions to the parks, no more rowboats and picnics. His jokes and riddles. I pressed my lips together and stifled my sobs so my sister Ruthie wouldn't wake up and find me crying.

Mrs. Lindenbaum was right. He stayed.

XVIII

The Candy Store Across the Street

My mother's two younger brothers, Zalman the junk dealer and Max the milkman, bought a foreclosed farm in the mountains for a song. The bank needed to get rid of it. They planned to collect junk, buy into a milk delivery route, and grow vegetables while their wives raised the children and tended the chicken coops and rented out rooms in summer. Zalman's wife Anna, stolid and silent, was from the Old Country and was used to hard work. Aunt Eva, Max's wife, was a city girl who dressed in style and liked a good time. With tears in her eyes she gave her fur coat to my mother, a three-quarter-length monkey fur that my mother's oldest brother, ShmaFayvl, had bought her years before as an extra wedding present. The coat, with its long black silky strands that swayed as you walked, looked ridiculous on my stumpy little Mama, and she had to keep sewing the skins together, and the lining was in shreds, but she wore it gratefully against the winter cold.

Some crabby neighbor, probably a Republican, snitched to the Home Relief Bureau. An investigator rang the bell.

"We have a report that you bought a fur coat while you were receiving money from the State of New York as a needy family. Will you please allow me to see your clothes closets?"

My mother walked her to the girls' bedroom, took the monkey fur off the pile of coats on the sewing machine, and threw it at her feet.

"Here, I give you this *shmata* for a present. Let me see *you* wear it!"

And that's how we were thrown off Home Relief and lost seven dollars a week.

We couldn't make out without the seven dollars. It wasn't even enough. My father's garment factory got shut down in the Depression. His part-time job as a janitor at Lavanburg Homes didn't bring in a dime; it was for working off the rent. For a little extra money on the side my mother bought toy American flags from the Betty Boop store on Ludlow Street and my father sold them at parades. He took Sidney to sit up on his shoulders and wave two flags above the crowd. And my mother took me to sell peanuts with her at the Statue of Liberty line in Battery Park. She kept the peanuts hidden in two leather shopping bags and I sold them from my own wicker basket. I wore Mama's big shawl from Russia so I could cover the basket when cops came by because we didn't have a license to peddle.

But we could only sell flags and peanuts on weekends and holidays and only in good weather. The rest of the time we had just the Home Relief money and a little rush-work my father sometimes picked up from his friend Mister Toperick who made the shopping bags. "What I need now to make out," Mama said, "is a regular full-time job. Only Feyga is in the way."

I was six years old, in first grade, when my mother threw the monkey fur at the Home Relief investigator. Before Mama could go look for a full-time job she had to find someone to take care of me when I came home from school. My brother Sidney, age seven, went straight from school to the Jewish Center on Stanton and Essex streets, where he studied for his Bar Mitzva, which would make him a man at age thirteen. My sister Ruthie, already thirteen, had after-school activities with her friends and Mama wouldn't let her give up her life to stay home with me. Fifteen-year-old Maxie went his own mysterious ways. We never saw him before supper. My father dressed and left the house every morning as if he were going to work even while he was the janitor. Ma said he sat all day in the coffee houses with his friends. He never came back home before supper either.

I said, "Mama, I can be home by myself. Just give me a key and I'll go right home and stay in my bedroom, I promise."

"Remember what happened to your friend Phyllis when she wore a key from her neck? Remember how she got a hundred and four degrees in fever and almost died from pneumonia till somebody came home?"

I remembered that time. I was in the vigil under her window when Doctor Steinmetz stepped out of the building with his satchel and said the crisis was over.

"And remember down Goerck Street the four Italian girls what got burnt up from playing with matches?"

I remembered that also. Their bodies were found under the bed, piled up together. My gang got on line to see them in their coffins in the window of the Grand Street Funeral Home. Their faces were made of wax with painted-on eyebrows and shiny red lips. It was in the Daily News, front page. The mother had just run out to the store for a second and she got all the blame. They said she wanted to kill herself except she was Catholic and it was not allowed.

I said, "So let me play outside. When it rains I can sit on the steps in the hall. My friends do it." She said, "Leave the stupid mothers to take a chance with their young ones. Who knows what can happen next?"

A full-time job came up suddenly through my mother's second-eldest brother, AlyaLeyb, a trembly mouse whose name means "lion" in Hebrew and "lion" in Yiddish. He had been dressed as a girl in Russia to escape service in the Tsar's army but he was found out and drafted anyway. With that miserable exception from which he barely escaped in one piece,

AlyaLeyb's only job in his life was as house-painter's helper to their eldest brother ShmaFayvl.

But now there wasn't enough work for the two of them so ShmaFayvl let him go. ShmaFayvl, who lived in expensive Washington Heights and whose son was studying to be a lawyer, fired his own brother who had to support a wife and two growing children. Nobody dared to tell my grandmother.

While Mama brought a big jar of chicken and soup to his wife Pulla and showed her how to apply for Home Relief, AlyaLeyb went to 14th Street, and starting at Avenue D and going blindly from store to store on both sides of the street for more than seven long avenues, by some miracle found a job all by himself, in the Automat just before Union Square, clearing used dishes off the tables onto trays and placing the trays onto the dumbwaiters. He was there less than a week when just at suppertime he rang our doorbell like a fire alarm, making us all jump and run to pick up the newspapers covering the floor, but before we could hide them he burst into the kitchen quivering with excitement. He had found my mother a job where he worked! A second miracle!

The job was in the basement, taking the trays off the Automat's dumbwaiters, scraping off the garbage, and stacking up the dishes for the dishwasher men. The woman who had been doing it had an accident and she was taken away by ambulance. In the midst of that commotion AlyaLeyb, who could hardly speak a dozen words of English, had found the courage to step up to the boss and recommend my mother.

In the morning my mother went with me to Mister Seltzer's candy store across the street to ask if just this once would he please let me stay in the store after school until she got home. He said sure, I could sit at the table in the back. She paid for a double-scoop chocolate malted. She made me promise to go straight from school to the candy store and stay in the back out of the way of customers and drink up the whole malted until she came for me.

At three o'clock I squeezed past the crowd of boys in the front part of the candy store and I sat down at the table with my pencil box near where the back room started.

The tabletop was white porcelain with blue-checked triangles in the corners, just like the table we had at home. Beyond the table was the pinball machine and after that was the telephone booth and then the back room started.

Across the narrow aisle from where I sat was the mahogany-and-glass case where I could look as long as I wanted at the beautiful women and the noble men on the cigar boxes, at the celluloid cupie dolls, at the rubber balls, the yoyos, Hi-Lo paddle sets, marbles, jacks, jump ropes, pick-up sticks, chalk, and an opened box of balloons in all colors.

After the three o'clock crowd emptied out and the store was quiet, Mister Seltzer brought me my malted. He poured it from the polished steel mixer into two tall glasses and set down two straws. While I was struggling to drink it all, Nelly, old Missus Heinbach's Irish setter dog, came in by herself carrying a change purse in her teeth. Mister Seltzer took the purse and gave her a rolled-up Daily Mirror in its place. She held the newspaper daintily between her teeth and went back out.

All my life I had seen Nelly tiptoeing along the street from the corner building with a change purse in her mouth and coming back with a newspaper in her mouth. This was the first time I saw how the trick worked. Mister Seltzer looked at me. "Do you go to the grocery store for your mother?" I said yes. It was a few doors away.

"Then do me a favor and take this pocketbook over there. It has an order from Missus Heinbach."

I skipped out with Nelly's change purse and watched as the grocer filled a brown paper bag with the order. He took money from the purse, dropped the purse into the paper bag, and his delivery boy took the bag and left the store, Nelly following with the newspaper still in her mouth, back to Missus Heinbach's corner building. So then I learned the whole trick.

When I finally finished my malted, Mister Seltzer took the two glasses away and brought over a Shirley Temple coloring book with a torn cover. He told me to keep it. I spent the next while coloring with the six crayons from my pencil box.

Sometimes the store was empty and sometimes customers came in all the way up to my table. In my part of the store, only a few grown-up men went past me to the back room and only a few boys clumped around the pinball machine.

The telephone rang. A man from the back room answered it. He called out to the boys at the pinball machine, "Who wants to get Rozzie Harris, F32?" The letter F was the name of a Lavanburg building and the number 32 meant the third floor second door. The two youngest boys jostled each other. The man chose one and told the other, "You'll go next." Miss Harris came running to the phone without a coat, her hair in curlers. You only got five minutes and then the nickel was up and the caller had to deposit another nickel. I could see her through the glass door of the telephone booth, twisting her shoulders and making all kinds of facial expressions while she talked into the speaker, so I knew it was a date. When she hung up she gave the boy a tip.

I had to go to the toilet. I raised my hand like I had learned to do in school, until Mister Seltzer noticed me. "May I please leave the room?" He said, "Go in the back. It's after the sink."

In the back room, the men were playing cards. They were tossing pennies in the kitty to start a round of poker. One guy watched with his chair turned backwards, his chin on his folded arms. Another guy was leaning against a wall of soda cases. I had to squeeze past between them. I said, "Please excuse me," which I had also learned in school. The man against the soda cases said to the man in the chair, "You hear the kid? Why don't you ever excuse yourself, eh?" When I came out of the toilet the first man was in the game. He called out, "C'mere kid, sit next to me and bring me luck." He showed me his hand. No matching pairs, no high cards. But instead of folding the hand, he kept the three diamonds and discarded two cards. He drew two more diamonds for a flush and won the pot. He said, "Hey, you really brought me luck," and he slid two pennies in front of me with his fingertips. I scooped them into my coat pocket. His name was Babe. Every time Babe won he slid some pennies in front of me. Then the other winners got into the spirit and slid pennies my way too. Sometimes the pot was big and I got a nickel.

When my mother came for me, Mister Seltzer said I was no trouble at all, I could stay in the store after school every day if she wanted. She paid for the next day's double-scoop chocolate malted and he put the Shirley Temple coloring book behind the counter for next time.

Upstairs I told my mother about the back room and showed her both of my coat pockets stuffed with coins. "*Ay, ay,*" she laughed, "*a kliga kup.*" A clever head. "From my mother's iron milk I made a girl with an iron head." She knocked on my head as if to knock on wood for good luck, and she said *kunahora* and pretend-spit at me three times, "*ptu ptu ptu,*" to make me seem worthless so as not to attract the Evil Eye of Envy. "Keep the money for yourself," she said. "Save up for your own expenses. That will be the biggest help."

Then she gave me a tin Swee-Touch-Nee Tea treasure box and said to keep it in the dresser drawer behind the underwear. She said, "Don't tell nobody you make tips. Nobody needs to know your business." Then she said, "Listen to me. Don't spend none of this money in the store. Mister Seltzer also don't want to know."

Next day in the candy store, Babe and Sugar, the guy who had been leaning against the soda cases, were the only ones in the back room. Sugar said, "Hey, kid, I'm gonna show ya somethin'. I'm gonna teach you solitaire. Once you know solitaire, you don't need to wait for nobody to come along. You can play by yourself."

"If he teaches you," Babe said, "you're gonna lose, guaranteed. Sugar is the biggest loser. You shoulda seen him lose last night."

"What are ya yappin' about?" Sugar said. "If I didn't lose last night you wouldn't have a dime today."

The telephone rang. Babe looked up at the clock. There were phone calls at certain times that he wanted to answer himself.

This time he said to me, "Go ahead, kid, take the call, make yourself some tips. Do you know how to find apartments?" I nodded yes. I stood on the milk box to reach the receiver. "Hello?" The operator said, "I have a call for Miss Beverly Cohen at 126 Goerck Street, Apartment C43." That meant the C building fourth floor third door. I ran to the building, rang the downstairs bell, and yelled while I ran up the staircase, "Beverly Cohen, telephone!"

She flew past me before I reached the fourth floor. After Miss Cohen finished her call she gave me two cents. I took another call until the pinball-machine boys came in, then Babe came out of the back room and told them I was included in taking turns. The boys told me if somebody gave only a penny, not to call them to the telephone any more.

I went back to playing solitaire with Sugar. "Why do they call you Sugar?" I asked.

"Because I'm sweet."

"Because he's *mishuga*, crazy," Babe said. "You're Jewish, right? You know that word *mishuga*? That's his real name, Shuga for short, ha ha ha."

"Ask him why he's called Babe. Because of his mentality, ha ha ha."

More men came in: Farmer, Mike, and Peewee, who was really the biggest. The poker game started up. Farmer said to come sit next to him. Sugar, leaning against the soda cases again, said, "Ask him how he got the name Farmer. Because he's saving up for a farm. A horse farm. Go ahead, kid, bring him luck, he needs it."

I got tips out of every pot and extra money when Farmer won, besides the telephone tips. I went home with full pockets.

Every day was the same in the candy store, but new things happened also. When I finished the Shirley Temple coloring book, Mister Seltzer gave me a book of cut-out Paris fashion dolls and a pair of scissors. One day Nellie came in the rain and Mister Seltzer put her newspaper in a paper bag. Once my boyfriend Joey came by while I was on my way back from the grocer, and I treated us both to the moving picture in the nickelodeon machine before going back inside. You put two pennies in the slot and then you look through the metal peep-box while you turn the handle on the side of the machine. The handle flips picture cards over a roller and that makes them move just like the movies. You go as fast or slow as you want. I took the first turn. I saw a beautiful hula dancer with very long hair. She had on a grass skirt and a necklace of flowers over her bust, and as she wiggled, her necklace swayed and her thighs split her grass skirt right up to the waist and you almost saw her private parts.

Then it was Joey's turn. He giggled and said it was a dirty picture show. I gave him a knuckle punch in the arm and ran back into the candy store.

By the end of the week my treasure box was almost full. I had more than three and a half dollars. My mother took my coins and gave me four one-dollar bills. She said, "It's a tip from me included, to give you a good start."

On Saturday after the Cannon Street movies I went to Clinton Street with my sister Ruthie and I bought myself black patent leather tap-dance shoes with grosgrain ribbons, and white lisle socks to go with them. The taps on the shoes were thick and shiny bright. The grosgrain ribbons tied into big bows that didn't come undone. The socks didn't wrinkle and slip under my heels. The shoes and socks together cost two dollars and fifteen cents. I put a dollar bill back in the treasure box and I put the coins, eighty-five cents, back in my pocket for spending money.

On Sunday I put on my dazzling new tap-dance shoes and white socks and ran outside to look for my gang.

I rounded up Celia, Enela, Phyllis, and Lovie for frankfurters and soda, my treat, at Belitz's delicatessen, three blocks away on Rivington and Cannon streets. We linked arms five across. And for the first time in my life I was in the middle, clicking the pavement smartly with my tap-dance shoes instead of stumbling along at the edge of the curb getting a shove or a punch from people who would get mad at us for taking up the whole sidewalk and forcing them into the gutter.

All the way to Belitz's deli we sang at the top of our lungs "The Song of the Goerck Street Girls." The song had been passed along from the last Irish girls who moved off the block to the first Jewish girls who moved in.

In Jersey City where I did dwell
A butcher's son I loved so well
He stole my heart away from me
And now he thinks no more of me.

He sits the girls upon his knee
And tells them things he won't tell me
And now I know the reason why
Because they have more gold than I.

Gold can vanish and silver can fly
And then they'll be as poor as I
As poor as I they'll never be
Till apples grow on the cherry tree.

I wish, I wish, I wish in vain
I wish I were sixteen again
Sixteen again I'll never be
Till apples grow on the cherry tree.

My life in paradise was not to last. One day a girl from my building ran up to me in the candy store and said my mother wants me home. I found her sitting in a chair in the middle of the kitchen with blood sploshed all down her slip and a blood-soaked bandage on her head. I dropped to my knees. "*MA-MAH!*"

"Don't worry it's nothing," she said, "I have a case!" Her eyes gleamed and her face was lit up with joy. "I have a good case! A lawyer is coming, it could be worth hundreds!"

"Mama, what *happened*? You're *bleeding!*"

"Don't worry I'm all right. The *bestias* wouldn't even call an ambulance, they sneaked me to their own doctor not to make a case. They'll find out who they're dealing with! I will sue them for plenty."

"Mama, who *did* it? What *happened*? *Tell* me!"

"Excuse me I'm all excited. The trays from the Automat fell on my head. They tumbled down from the dumbwaiter and the knifes and forks stabbed into my head while I was leaning in to take out a tray, the same thing what happened to the lady before me."

I started to cry.

"No, no, there's nothing to cry for, it looks worse than it is. I don't even feel it. I'm just waiting to take pictures." She sat up rigid in the chair as if she were already posing before the camera. "You want something to eat? Go look in the refrigerator."

"I'm not hungry."

"Nobody has to know what happened, you hear? Bite your tongue. It should stay between you and me and Ruthie. Don't mention to Papa, all right? Ah, do I have a case! At least maybe three hundred."

Soon after, the lawyer came in with a photographer. They took pictures, then the lawyer went downstairs and phoned for an ambulance. Ma said to me, "Don't worry, you hear? Be good. Go play in your room. Ruthie will come home any minute."

The ambulance men came with a stretcher and put a gray blanket over my little Mama and took her away. The lawyer and photographer went with them, carrying a paper shopping bag she had prepared in advance for the trip to the hospital. I waited alone in the kitchen, my lips shivering, scared she would bleed to death.

When Ruthie finally came home I rushed at her bawling, "Mama was taken in a ambulance. Bleeding from her head."

Before I even started to say what happened Mama was back in a fresh housedress and a kerchief over her hair, tied at the back of her neck. She told Ruthie the whole story from the beginning all the while they both started getting supper ready as if nothing happened.

I didn't have to wait for my mother in the candy store any more. She couldn't work at a regular job until after the lawyer had claimed damages. I went anyhow, almost every day, until spring lured me away and I gave up the money for the freedom of the street. When I did show up in the store Babe made the pinball-machine boys give me turns on the telephone run. Sugar, Farmer, and all the other guys were always glad to see me but I didn't sit in with them at the poker games. It's different when you're just visiting.

Early next winter my uncles Max and Zalman came back from the mountains with Eva, Anna, and their children. They got apartments near each other in Brooklyn and started up their old businesses again. People who knew them from the mountains said they had nearly starved and the bank took back the farm.

Aunt Eva came to visit. My mother had a surprise welcome-home present for her: the monkey fur coat, restitched and relined in red satin by Hymie the furrier, my uncle on my father's side. "It's too much," Aunt Eva said, in tears again. "Your mother is an angel," she said. "You have no idea. Did she tell you how she rescued us?" My father was in the next room. My mother blinked her eyes and twisted her lips at Eva, which I knew was her signal not to mention it, not to say another word. And I never heard another word about the three hundred dollars my mother had said she would get from her case.

XIX
The Death of Baba

On a freezing cold day in January I got home from school to find Baba in my bed, the bed I shared with my sister Ruthie. She was lying under the huge feather quilt that came with her from Russia. The quilt—called the *iberbet*, "overbed"—had been taken out of the dining room closet behind the piano. Our American quilt was folded up on top of the sewing machine. Baba's body made no impression under the billowing feathers. Her small round head was sticking out at the top of the *iberbet* like a broken-off doll's head. Her brown hair looked fake on top of her pale face. She lay at the wrong end of the bed, the way Ruthie and I did in order to see out the window. Light barely entered through the steamy fog made by the warm room on the cold window panes.

Baba turned her head to me and smiled. "*Fey*gela," she said, pronouncing my name like a caress. Her hand came out from under the *iberbet*. I took it. She drew me toward her and said, "One two tree push*kutt*i." We used to beg her, "Baba, say spaghetti," and she would say "One, two, tree," as if preparing to jump into cold water, and then "pushKUTTi," making it come out like a sneeze. We would laugh and clap our hands, and she would laugh with us. She knew no English and never had much else to say to me, though she always patted my head and gave me poppyseed cakes and two pennies.

When I was very little she would let me climb onto her lap and play with the pea-sized growth at the inner corner of her eye. I can remember her playing with my fingers, wiggling each finger in turn, starting with the thumb, as she pronounced in Russian:

Sorinka, sorinka, ootsi kootsi porinka

103

At "porinka" she'd reach my pinky, then continue in Yiddish:

Meezela mayzela, meezela mayzela

"Little mouse, little mouse," as her fingers walked up my arm.

Kut kut kut kut kut as she tickled my neck.

Now that I was seven and losing my baby teeth, I would bring along a tooth when my mother took me to visit her on 8th Street. She would circle the palm of my hand with it as if she were casting a spell, and she would say,

Meezela mayzela Meezela mayzela
Na dir a beyndela Git mir on ayzena

Little mouse, little mouse,
Here is a bone tooth Give me an iron tooth

She would put the tooth in a glass jar marked with my name and she would put a nickel in my hand. These few words are all I remember my dear Baba saying to me, my Baba who was, more than anyone I have ever seen, just like the round-bottomed jolly Russian doll who could never be knocked down and who has inside her another doll, then another, and another.

That night I had to wait up while everyone decided where Ruthie and I were supposed to sleep now that Baba was in our bed. Maxie and Sidney, my brothers, had the big bedroom and shared the other bed. My father and mother slept in the dining room in a folding bed. They rolled it out on its wheels at night from behind our girls' bedroom door. That night Ruthie slept with my mother in the folding bed, my father slept with the boys three to a bed, and Mama made a bed for me in the kitchen. She placed pillows on three kitchen chairs alongside the sink, alternating the chair backs like musical chairs to keep me from falling out. Then she gave me Baba's maroon shawl for a blanket, the very shawl that Baba had wrapped around Mama when she was a little girl in Russia.

We had mice in the kitchen. I could hear them scuttling, and I was afraid to fall asleep. A small lightbulb stuck straight out of the wall over the sink; it was always kept on all night. I played with staring at it, shutting my eyes to see a round green moon, and staring at it again.

Mama woke me early next morning to take the chairs away. "I have to get ready for Doctor Steinmetz," she said. I finished sleeping at the kitchen table with my head on my folded arms.

After school next day I went straight to the bedroom to my Baba. Her bed had been pushed closer to the window and up against the dresser, making space for a chair and for an end-table full of sick-bed supplies. Baba reached for my hand. I climbed up onto the bed and we kissed.

"Should I sing *Papirossen?*" I asked.

"*Yeh, yeh. A zisela kind*"—a sweet child.

It was my best song, about an orphan boy who sells cigarettes in the rain and sleeps on a park bench. I knew all the stanzas.

When I came back from my friend Celia's house at supper-time, no one was in the kitchen. Just inside the door of Baba's room, on the floor, I saw leeches on a newspaper, each wriggling in a blot of blood. Doctor Steinmetz was leaning over Baba, pulling off a leech from behind her ear. He dropped it onto the newspaper and poured salt on it. Blood flowed into the salt and onto the newspaper as the leech shriveled and died. There were more leeches in a jar. Mama was standing by the bed. Ruthie, too. I think Maxie might have been on the sewing machine bench. Ma said to me, "Doctor Steinmetz is thinning Baba's blood to make her feel better." Her voice was confidential, almost obscene, as if she were talking about woman-troubles. She told me I was to go to Aunt Becky's house, on Papa's side of the family, till Baba gets better, that Sidney had already been sent to Uncle AlyaLeyb. Mama said I should be a good girl, listen to everyone, and eat what they give me, and when I come back she'll take me to the movies.

A small cardboard valise was already packed for me. I didn't even take my hat and coat off because Papa was waiting to walk me over to Aunt Becky's.

I didn't go up to Baba to kiss her because of the leeches on the newspapers, and because she had her eyes almost closed and her mouth open and was breathing with sounds. I ran out of the bedroom and out of the house ahead of Papa.

Uncle Hymie Goldberg, Aunt Becky's husband, had a fur store in the same building as their house. They lived on Willett Street on the other side of the Williamsburg Bridge. I used to stay in Hymie's store while my father went visiting upstairs, because my mother was mad at Papa's family and didn't want her children to be friends with them, not even with my other grandmother. But she was good friends with Hymie because she knew him from before.

I would always make Papa stop outside first so I could look in the fur store window. A bushy-tailed fox on a tree limb stared out at me in the early evening dusk, its brown glass eyes glowing in the lamppost light. A green-eyed lynx crept along a green carpet. A plaster-haired dummy with pointy red lips and white teeth wore a Persian lamb coat. A squirrel sat up in front of her painted shoes.

Aunt Becky answered the downstairs bell from the open door of her apartment one flight up. I ran up the steps and stood in front of her. She took me through her entrance foyer to the front room on the left and showed me where I was to sleep, on a large plush sofa with a crocheted throw that she told me to use for my blanket.

I looked at the walls around me. They were filled with my cousin Henry's black velvet paintings of Palestine: palm trees and domed houses, hills.

Some paintings had an orange sunset, some had a yellow crescent moon in a purple sky. Through the open front-room door on the right, on the other side of the foyer, I could see all four of my Kessler cousins, all grownups, sitting around the kitchen table playing cards. Aunt Becky told me the bathroom was at the end of the foyer. "We have business to talk over in the kitchen," she said, "so I will leave you now. Sleep well." She shut my door. I forgot to tell her I didn't have supper.

I opened my valise and saw my next day's dress and panties, an extra sweater, my toothbrush, two safety pins, and extra rubberbands for my stockings. There was also a towel. That meant I shouldn't use their family's towel.

That night I slept, as usual, in the slip and undershirt I had worn during the day. We didn't have pajamas or nightgowns or bathrobes in my house, and except for panties and socks I only changed my underwear at Saturday bath time. I had to lie still on Becky's couch to keep from mussing my long hair because I couldn't comb and braid it by myself.

I dressed very early next morning, while it was still dark, so as not to be seen in my slip. I listened to the clip-clop of the horses bringing milk and coal down the street, and the put-put of a car trying to start up in the cold. I watched one painting after another come to life as daylight gradually entered the room.

I waited for Aunt Becky to open the door.

After everyone else had gone to work, and I had gone to the bathroom, Aunt Becky brought me into the kitchen for a breakfast of orange juice, Rice Krispies with milk and banana, and chocolate milk with a graham cracker. Back in the living room I looked through some picture magazines and again at the paintings. Then I sat up on my knees at one of the two window seats and watched the street. A horse-and-wagon waited at the curb. Sparrows were flitting down to peck at the oats in the horse droppings. Snow began to fall again.

I loved the silence of Aunt Becky's front room. I loved having a day off school and being by myself with no one calling me to do things. I didn't think it odd that I was left alone. In those times children didn't expect grownups to provide things for their amusement. I didn't know that I was being set apart out of respect for my dying Baba, that I was being protected from the unseemliness of playing or having fun while she was passing away. Although I hoped Uncle Hymie would invite me down to his store, it would be rude to ask. I didn't know that he had been traveling all night long to my Baba's other five children, first trudging through the snow to my mother's brother AlyaLeyb on East 4th Street, then to Mama's younger sister Dora on East 8th Street, and then by subway to Brooklyn to her younger brother Zalman and the youngest brother Max, then way over to Washington Heights in upper Manhattan to her eldest brother ShmaFayvl, waking up one after another and sending them all to Baba's bedside.

Then Uncle Hymie got off the subway at 14th Street and walked back through the snow to 8th Street to call on Baba's synagogue attendant, Baba's next-door neighbor, and the secretary of Baba's Friendship Society, then back to my house to sit with Mama and hold her hand.

For lunch I had tunafish on rye bread and tea with a raisin biscuit. Aunt Becky gave me tea the grown-up way, in a glass, stirring in the sugar cube with a spoon. At home I took tea from a saucer, sipping it through a sugar cube between my teeth. From then on, I always took my tea in a glass.

In the afternoon Aunt Becky took me to an upstairs apartment to visit my other grandmother, BashaLeya, whom we called "Baba from Willett Street," or "Baba on Papa's Side." Aunt Becky brought me into the dining room and said, "Mama, here's Benny's daughter Fay," and left me. Papa's Baba sat in a corner by the window, in a tall armchair. I had to walk all the way around the dining table to get to her. The table, of polished mahogany, filled most of the room. Tall mahogany dining chairs, their high backs upholstered in tapestry, were tucked in all around the table. White lace runners covered the bureau and end tables. Photographs in fancy silver frames stood on them. More photographs were in the china closet with the glassware. Baba BashaLeya sat in her armchair, a welcoming smile on her face. The sun shone in through the snow, casting light on her corner of the room, on her thin white hair, on the fine lace shawl around her shoulders, on the doily and cut-glass bowl on the table beside her.

"Kenst du redn eedish?" she asked. Can you speak Yiddish? *"Yeh, Baba, ikh red a bisl nor ikh farshtey a sakh."* I speak a little but I understand a lot. With a nod and a graceful hand she offered me a Hershey's kisses from the bowl. I unwrapped the silver paper carefully, and put the chocolate in my mouth carefully, afraid I might smear my fingers. She took the silver paper from me and set it in a china bowl, also on her table. She said, "Take one for later." I didn't know whether to take it because she was my grandmother or refuse it politely because I was company. She smiled and put the second kisses in my pocket. Then she held onto one side of the armchair and lifted herself up and took me by the hand to see the photographs. I saw graduation pictures of the cousins who lived downstairs. My father in a straw hat and bow tie. A portrait of herself in a high lace collar. Another of my grandfather, my Zeyda from Willett Street, next to a bookstand with his elbow resting on the book. Only my Zeyda, with his short pointed beard, looked like the same person I knew. I would sometimes be

109

able to watch him from the women's balcony of the Willett Street synagogue as he stood below, praying next to my father. In other photographs I saw boys in velvet vests and knee pants, girls in sailor dresses, grownups in stately black suits or long skirts.

As my lovely Baba from Willett Street pointed out my relatives on my father's side, I listened to her melodious Yiddish, so unlike any other Yiddish speech I knew. Her consonants were soft and flowed into her vowels.

I felt privileged to be alone with her, to have her speaking directly to me. At the china closet she opened the glass door and took out a small oval portrait, faded and creased. "This is my mother," she said. "Your father's Baba. She is gone a long time, may she rest in peace. I used to miss her like a stone was in my heart, *vie a shteyn in hartz,* but now I have my loving memories." Then I asked, almost whispered, the question that never got answered:

"Where did she go, Baba?"

"She is with all good souls, who knows where, waiting for the *Meshiyakh* to come." She put the portrait back in the china closet.

BashaLeya. I said her beautiful name to myself over and over. Later I gave her name to the beautiful lady doll on the boys' bedspread, and still later to my beautiful daughter.

The next night I had supper in the kitchen with the family. Big portions of breaded veal chops, mashed potatoes, green peas for everyone. Seltzer, pickles, and sauerkraut on the table. Apple shtrudel waited in the corner for tea. All four cousins were there—Max the good one, Ruby the bum, Fay the teacher, and Henry the hunchback. I knew all of them from listening while Uncle Hymie talked with my mother on his tea rounds. Fay said, "Come sit next to me. We have the same name." I sat between her and Henry. I liked him because he was famous—his velvet paintings were on sale in all the furniture stores on Grand Street—and because his hunchback made him almost as small as me.

My cousins spoke little, mostly about the snow coming down, and the men started their card game before the dishes were off the table while Fay passed around the shtrudel on plates with pretty flower designs and Aunt Becky brought out nuts and wrapped candies. Max lit up a large pipe. Ruby smoked a cigarillo. Then Fay joined the card game. She and Henry had separate packs of Old Gold. I proudly struck the matches and lit their cigarettes for them.

My father came for me the next afternoon. He couldn't stay for a glass of tea. He explained that we had to be home early, before Friday *Shabbas*. We packed my valise and I kissed my Aunt Becky goodbye.

Outside it was snowing harder. On the way along Willett Street, Papa asked if I had a good time in Becky's house, and what had I done there. It was nice to be able to talk freely again. I felt like skipping. But he wasn't listening, and rushed us on.

Crossing under the Delancey Street bridge we saw the snow-plow trucks of the Sanitation Department moving out of their garage. On Rivington Street the pushcart peddlers were flinging heavy covers over their drygoods and produce. As we turned the corner of Willett into Stanton Street, a gust of sharp snow blew in our faces. Five more blocks: Sheriff, Columbia, Cannon, Lewis, Goerck.

I couldn't wait to get home. I remembered that my mother had promised to take me to the movies. I loved going to the movies with Mama. We went at night. That's when they gave every customer a piece from a set of dishes and put on the lights between pictures so we could buy candy and play Bingo, and we walked back very late through empty streets, holding hands like friends.

At home, Papa and I were stamping the snow off our feet in the vestibule when Mama opened the dining room door and stood there in the threshold, her face lifeless. "Feygela," she said, "I have to tell you. Baba died yesterday." Behind her I saw a crowd of relatives and strangers, sitting and standing everywhere, all of them staring at me. "I don't care," I screamed. "I want to go to the movies! You promised! You promised!" I stamped my feet and cried like a baby in a tantrum. Mama tried to shush me. Then Ruthie came out and yanked me into the kitchen and shut the kitchen door. My shame at myself made it harder for me to stop.

The house emptied out soon after, everyone hurrying to be home by sundown because it was forbidden to be traveling on *Shabbas*. In the kitchen, Ruthie set out the funeral meal brought over by Baba's Friendship Society. She sent me to the dining room for the wine. Mama was sitting in the middle of the room on a milkbox, in an old housedress and stocking feet, hugging herself and swaying. The dining room table was pushed against the far wall, the chairs lined up against the near wall. I grabbed the wine bottle and rushed back to Ruthie. Papa yelled to Mama from the kitchen, "Come get up and light the candles. You're not allowed to sit *shiva* on Shabbas." No answer. Ruthie lit the candles.

Papa told us that besides the seven days of *shiva* Mama had to be in mourning for thirty days of *shloshim,* which meant no music or weddings and the bedroom where Baba died had to be closed. I would have to sleep on the chairs in the kitchen with the mice all month long. I thought it was fair punishment for my acting like a baby in front of everyone, and I promised myself never to complain about anything ever again.

Ruthie and I cleaned the house spotless on Saturday. We covered all the mirrors with a paste made with Bon Ami scouring powder and water because Mama was not allowed to see her reflection. On Saturday night, *shiva* started. Until Thursday at sundown Mama sat on her milkbox while Pa left the front door open for visitors. They took off their galoshes and shoes in the hallway, walked in without greetings, put a dish of food or a bottle of whisky on the dining room table, put their coats on the backs of their chairs— some of them folding chairs borrowed from the neighbors—and sat down, all in silence. One at a time they took the chair beside my mother's milkbox to share a remembrance of Baba. With each new visitor Ma had ready a fresh gush of tears. "I lost my best friend, my best friend."

In that week of *shiva* I learned of the Baba I never had a chance to know. Her name was HayaReyzl. She was born in 1872. She had been a girls' Hebrew teacher in Russia. In summer on warm Saturdays she would sneak her pupils out from behind the curtained women's section of the synagogue and swim naked with them in the stream. I learned that she sold potatoes and chickens from her backyard garden to Gypsies, that she spoke Romany, the Gypsy language, and that when my Zeyda wasn't home she got my mother to sing Gypsy songs at the window and draw customers with her voice like a bell. In America, Baba earned good tips in the cemetery by leading mourners in the graveside memorial prayers. She was the only woman who dared to compete with the bearded scholars waiting at the gate, and she was the most in demand. And when my mother had to work on Saturdays to get a job, Baba consoled her. "God understands, you have to live in *this* world." I learned that she had been married off at age fourteen, that my Zeyda had a fiery temper to match his red hair, and that he used to "throw her around." My little Baba!

My father bought mousetraps. Night after night I jumped awake when one snapped and set off horrible squeals. I'd run to the bedroom to wake him up and then run back to the kitchen so as not to hear him flushing it down the toilet. Then he'd come back and set the trap again. But he never got rid of the mice.

After the month of mourning, my mother stopped keeping a strictly kosher kitchen and began talking to everyone in English. Liberated from her close ties to her mother, she set about, like most of the immigrants, to Americanize herself. She put on lipstick and sheer stockings and asked to be called Bessie, not Pessa. But every time some new sorrow or slight or injustice brought tears to her eyes, the tears were not wasted. She would say, "Oh, how I miss my dear mother," or "Oh, if only my mother were alive," or "I lost my best friend, my best friend." The rest of us would roll our eyes, exasperated, and I would say, "Ma. Stop!"

One night in early March, Mama took me to a Mothers Club anniversary party in our Lavanburg Social Center, to sing "Ol' Man River" as part of the entertainment. It was a lively party with delicatessen sandwiches and with whisky and beer alongside the sodas. Everyone loosened up and started remembering their good times in the Old Country. Mama began an old Russian song:

> *G'de ota ulitz g'de ota dom,*
> *G'de ota barishna shto ya lyublon*
> *Nyet etoy ulitzy, nyet etoy dom,*
> *Nyet etoy barishna shto ya lyublon.*
>
> *Where is the street, where is the house,*
> *Where is the lady whom I once loved?*
> *Gone is the street, gone is the house,*
> *Gone is the lady whom I once loved.*

Her voice had a burr in it, and before she got to the end of the first stanza it cracked and went off pitch. Other women picked up the song. I was so embarrassed for her. I remembered how beautifully she used to sing. Now no one would know how lovely her voice had been. Tears almost came to my eyes, and I thought, she has lost her voice crying for her dead mother.

Snow fell all winter and into spring. New snow piled on old until the curbside mountains got so high that the children swooped down them on cardboard sleds. One day my gang was having a snowball fight, boys against girls, and my boyfriend Joey hit me on the ear with a hard-frozen snowball. It stung so much I couldn't stop the tears but I didn't want to be called a cry-baby so I ran into the hallway of a building across the street. Joey ran in after me to ask if he had hurt me.

"No," I said, "I'm crying because my grandmother died and I didn't kiss her goodbye." He put his arms around me and my crying turned to sobs against his shoulder, my face buried in his wet wool coat. Within his arms I felt a great surge of love and sorrow. Then, after awhile, we went back outside hand in hand, and then I no longer felt the stone in my heart.

XX

Ma's Stories

My mother didn't read stories to us. She didn't tell jokes or anecdotes; she left those to the men. Like most Jews who had fled from the pogroms, those rounds of slaughterings from the Tsar's Cossacks who swooped in on horseback with flashing swords, she seldom talked about the Old Country. She was also glad to have left behind all the "we must nots" and "we're not allowed tos" of her own people. Her tales to her children were of daily-life calamities gathered from gossip and from the Yiddish newspapers my father brought home from the subway trash cans. Her true talent in story-telling came out in the telling and retelling and further retelling of Yiddish plays and movies, to which she was devoted. She mixed up the plots and added her own twists until you couldn't tell where her stories had come from, but she told them eloquently, using a stock supply of poetic expressions that may have come down from the Jews of Persia to the Jews of New York by way of Second Avenue love songs.

My favorite stories were a folk version of "King Lear" and a Passover story about a strange guest. The main source of my mother's "King Lear" was probably the movie "Yiddish King Lear" of 1934, but she had also seen "King Lear" staged by a Shakespeare company of Jewish actors who traveled throughout Europe. They performed in a dozen languages and altered the plot to accord with the local audience's level of sophistication.

My mother's "Passover Guest" story is probably a blend of an old tale for children and a 1937 movie called "The Vow," itself based on a blend of old tales. I used to think "The Passover Guest" was part of the regular Passover ritual, because that's

117

what it was in our home, but it turns out that no one I've come across has ever heard of it.

"Yiddish King Lear" and "The Vow" both played at the American, a dinky old movie house on East 3rd Street between Avenues D and C that showed third-run Hollywood movies and occasionally ran Yiddish film festivals for a whole week. Here is how I remember my mother telling these two stories.

Ma's "King Lear"

Once there was a great king who had three daughters. He was a vain and haughty king who liked to be flattered. One day, just to amuse himself, he called his daughters to his throne and asked them, first the eldest, How much do you love me? The eldest daughter answered, I love you as a flower loves the golden sun that warms it and brings it to life. Without you I would wither and die. The king thought this was a pretty answer, so he kissed his daughter and promised to give her a castle and a casket of gold and a garden full of flowers.

Then the king called his second daughter and asked her, How much do you love me? The second daughter answered, I love you as the wanderer in the night loves the moon that casts its silver light over the darkness. Without you I would lose my way and die. The king thought this also was a pretty answer, so he kissed his daughter and promised her a castle and a casket of silver and a forest of splendid trees.

Then the king asked his youngest daughter, How much do you love me? The third daughter said, I love you as meat loves salt. What? said the king. That's a crude joke. Come, tell me how much you love me. The third daughter said again, I love you as meat loves salt. What does this mean? said the king, getting angry. Why does my daughter speak such ugly words to me?

The third daughter said, I'm sorry Father, I can't say you are my sun or moon, or use the language of lovers when speaking

118

with you. It is not fitting or honest. I love you as is your due. I love you as meat loves salt.

The king got so angry that he shouted, Salt is it? Salt tears you shall have. Go, and never let me see you again.

Then the king gave up everything he had to his two other daughters. He gave them the castles and caskets, the garden and forest. Then he got old and blind, and they had no further use for him, so they threw him out.

Then the king went wandering on the road like a beggar, half naked, sleeping on haystacks in the fields and begging for a bite to eat. One day he came to a town where he was brought to the house of a great lady who was said to be very kind. So it was. He was taken into the house and treated with great respect. He was bathed and dressed in fresh garments and brought to the table to eat with the family. All the while he wondered, Where have I come to? What kind of people are these who treat a poor blind stranger like a king?

Then he was served a plate of boiled meat. He began to eat eagerly, he was as hungry as a wolf. To his surprise, the meat had no taste at all. It tasted like wood. He put down his fork and began to cry. The great lady asked him, Why are you crying? The king answered, Once I had a daughter who told me she loved me as meat loves salt. But I did not understand her. I told her I never wanted to see her again, and now I think that God made me blind to punish me for my foolishness. I gave everything I had to my two daughters with false tongues, and they turned me out to wander in the world like a beggar. Now I know that meat without salt is as tasteless as life without love, and there is no more use in living because I have lost my one true daughter forever. And he cried until the tears flowed like rain out of his blind eyes.

Then the great lady came up to him and said, Don't cry. I am your daughter. You have found me again after all. You have understood me and have made me happy. I beg you to stay here with us and make our humble home your own.

Then the king clutched at her and felt for her face and he kissed her, and they both cried so much that the meat was well flavored with their salt tears.

So the king had a fine meal and lived with his faithful daughter and her family, with all his grandchildren and great-grandchildren for all the rest of his long and happy life. And he believed that God had made it up to him for his sufferings by allowing his story to reach to the fourth generation.

"The Passover Guest"

Once there was a rich man, the richest in the whole town. His large family wore fancy clothes even on weekdays, and they were very stuck up. They lived next door to a poor family and they walked past with their noses in the air, pretending not to see them so they wouldn't have to say hello.

When Passover came, this rich man made a very big seder, the special feast on two nights to celebrate the escape of the Jews from slavery in Egypt. He invited the richest people from the town so they could come and admire his plates and finery. He was so rich that nobody dared refuse him.

On the first night of Passover the table was set with lustrous white linen, gleaming silver, sparkling crystal. The wine was a deep ruby red, the food was abundant. At the proper time the golden jewel-studded wine cup for Elijah the Prophet, Angel of Hope, was filled to the brim and the youngest child flung open the door to let the invisible Angel fly in on the breeze and sip from the cup. There in the open door stood an old graybeard in tattered clothes, squinting in the brilliant light. Everyone burst out laughing, and the rich man called out from his seat at the head of the table, "You've come to the wrong house. Go next door, you'll be welcome there." And everyone laughed again. The tattered man turned around and disappeared in the mist like a gray ghost.

On the second night of Passover the table of the rich man was set with fresh white linen, the wine flowed freely, the food was just as abundant. The wine cup for Elijah the Prophet was filled again, and the youngest child flung open the door. Everyone gasped and fell silent. There stood a tall man with a splendid white beard, dressed in a white satin caftan embroidered with gold and silver. Their eyes hurt to look, his garment shone like a hundred candles. The rich man rushed up to escort the stranger to the table, calling him Honored Guest. He pushed people aside to make room for the stranger to be seated next to him, at his right hand. The servants brought a new setting, and the host gave the stranger the most splendid wine cup he possessed, the one meant for Elijah the Prophet. Then he commenced with the seder. They all said the blessing over the wine and, as required, took a sip from their cups. The stranger lifted his jewel-studded cup, but instead of taking a sip he poured the deep red wine down the front of his beautiful satin caftan. Everyone was stunned but said nothing. At the second blessing, the stranger again poured the wine on his caftan, and at the third of the four blessings the same. The rich man could no longer restrain himself. "Tell me," he asked, "why are you pouring my Passover wine all over your clothes?"

The stranger answered, and his voice rumbled like a boulder rolling down Mount Sinai: "You refused to invite me to your table yesterday when I was dressed in rags. Today you invite me because I am wearing fine raiments. Therefore you did not give the wine to me but to my raiments."

Then Elijah the Prophet, for that's who he was, got up from the table and flowed out of the open door as if in a dream, and he went to the seder of the poor family next door, where the day before he had been treated respectfully and had been invited to the seder though dressed in rags.

121

From that day on the poor family became very lucky and happy and rich. The fortune of the rich man declined, and his family ended up quarreling with each other at every meal.

"The Depression of Boris Thomashevsky"

Just one time Mama said, "Now I'll tell you a true story. You know Boris Thomashevsky is the greatest actor in the Yiddish theater. Well, one day I was shopping on Stanton Street and I recognized him sitting on a stoop like a bum in dirty clothes and everything. So I said, "You, Thomashevsky, what happened? Why are you sitting here?" He didn't answer me. He looked confused. So I begged him to let me help him get back on his feet. I took his hand and he came home with me. The children were still in school. I sat him down in the kitchen and I brought him out a nice plate with chicken and cole slaw and potato salad and a nice pletzl. He ate slow, not like he was hungry. He didn't say nothing so I had to keep talking, so I told him how we went to the mountains in the summer to his sister Jenny and what a good time we had in her swimming pool. Then when I saw he stopped eating I led him to the bathroom to wash up. He was there for a long time so I got nervous and I called through the door, "Are you all right?" No answer. So I opened the door and I saw him with a razor in his hand. His hand was shaking and his other hand was open at the wrist. He was trying to get up the nerve to kill himself. So I yelled at him, "Shame on you. Is this how you thank me for inviting you to my house, my children should come home from school and see you on the floor covered with blood?" He put down the razor and started to cry and he pushed me out of the way and ran out of the house.

I never told nobody. Then it came out later that this great man lost all his money and got into a depression.

XXI

The Chicken Market in the Williamsburg Bridge

My mother always found a way to bring money into the house, even in the worst Depression years. When her summer season of selling peanuts in Battery Park was over, when she had spent too generously on new fall outfits for her four growing children, when she could not, after an exhausting battle, squeeze an extra penny from my father for the High Holiday expenses, she spat out: "All right! I know what I can do." She shoved a hooverette apron into her leather shopping bag. "I'll go pluck chickens!"

In the middle of the night we were jolted awake by the door slamming shut so hard that the windowpanes rattled and the next-door neighbor's dog barked. It was my mother, off to the live poultry market under the Williamsburg Bridge, to sit among the pluckers—*flickers* in Yiddish—for five cents a head. For a Jewish wife, plucking the feathers off chickens was the lowliest job next to being a cleaning lady, and she hoped word would get back to my father to shame him, for he was the respected Recording Secretary in four organizations. He wasn't shamed. He never spoke of it. Maybe he pretended not to know. Anyway, she stayed on to become a regular.

My mother had a flair for plucking chickens. Gentile women have the luxury of loosening the feathers by dunking the bird into a washbucket of boiling water. By Jewish law, to use hot water means to cook the chicken before the koshering has been done, before the salting and soaking and rinsing that draws all the blood out of the flesh. Thereby evolved this peculiar specialty of Jewish wives, this unappreciated culinary skill. To do it right you have to spread the bird's skin with one hand while yanking out the feathers with the thumb and middle finger of the other hand, briskly, in the exact direction of growth, and to get the job done you want to pull out as many feathers as you can grasp at a time without ripping the skin, a talent at which the women in our family excelled.

The Farmers, The Slaughterers, The Pluckers, The Clean-up Men

The live poultry market was open only three weeks a year, from before Rosh Hashana the Jewish New Year, through Yom Kippur the Days of Atonement, to the end of Sikkus the Harvest festival. During this time a frenzy of cooking and baking more than doubled the need for poultry and eggs.

Year round, New York's kosher butcher shops and butter-and-egg stores were supplied by distributors who drove their flatbed trucks along the dirt and gravel roads of the Catskill Mountains picking up crates of live poultry and eggs from the small Jewish farms. At holiday time the crates were stacked so high they teetered at the top and had to be lashed down with ropes.

To take advantage of the extra demand, some fifteen to twenty farmers borrowed or rented trucks themselves, to sell their own stock at bargain prices.

A few farmers from the specialized poultry farms around Lakewood, New Jersey, joined up with them at Sloatsburg, where they stopped for early breakfast at the all-night Red Apple Rest before entering the city.

The chicken market was held inside the base of the bridge at Pitt Street, in a vast unused space rented from the Department of Markets. A twin base farther down Delancey Street, close to the East River, was used as a garage for Department of Sanitation snow plows. My mother, a lover of action, a born insider, would get to the market by four-thirty for the arrival of the farmers' trucks, to be there for the clatter of crates being stacked on the street, the chucks and squawks of the chickens, the festive sight of their heads poking through the bars, peering this way and that, bobbing up and down, red combs flapping, beaks gaping.

The farmers moved along the wall of stacked crates, discarding the birds that had died of stress, while they waited for the health inspectors to spot-check for poultry diseases. After the stacks were inspected and tagged, the farmers carried their crates inside, to be arranged as booth partitions.

Some farmers specialized in eggs. Some brought in live ducks and a few geese along with the chickens. There were also pullets, called spring chickens, and roosters, called roasters. Most of the load, though, were soup chickens, four-to-five-pound hens. They cost twenty-five to thirty cents a pound, almost twice as much as stewing beef.

When the farmers had set up their booths and put out their folding tables and scales and were standing around with coffee and buttered kaiser rolls, my mother would join them, have coffee with them, gather the news of the Catskill farms, the cook-alone guest houses, the boarding houses and hotels. She would amuse them with aptly phrased comments as she listened, for they were all former city boys who loved gossip and lively talk. All the while she speculated on how she might turn these contacts with the farmers into an opportunity to make a little extra money.

Three or four *shoykhets*, ritual slaughterers, arrived at about a quarter to five. Religious men with skullcaps and long beards, they didn't mingle with the farmers but went straight to their long wood-slat platform opposite the booths, put on white canvas coats buttoned down to the ankles, and got out their knives and sharpeners. Their knives resembled straight razors with a curved tip. Behind the shoykhets was an iron stand that had clamps at the bottom, holding it to the back of the platform, and hooks at the top for hanging the fowl.

The chicken pluckers arrived soon after, about ten women. They put on wrap-around hooverettes over their dresses, then they put on butcher aprons over the hooverettes, then they covered their hair with kerchiefs. One fat old-timer had fashioned for herself a covering of heavy duck fabric with cut-out holes for her head and arms. She put a big red-print kerchief on backwards, knotting it on her forehead. The end pointed toward her nose and the two folds stood straight up over her ears. Behind her back she was called *der Alta Genzl*, the Old Goose. She was the best plucker in the market.

The farmers disdained protective clothing. They remained as they were, in baggy serge pants, plain cotton shirts and dark plaid overshirts, caps set straight across the brow.

The pluckers dragged all kinds of chairs from the back of the cavern and took up places in the middle of the hall. Ma secured a spot next to the Old Goose to get the overflow of her customers. The Old Goose sat on a milking stool, covering it with her tent and looking just like she was setting a clutch of eggs.

While the farmers, shoykhets, and pluckers were getting into place, two hired clean-up men from The Bowery had been filling buckets of water from the fire hydrant outside and lining them up at the sides of the entrance. When everyone had settled down, they began to sprinkle the floor with fresh sawdust from burlap bags. All fell silent, as if a stage curtain was about to rise. Even the chickens seemed to lower their squawks.

That's when you noticed how cold and damp it was inside the bridge. The rough cement floor was often still wet from the previous wash-down. The small windows, high up in the stone walls, were black with soot. The bridge overhang kept daylight from penetrating through the entrance; the market was lit by naked light bulbs hanging from the darkness above. Eyes fixed on the ticking wall clock next to the entranceway.

At five o'clock exactly, customers swarmed in as if invisible guards had opened invisible gates. They paced up and down the aisles, stopping at one booth after another to peer into the crates, point out a likely chicken, get the farmer to hold it while they poked and prodded, made him put it back, moved on, came back, bargained over the price. They were *mavens*, experts. They argued with zest. They were proud to be up so early, to be so clever, to be getting the freshest chickens in the city at such bargain prices.

When a purchase was settled the farmer would open the crate door, grab the chosen bird over the wings, and clutch it to his chest with one hand while closing the door then tying its feet with the other hand. Sometimes a bird escaped. There were always a few chickens wandering around on the floor.

The weighing, the final price, the tying of the feet dealt with, the farmer would take his money and walk his customer across the hall.

The shoykhets worked fast. They inspected each fowl under the wings, under the legs, around the tail, along the neck, and worked their fingers under the body feathers. Any flaw, blemish, or break in the skin would make it unacceptable. They forced the head way back and slit the neck vein with their curved knife, ducking to one side as the blood spurted up. They hung the bird head-down over a tin funnel, which drained the blood into a barrel. The customer waited around until the bird was dead. She paid the shoykhet a nickel.

Then came the plucking. The pluckers steadied the chickens in their laps, the bloody head hanging over a thigh, and, with their feet planted square on the ground, pulled out fistfuls of feathers. In no time a mound of feathers surrounded each chair, crept toward the aisle, and drifted like snow as passing customers stirred the air.

The clean-up men from The Bowery were in constant motion, filling barrels with feathers and rolling them out, flinging buckets of water across the floor, and sprinkling on more sawdust to keep the fallen feathers from flying. But the down, the tiny weightless feathers from the underside of the birds, could not be subdued. They formed a floating, drifting fog of fluff that got onto eyelashes, up nostrils, into shoes. Almost as pervasive were the displaced lice. They crawled over and under and into everyone's hair and clothing, eventually abandoning the humans to search for the warmer flesh of the fowl.

My mother sat next to the Old Goose, eyeing her, challenging herself to keep up with her. The Old Goose sat unperturbed. Both had steady work. Both could clean a big hen of its feathers in only ten minutes without tearing a bit of skin. My mother often earned a dollar and a half, even more, before her arm cramped up and she had to stop for the day. The Old Goose always outlasted her. But at the courtesy discount the pluckers received, my mother had earned enough for a hen, a pullet, and a three-dozen carton of eggs, and she had enough money left over for potatoes and soup greens on the way home.

The market began to peter out by seven-thirty. The farmers had to close up and be ready for the four-hour ride back upstate. The housewives had to get home to wake the children, make breakfast, pack lunches, get their husbands off to work and the children off to school. Some older women hung around to the end, waiting to buy cracked eggs, waiting for the last-minute slash in prices, for the farmers hated to return stock to the farm. The last chickens were of the poorest quality, and so were the clothes and shoes and general appearance of the last customers as they shuffled down the disappearing aisles among the last of the crates and the remaining clumps of sticky-wet sawdust mixed with chicken droppings and blood-streaked feathers. The chicken pluckers left before the end, knowing these women would not spare a nickel to have the feathers removed, not when a nickel could buy three rolls or a pound of potatoes or, with one or two pennies more, a quart of milk.

My mother hung around with the farmers outside as they waited to reload the trucks. She took a particular interest in the egg farmers. One day she pointed out some leftover egg cartons and said to the farmer, "Let me have these eggs on consignment. I'll see if I can sell them for you door to door, fifty-fifty split, all right?" He agreed, and thus began a respectable new business for Ma: customer peddling.

The egg farmer made a stop at our house every Friday on his rounds of the butter-and-egg stores. He left thirty-six cartons of dozens. At seventeen cents a dozen, eight-and-a-half cents for her, she could have earned up to three dollars a week except that we used up two cartons ourselves and also some of the eggs had to be returned.

We had to candle the eggs before they could be sold. Another job for my sister Ruthie and me when we got home from school. The farmer lent us a candler: a bright electric light mounted on a wood platform. You put a carton on the platform and held up one egg at a time in front of the light. If you saw a blood spot, the egg was unacceptable, not kosher, and it went into a reject carton. The farmer took the rejects back, to be mixed with animal feed.

The Chicken Farm in Lakewood, New Jersey

My mother was invited to visit the farm. She took Ruthie and me with her for a chance to get out of the city. We went by Greyhound Bus to Lakewood, New Jersey, and the farmer picked us up at the station.

It didn't look like a farm. I was disappointed. There were only long low chicken coops, all in rows, and scrabbly dusty grass that you couldn't sit on. We came upon a Japanese examiner in one of the incubator rooms at the end of a coop. He wore a white jacket like a doctor's, and he had a friendly round face. He examined day-old chicks to separate out the males. He could tell by a certain tinge of color in the eye. He kept just a few robust-looking male chicks for breeders and roasters and drowned the rest in a washbucket because, he explained, roosters produce no eggs and cost more to feed than the money they could bring in at the market. The drowned chicks floated on the water, feet dangling, wormlike bodies attached to ugly heads, their eyes bulging through closed blue lids. The Japanese man wanted to give me a live chick to hold, but I wouldn't put out my hand.

Door-to-Door on Consignment

In time, my mother expanded her door-to-door egg-peddling business to include housedresses, and then also linens. She picked up her merchandise on consignment from two Rivington Street stores, sold up and down the stairs in another neighborhood where our family wasn't known, and brought the unsold goods back to the stores. My father never found out about her new source of money. She took out a bank book from The Bowery Savings Bank and began to look at the modern-style living room suites in the windows of the furniture stores on Avenue A. She began to dream of replacing our helter-skelter old-fashioned dining room pieces in time for Ruthie's sweet-sixteen party, when she would be allowed to wear black and eligible boys would start coming to the house to take her out on dates.

Along with her new business as a door-to-door peddler, my mother continued to pluck chickens during the High Holidays for the extra money and also to keep up her contacts with the Catskill farmers, for now she planned to bring her children to the mountains every summer for the fresh country air and pay for it by peddling merchandise along the back roads.

Strike Down My Sins

My mother wouldn't let me go to the chicken market with her when I was little. She said that it was too early to wake me up and that it was too crowded and filthy. She left Ruthie to take care of me until she got home to prepare breakfast and lunches. But she made one exception, for the day of *Shlugn Kaporis*, the Striking Down of Sins. It came before the fast of *Yom Kippur*, the Day of Atonement, at which time we had to atone to God for all the bad things we did during the year. *Shlugn* means hitting. *Kaporis* is for putting our sins on the heads of others before we had to account to God. These others were chickens and fish: a live hen for women and girls, and a live rooster or carp for men and boys.

My two brothers refused to use a rooster; they demanded a carp. Ruthie and I had no choice. We had to swing a hen over our heads while holding tight to its legs to keep it from escaping. Ma, Ruthie, and I used to do it together. I would hang onto the feet, Ruthie would wrap her hands around mine, and Ma would hold down the wings while all three of us bent over the table to read from the prayer book. You had to circle the struggling, squawking chicken three times for each of the three

131

lines in the prayer, and then you had to say the whole prayer again, which made it ten times.

This creature is instead of me, on account of my sins,
to make amends for me.
This hen shall go to her death for me. And may I
have a long and healthy life.

Then my two brothers and my father would each have to take his turn holding the slippery carp in a dish towel, and they would have to say, "This carp shall go to his death for me," otherwise it was the same.

As a special treat my mother allowed me to come to the market at *Shlugn Kaporis* time and pick out my own personal chicken. She would go at her usual time, half-past four in the morning, and my sister Ruthie would bring me later. Some of the other chicken pluckers and a few customers would bring their young daughters too. The farmers gave each girl a hand-ful of celluloid chicken rings in all different colors. They were for putting on each chicken's foot to identify the owner. When you put a chicken ring on your finger you made it fit by squeez-ing the band tighter. I saved a pair of golden yellow rings for myself and my boyfriend Joey, and the rest I gave out to the girls in my gang.

One time my mother said Aunt Dora would be coming to pick out a *Kaporis* chicken with my cousin Pearlie, who was almost as old as my sister, and my cousin Sylvie, who was almost as old as me. I was thrilled. I ran along all the crates, finding the ducks and geese and picking out the best hens to show them.

But by the time they came, around six-thirty, the aisles were already jammed with customers and they were over-whelmed by the stench, the din, the dead birds on hooks, the feather fluffs all over the place. My cousin Sylvie hid under a table at the back and wouldn't come out until Aunt Dora and Pearlie were finished. They never came again. When Ruthie started high school she didn't want to bring me anymore either.

From that time on my mother woke me while it was still dark and took me with her for the four-thirty caravan of trucks. I liked that the best because then I could see the market from the very beginning and drink coffee with the farmers while my mother kidded around with them, and I would feel the thrill of being an insider.

The Red Rooster, The Speckled Hen, The Golden Carp

One year when I went to pick out a *Kaporis* chicken, I tried to find a bird like the one in Hilda Conkling's poem "Red Rooster." It was in a poetry book, Louis Untermeyer's children's collection called *This Singing World,* which I stole by accident from my second-grade classroom when I was seven years old. Copies were kept in the book closet and were only passed out once a week, and one day I didn't hear the teacher say to pass the books back, and then she locked the closet door and it was too late; I was too embarrassed to tell her I wasn't paying attention. Hilda Conkling wrote the poem when she was also seven.

> *Red Rooster in your gray coop,*
> *O stately creature with tail-feathers red and blue,*
> *Yellow and black,*
> *You have a comb gay as a parade on your head:*
> *You have pearl trinkets on your feet:*
> *The short feathers smooth along your back*
> *Are the dark color of wet rocks,*
> *Or the rippled green of ships*

When I look at their sides through water.
I don't know how you happened to be made
So proud, so foolish,
Wearing your coat of many colors,
Shouting all day long your crooked words,
Loud . . . sharp . . . not beautiful!

I walked all around the crates looking for red roosters. Most were white. Of the red ones, none had colored tail feathers and green sides, but I chose the largest rooster with the most uneven colors. It had fierce eyes and a huge comb and it stood up high on its legs. "I want this one," I said. "It's a beauty," my mother said, "but it's a rooster. You have to have a hen." I hung my head. "Well, all right, I'll take this one for Papa, and the boys will have the carp."

I stood by the red rooster, watching it, until Ma was ready to leave. It shifted a lot, and cocked its head in every direction, and stretched its neck and wings, but it wasn't fluttery. As soon as she put it in the dark of her leather shopping bag it lay perfectly still. Ma added a plump little speckled hen for Ruthie and me, and off we went to buy the live carp.

At *Kaporis* time, dozens of peddlers up and down Rivington Street filled their tin-lined pushcarts with water and converted them to carp tanks. The prices were much lower than in the stores but the water was shallow and the carp hardly had room to move and didn't look very lively.

Ma took me to Manny Fisher's mother's store on Rivington and Sheriff streets to buy the carp. She was a regular customer there; she would buy a chunk from the belly of a fish and ask for a pile of free heads to use for soups. This time Ma walked around the carp tank quietly and thoughtfully, shading her eyes and peering into the water from above, trying to see every fish. I wanted to get home to take the chickens out of the shopping bag. She said, "What do you think?" There were more than two dozen carp in the tank, stacked several layers deep, going back and forth, back and forth, their heads swaying from side to side, feeling with their barbels. They cast deep shadows in the water. How mysterious it was to see into their dark, silent, drifting world. I pointed out a fish that was nudging a wider path for itself. It was not the biggest but not too small either, round in the belly and with gleaming scales, more golden than the others. Mama peered down. She agreed with my choice. "You're a better maven than me," she said proudly. "Chicken and fish, you beat me in pieces."

Ma wrapped the carp in wet newspaper and I carried it home in a paper bag while she took the leather bag with the two chickens.

At home we settled the carp in a bathtubful of cold water and I covered the bathroom floor with newspapers. Then Ma got a ball of twine and the leather shopping bag and sent me out of the bathroom. What a commotion of flapping and squawking and fluttering I heard through the door! But soon enough she had the hen and rooster tied to the base of the toilet, each by one leg. And there they had to stay for two days, feeding off scraps in one tin dish and knocking over the water in the other tin dish, while we had to use the toilet without getting our legs pecked at.

The bathroom was narrow. The sink was in front, at the head of the bathtub, and the toilet was next to the end, by the small window. I walked along the top edge of the tub, reaching out with my hands to balance myself against the tile wall on the other side of the tub, and then I had to hang onto the window sill and climb down to the toilet seat without letting my legs dangle down.

I went into the bathroom as often as I could, to stay with the chickens and watch the carp in the bathtub. I changed the newspapers and gave the birds food scraps and fresh water. I read to them out loud to keep them company, and I recited Hilda Conkling's poem to the red rooster. The birds settled down. I was able to pat them and stroke their backs from above, with my feet tucked under. I made up a poem for the speckled hen so she could have one also:

> Speckled hen, speckled hen so far from home
> Your eggs are stolen, your nest is gone
> Your little yellow chicks are dead
> And I must swing you over my head.

The carp got no food. It swam back and forth, back and forth, hour after hour. It had to flip its tail and fold its middle to turn around at the ends of the narrow tub. If you startled it by moving quickly, it would thrash its tail and bang its head against the tub. The water got murky with carp dirt. I drained and refilled the water very gradually so as not to alarm it. But every so often it shuddered and thrashed. I sat on the toilet lid with my feet up on the edge of the tub and watched its mouth open and close, open and close, its barbels twitch. I looked into its mottled yellow eyes—first the left eye as it swam toward the sink, then the right eye as it swam toward the window. I made up a poem for the carp also:

> Yellow carp with an old man's eye,
> Gulping and thrashing
> Do you think? Do you cry?
> You were swimming free
> Then suddenly
> Yanked through a splash to the sky
> To the air
> To a world of despair

Kaporis came the next day before sundown. My father got home from work early and we went through the ritual at the kitchen table.

Ruthie and I swung the speckled hen over our heads with my mother. Then my mother climbed up on a chair while holding the rooster's wings and handed it to my father. He tried to swing the screaming squawking rooster while Ma stayed up on the chair and fought to control the wildly beating wings. I hid behind Ruthie and she covered the frightened little hen until the prayer was over. Then my father, mother, and sister forced the chickens into my mother's black leather shopping bag and hung the bag on the kitchen doorknob. Then the boys took their turn. Each swung the golden carp over his head ten times and said "this creature instead of me" while it squirmed inside the towel, its tail sticking out and flapping desperately. When they were finished Ma threw the carp onto the bread board and smacked its head with her rolling pin and wrapped it in wax paper and put in the refrigerator. Then she picked up the leather bag and rushed off to the slaughterer with the proud red rooster and the little speckled hen.

My Vow

In the eyes of God a girl's sins are on her mother's head until the age of nine. I was eight years and two months old. That's why I had to give my sins to the little speckled hen or they would have gone to my mother. On Yom Kippur Eve, when we said the Prayer of Reckoning in the women's balcony of the synagogue, I swore to God that in my next year I would take all my sins unto myself and never ever give them to any animals any more.

XXII
Dance Lessons

Dancing in the Street

In summertime everybody showed up for the Friday night dances on the Stanton Street corner of Goerck Street. The latest big-band hit tunes blasted out from a loudspeaker tied to the corner lamp-post. Traffic was stopped and the street filled up with dancing couples: grown-up boys in jackets and ties, grown-up girls in make-up and silk dresses, doing the latest dance steps. The old ladies leaned out of their windows to watch, their elbows on pillows. Little girls in fluffy skirts stood at the top of the front stoops and wriggled their hips to the music with their pinkies in the air. My gang of nine-year-old girls clustered by Starkman's cleaning store across the street from the lamp-post, trying to look indifferent, knowing what would happen next. Next our boys' gang ran up and dragged us into the street while we squealed and squirmed and pretended we were being captured. They pulled us over to the lamp-post and cleared a space for us to dance, though none of us really knew how.

Not just our block, but the whole Lower East Side was doing Friday night dances, though not in the street.

Dances were going on in three other settlement houses: the Educational Alliance, Madison House, and Christadora House, and in the Labor Temple on East 14th Street, and all along the side streets in the boys' basement social clubs. And when the dancing was over we all went home and turned on our radios and listened to the Midnight Matinee and the latest Hit Parade songs and danced some more.

Mister Goldfeld, the administrator of Lavanburg Homes where I lived, worried about holding dances in the street on

Friday nights because it was the Jewish Sabbath. But the Fathers Club and Senior Boys took it over without even asking him because they said he didn't rule the streets. Yes we did light the Sabbath candles at sundown, and yes we did shut the electricity while the candles were lit, but except in the very few very religious families we didn't have to stay indoors sitting in the dark all night.

Lavanburg's First Dance Class

When summer was over a lot of girls, maybe fifteen, waited in Lavanburg's South Hall for our first dance lesson. Dance class was a new junior activity of our basement Social Center. It was for ages nine through eleven. My whole gang signed up: Celia, Phyllis, Enela, Lovey, and me.

Our boys' gang was in the back alley peeking in through the basement windows on their knees and elbows, making mashed faces against the window panes. They wanted to learn the dance steps as much as we did— the Lindy hop, the Manhattan, a whole bunch of new Latin dances—but they would never be caught taking dance lessons, oh no.

Teacher was late. We spent the time guessing what she would look like and how she would be dressed. Would she show up in spike heels? Would she have blonde hair? Curly bangs? Would she be wearing the latest red satin-lined circle skirt? Phyllis was wearing one, black with a red satin lining that flashed when she did the dips and flips of the Lindy hop with her boyfriend Freddy. That's all the Lindy he knew, dips and flips. I myself loved the rhumba best. I wanted teacher to be wearing ruffled sleeves and show us how to shimmy and shake our shoulders. Celia, my best friend, wanted her to be wearing a white satin blouse with black satin shorts and tap shoes, but she had little hope of learning tap. For that you had to go to a private dance academy, and it was expensive.

We were getting impatient. Sylvia, one of the older girls, started singing the latest Hit Parade song by Irving Berlin, then she grabbed the girl next to her and danced a slow Lindy. In a split second we all grabbed a partner and joined in:

Come get together
Let the dance floor feel your leather
Step as lightly as a feather
Let yourself go.

Come hit the timber
Loosen up and start to limber
Can't you hear that hot marimba
Let yourself go.

Let yourself go, relax
And let yourself go, relax
You've got yourself tied up in a knot
The night is cold but the music's hot so. . .

The South Hall door flew open and there she was, our dance teacher. We froze in place and stared. She wore glasses and had no makeup on. She was dark, olive-skinned. Her nose was too long. Her hair was just pulled back with a barrette and left to hang down loose. And her clothes were *really* strange. She wore a long black cape and had a big leather pouch slung over it, and she wore ugly round-toed thick-heeled shoes with old-fashioned ankle straps. Without stopping she said over her shoulder, "Sorry I'm late, class, I had the wrong directions," then she turned left and made for the near end of the bench that ran all around the walls. She reached it so swiftly, and with such ease—a smooth stride, chest high, head up—that there was no mistaking her for anyone but a real professional dancer, though what kind was a mystery.

We watched in silence as teacher flung off her pouch and cape and tossed back her hair. Her dress was even more surprising: a calf-length maroon wrap-around skirt over a tight long-sleeved maroon top, both of a clinging jersey fabric. She pulled a hand drum out of the pouch along with a cotton-tipped mallet and gray T-strap slippers. She tugged open her ankle straps and flung off her shoes and put on the slippers over thick tan stockings. She strode to the middle of the hall, faced us, folded back the front of her skirt, and sat down right on the dirty floor with her legs spread apart so we could see that her maroon top came all the way down to cover her crotch like a bathing suit. Later we learned that this was called a leotard and that her stockings were actually tights like those on circus performers, and also that her ugly shoes were for flamenco tap dancing.

"All right class," she said, "come up front and spread out at arm's length in two rows." We shuffled forward, glancing around at each other. "Sit facing me." We looked at the floor. It got mopped and sprinkled with talc before the South Hall's Friday night dances to make the painted cement slippery. The rest of the week it built up a filthy black film of old talc mixed with dirt and coal dust. "Oh, I see," she said. "You didn't come prepared. Well, all right. Sit on the bench for now. Next time please come to class in shorts and an old shirt. No dance slippers. You'll work barefoot. I'll see that the floor gets washed."

Normally we would be all over a new teacher in the Social Center with questions and protests and demands. Normally she would have had to shout for minutes to bring us to order, to insist that we speak one at a time. But, I don't know how, this teacher went from one thing to the next to the next that left no room for us to interrupt. She told us her name was Beatrice Baronofsky and we could call her Miss Bea. She made us say our first names three times around. She said "I'll ask you to repeat your names at the beginning of class for a while because I have to call out directions while you're dancing."

Then she told us class is in four sections: warm-ups, coming across the floor, improvisation, and composition. "We'll do some folk dancing too when we have time. Any questions?"

Silence. We looked around at each other. More silence. Finally the new girl from Germany spoke. "Vill you learin us de Lindy?" Giggles here and there, then we all broke down in wildly uncontrollable laughter. The boys outside picked up the mayhem and banged on the windows. Miss Bea watched us as if in deep thought. The laughter subsided. She picked up her drum and rose straight up from the floor and landed with her feet apart. I wondered how she did that. "Class, notice what you did while you were laughing." We didn't know what she meant. The boys kept up their banging. "Don't pay attention to the boys outside. They'll get bored and leave. Now, you did some very interesting things. Stand up. Spread out." She began a soft pulse on her drum: *tum, tum, tum, tum.* "Celia, you were bent over, clutching your stomach. Will you do that now? Fay, you had your right hand over your mouth and your head turned to the left. Sylvia, you had both arms in the air, elbows and head bent. Gladys, you lifted your shoulders to your ears. Good. The rest of you take your laughing position or make up a new one." The German girl who had provoked the laughter—her name was Bertha—had a slight smile on her face and a look of confusion. "Bertha, you come and stand beside me. The rest of you, now listen carefully, you're going to the opposite of this position and back again, and away again, and back again. Celia, come up and demonstrate." Celia slowly shuffled over. Miss Bea put down her drum, took her by the shoulders and turned her to face the class. Celia rolled her eyes. "Bring your arms straight out from your belly while you stand up straight, then bend over and clutch your belly again. Now: *Open* two three four, *return* six seven eight. Okay, go back in line and keep that up. Fay come up. Bring your right hand away from your mouth while you turn your head to the left. *Away* two three four, *return* six seven eight. Now everybody: Take your laugh position and follow the beat. *Away* two three four, *return* six seven eight, *continue* two three four, *keep-it-up* six seven eight." She tapped her drum softly. "Now slow down. Slower. Still slower." She picked up her drum. *Tum, tum, tum, tum, ta-rum, tum, tum, tum.*

I glanced around. Each of us, confined to only two slow repeating gestures, looked like the wax Gypsy in the glass booth on the Coney Island boardwalk who breathed in-and-up, out-and-down, and picked up your fortune. We looked like a collection of wax Gypsies. Scary.

"Bertha, you walk around among the dancers as if you landed in a strange world with strange creatures in it. When you come to the end, take a place and do a laughing gesture too." She kept the drum going, slowly counting out, "*One* two three four, *return* six seven eight."

After a while she said, "Everyone, move about the room. Keep going, keep going." She watched.

"Now form groups of twos and threes. Relate your gestures to each other." We looked so spooky. A couple of girls got the giggles but suppressed them.

"Now let the space around you feel thick and heavy. It's harder for you to move through the space. Keep going. Push your way through the heavy space. Slow down. Slow down. Listen to the beat." The beat was slow and solemn. "Now look at each other and look away. Come back. Walk around. Slower. Slower. Turn the mood to grief." She gradually led us with her drum into slow ponderous motions.

Raising arms, clutching stomachs, hands over mouth, heads turning to shoulders, slower, still slower, we gradually came to look like we were witnessing the end of the world.

I could see and feel the grief. It was scary but somehow also beautiful.

Miss Bea said, "All right class, back to your seats." The mood of grief had gotten to us. We were quiet. The boys were gone. It was dark outside."Remember what you did. It was very interesting. Didn't you think so?" We looked around at each other and some of us nodded. I did. "We'll return to this scene later. I'll just leave you with this thought for now: Bertha asked to learn the Lindy. Here's my answer. The Lindy is a *social* dance. The steps are known in advance. The mood is driven by popular music. The beat is constant. You're on a dance floor with a partner, right? It's easy to pick up. What we do here is called *modern* dance. We'll talk about it more as we go along, but I'll just say this for now:

"The modern dancer uses her body as an instrument of expression in the medium of space, usually on a stage which acts as a frame. She's like a painter because she uses her body as if it were a brush, creating forms in the frame that have direction and motion and even suggest color because colors and gestures both have moods. And she's like a composer of music because she uses her body in the medium of time, with themes and variations and changing rhythmic patterns. The modern dancer is free to find her own movements according to what she wants to express and how she wants to affect her audience. And she coordinates these movements with those of her fellow dancers in all kinds of improvisations out of which fixed compositions emerge. You won't learn the Lindy here, but in time, not too long I would say, when you go to dance the Lindy, you'll see that it's a simple dance you can pick up easily by yourself, and you'll dance the Lindy gloriously. Okay Bertha?" Bertha looked back at her, adoringly.

Miss Bea gave us an assignment. "For next week I want you to notice people as if they were forms in space. Notice the way they walk, use their arms and legs, see if you can find rhythms, patterns. Play with them. Create different moods, the way we did tonight with laughter and grief. Next week we won't have to start from scratch. We'll be able to reach into a repertory of movement ideas. Okay, class dismissed. Remember to come on time, in old clothes. I'll see that the floor gets washed."

On our way along the corridor to the exit door, Celia stepped out in front like a parade leader and mimicked Miss Bea's swift stride but with knees bent like Groucho Marx. She turned around and faced us, walking backwards.

"All right class, now put your bottoms on the filthy floor and brush. Swish swish, come on, paint up the space. Bam Bam Bam Bam." She jutted her hips from side to side. "Now zombie time." She slow-motioned a monster with dripping hands reaching for us. We all cracked up laughing.

Phyllis said, "You know, she's really ugly." Celia added, "She's ugly and crazy! I'm gonna see what other junior activities are open Wednesdays. Who's coming?"

I said, "I liked her. I liked the way she made us dance and the way she didn't treat us like children."

Celia said, "Oh, Fay, you always want to be different." Her remark was so unfair. I didn't *ever* want to be different.

Sylvia and the other older girls moved on. The rest crowded around the Activities Board. I was left standing there while Phyllis, Enela, and Lovey all followed Celia to re-register for the Knitting Club.

Bertha, the new girl, came up to me. "I agree mit you. Miss Bea is a intra-esting lady."

I walked Bertha home. She lived across the street between the candy store and Frank Wing Hand Laundry, in an old building with broken-down rusty mailboxes. Her family was from Alsace-Lorraine, refugees from Hitler. I wondered if she had any friends. I wondered if I was still best friends with Celia, if I was still in my gang.

My Homework: Ruthie Setting Her Hair

My sister Ruthie was setting her hair at the dresser when I got home. I sat on the edge of the bed and handed her the curlers. She asked how was dance class. "Are you going to lindy and rhumba at my sweet sixteen party?"

"It isn't that kind of dancing."

"No? What kind is it?"

"Modern dance, not social dance. We're going to make up our own dances." I didn't tell her about the laughing dance that turned into a dance of grief. I thought of Celia. It was something you could make fun of, like reading a love poem out loud.

I watched Ruthie put her curlers in while she looked in the mirror. Her right hand was holding up a section of hair. She reached for a curler with her left hand and brought it to her right hand. Her arms met above her head in a diamond shape. She closed the curler over her hair and rolled it down to her head. That made her elbows go way out sideways and made her arms frame her face. Next curler. Reach up with hair in right hand, reach down with left hand, pick up curler. Left hand meets right hand above head. Both hands roll curler down while elbows bend out. Next curler. Next.

Ruthie set three rows of curlers and then I handed her the hairpins. She set them in pin curls across her forehead. In the morning when she combed out her setting, she'd have a crown of straight hair framed with soft curls. So pretty.

"My dance teacher has long hair," I said. "She clips it with a wide barrette, then she lets all her hair hang down in waves, and the waves don't get tangled or frizzy."

"She might be using fat rollers," Ruthie said.

"Can you try fat rollers on me? Then maybe I wouldn't have to wear braids."

"Sure I can. I have fat rollers somewhere. You go buy a wide barrette from Woolworths. Do you need money?"

"No thanks, I have enough."

Ruthie put a pink net around her setting and we got ready for bed. We slept on the same pillow. Ruthie read her True Romances magazine with her right arm around me and my head nestled in her shoulder. I got a hug every time she reached up to turn the page.

"You know what?" she said, "With rollers you won't be able to sleep on my arm."

"Will I be able to sleep on the rollers?"

"I'll tell you what," she said. "I can set your hair the minute I come home from school. I'll straighten it with a little bit of water and set it with gel, and I'll comb it out for you after supper. But you'll have to stay home all afternoon. Is that okay?"

"Okay. On Wednesdays."

She got up and shut the light and we kissed goodnight.

Down in the Dark and the Damp

Only eight girls showed up for class next Wednesday. Me, Bertha, a lively girl our age named Esther, and five older girls. Ruthie hadn't had time to set my hair so I wore my usual braids. We all came in shorts under our coats except Bertha, who changed behind the stage curtain and came out in her one-piece green bloomers from school gym. Miss Bea said, "Oh, what a good idea Bertha. With a gym suit you don't have to fuss about your blouse creeping up while you work. Class, if you have gym suits, wear them next time." Bertha beamed.

Miss Bea had managed to get the floor washed clean. We sat down and faced forward in two staggered lines with legs apart. I was in front. I discovered that I couldn't spread my legs unless I bent my knees. Even with my back slumped and knees bent I could only get them a foot apart.

And then, with our legs spread out we had to hold one ankle at a time and pull our ear toward it. I couldn't even get half way. I wished I had chosen the back row so I could hide. Then coming across the floor in a single line, I was so bad at leaping that I could feel my cheeks flame with embarrassment. Miss Bea called out for me to gallop instead.

Then she made everybody gallop, then skip, then run, then walk, so I managed to get through that part of class.

For improvisation we sat along the bench while Miss Bea gave us the theme: We were to be in a narrow tunnel: cold, dark, and muddy. The stage at the far end of South Hall would be the opening of the tunnel. "Spread out all across the room and begin to move toward the stage with your eyes closed."

She tapped lightly on her drum. *Tap, tap-a tap. Tap, tap-a tap.* "Let me see you feel your way along a wall with your arms, your toes, your back, your elbows. Feel the roof of the tunnel getting lower above your head. Feel the mud, thick and heavy, slowing down your steps. Listen. Is anyone near you? You hear trickles of water, a pebble dropping. Now add some movements you studied during the week."

I turned to face the imaginary wall and pressed against it. Using my sister Ruthie's arm movements, I reached for the roof overhead with my right hand and the wall in front of me with my left hand, then both hands up. I felt the tunnel getting lower, and muddy. I pulled my right foot out of the mud and sank with a bent knee. Then I slid the left foot toward the right and bent both knees deeper. My roof got lower and lower as the drum beat more urgently. I kept making Ruthie's diamond shapes as I sank slowly down. Miss Bea called out, "Very good Fay. Keep that."

Then she said "Esther, good change of direction. Remember that." Whenever she called out praise I had to keep myself from peeking. Then she said, "Feel for another person. Once you've made contact, don't lose it." Someone touched me. I clung to her and tried to raise myself. We stumbled and fell together. Then a third person lifted me. Miss Bea shouted, "Wonderful, the three of you! Keep that."

Then she said "Okay, now everyone, out of the tunnel. Stand up and open your eyes. React to the light." We looked around. We had all somehow reached each other and were next to the stage. We formed a chain and came slowly into the imaginary light. "Enjoy the outside," she shouted. "Run around! Jump! Leap! Reach for the sky!" She rolled her drum like gathering thunder then came to a sharp stop. *Slam*. "Excellent! Wonderful, class, all of you! Now gather round me on the floor."

Some of the girls sat up straight and spread their legs. I rolled over on my hip with bent knees, feeling clumsy again. Miss Bea said, "We've just done our first improvisation for a dance dedicated to coal miners. The intention of the exercise was to find our way out while a cave-in rumbled behind us. Remember what you did. We'll review and continue next week. We have a great start."

For the composition section of class Miss Bea read us a poem that was to accompany our dance, "Caliban in the Coal Mines" by Louis Untermeyer. She said we would emerge from the tunnel just as the poem reaches the last line. "Got that? Okay, here's the poem."

She beat the drum softly and steadily as she spoke the lines.

> *God, we don't like to complain—*
> *We know that the mine is no lark—*
> *But—there's the pools from the rain;*
> *But—there's the cold and the dark.*

God, You don't know what it is—
You, in Your well-lighted sky,
Watching the meteors whiz;
Warm, with the sun always by.

God, if You had but the moon
Stuck in Your cap for a lamp,
Even You'd tire of it soon,
Down in the dark and the damp.

Nothing but blackness above,
And nothing that moves but the cars—
God, if You wish for our love,
Fling us a handful of stars!

I was close to tears. I wanted to get up and fling myself back into the tunnel and start again. Miss Bea rose from the floor in her magical way and glided across the room to her leather pouch. She returned with photographs of coal miners underground, their faces smeared shiny black with coal dust and sweat. They had lamps strapped to their foreheads. She told us how hard the work is in the mines, how dangerous. "Whether or not God sent them, the handful of stars are there, outside the mines. They are the union organizers who are helping the miners to strike. That means the miners are refusing to work until the mine owners give them shorter hours and safer conditions. The union gives them enough money to hold out until their demands are met. It's called the United Mine Workers. So. Composition will start next week. For homework, remember everything you did in improvisation. Clean it up, add and subtract, clarify your movements, and bring it in as a solo dance. We'll watch one dancer at a time. Okay? Any questions?"

Sylvia asked, "Should we do it with our eyes closed?"

"Excellent question. Let's imagine we have a lamp on our heads and can see only a narrow beam of light. That might give some interesting results. Very good, Sylvia. Any more questions?"

Bertha asked, "Vill our lemps go hout?"

"Good, Bertha! Class, some very interesting things happened when your eyes were closed, especially the ways you found each other and found the stage. Yes, Bertha, let's have the lamps go out. More questions?" There were none.

"Class dismissed. Come on time next week."

Next week Miss Bea made us dance the last line again and again, leaping for the stars. I couldn't leap. I was so embarrassed. Miss Bea said, "Fay, I want you to kneel in prayer and offer thanks to God for the stars." She said it was a lovely touch. Then she asked me to stay after class and she started teaching me to leap. She said all I had to do was go down first and use my bent knees as a spring. I tried, and I felt myself hopping like a fat frog.

"That's a good start," Miss Bea said. "It takes time. The more you develop thigh muscles in the warm-ups the easier it will be to leap. Trust me, don't worry about it."

Saturday Rehearsals

One Wednesday Miss Bea told us that the mother's club had volunteered to make our costumes. "They'll be brown sateen knee-length shifts with a cowl neckline. Starting November we'll rehearse on Saturday mornings in addition to our Wednesday class. Who can't come on Saturdays? Raise your hand." No one did.

My father, a part-time porter at Lavanburg's, complained about Miss Bea wanting the floor mopped Saturdays. He already had to give it an extra washing on Wednesdays. I told him I would come with him early Saturdays and help by sweeping and moving the chairs. He shook his head but gave in.

Next Saturday morning Miss Bea came early and saw me helping. She admired my dedication. I told her I want to be a dancer when I grow up. "You already are a dancer," she said. "You have the mind and imagination and grace of a dancer. Trust me, the body will come along."

How I loved Miss Bea! And I clung to the words "you already are a dancer" from then on, and it helped so much. Just as rehearsal started Bertha's father pounded on the door and sent her mother in to get her. Her mother, wide-eyed, frightened, whispered "Shabbas." Bertha left the class crying and never came back.

Our First Performance

Eight weeks later we presented "Caliban" in South Hall at a December rally. The stadium benches had been rearranged to take the shape of the floor space that we had used in our rehearsals. Miss Bea called it a theater in the round although it was more like a square.

Art, Woodwork, Photography, Bookbinding, and Knitting all had exhibits at the back of the Hall, and the social clubs had put up posters of their activities. Miss Bea had warned us that the big shots who funded us would be there. "Let me tell you, you're going to be a sensation."

And we were! At the end the whole audience stood up and were screaming while they were applauding! It was the happiest moment of my whole entire life.

We left our costumes on and stood along the aisle to watch the actors from the theater club take over the stage. There were also actors sitting among the audience. The play was called "Waiting for Lefty" by Clifford Odets. Seymour Harris's mother, Mrs. Harris, was Edna the taxi driver's wife, and it turned out that she was a really good actress. At the end, when we find out Lefty was shot dead because he was trying to organize a taxi union, the actors on stage and in the audience raised their fists and yelled "Strike! Strike! Strike!" And the whole audience stood up and raised their fists also and yelled with the actors "Strike! Strike! Strike!" and then they all stamped their feet like they were marching. Tears were streaming down people's faces and yet everyone was joyous!

That night I sat on my windowsill and pledged my life to modern dance and to the cause of the laboring masses.

Guernica! The Lavanburg Dance Company!

Back in class next Wednesday, Miss Bea told us, "Our next dance will be about the bombing of ordinary people in the peaceful city of Guernica. Only last year a democratically elected government in Spain was attacked by its own army, backed by Nazi Germany, and there is now a civil war in Madrid, the capital city."

For the next month we worked on a battle scene set to a song about the war:

The four insurgent generals, the four insurgent generals,
The four insurgent generals, Mamita, mia
They have betrayed us, they have betrayed us.
Madrid your tears of sorrow, Madrid your tears of sorrow,
Madrid your tears of sorrow, Mamita, mia
We shall avenge them, we shall avenge them.

Miss Bea calls out the scene. We advance with machine guns. We hear planes above us. Miss Bea rattles her tambourine. We fall, we hide, we crawl through a trench. Miss Bea walks among us. She pokes at Alice with her mallet. "You have a bullet through your stomach." She tells Beverly "Lie down" and throws her shawl over Beverly's legs. She says to me "Blood is pouring into your eyes." To Sylvia, "You're shot dead." She stops. "You hear the planes returning. Run for your life, Run! Fay, you can't see. Beverly, your legs are pinned down. Someone help Lillie. Joyce, lead Fay. Run! Run for your life, Run! Blackout. Quick, back on the battlefield in pitch dark. Three of you are dead soldiers. The rest are women walking among the dead in faint light. Sylvia, you come in with a lantern and hold it up. Everyone freeze. Everyone stand up tall, move backwards like ghosts until you all disappear offstage. Lights up, listen for applause, come back for bows."

Then Miss Bea told us that we're The Lavanburg Dance Company, and that we'll be creating a repertory called "Dances of Protest." She said 'After Guernica we'll protest the chain gangs of the South and then the rape of Canton in China, and then we'll look at other injustices."

In my family only Ruthie came to our dances of protest, except one time Maxie came to see us do Guernica.

Next day he called me into the living room and showed me the radio station WQXR, where I could get classical music to dance to. He told me to keep practicing. My father just scolded me. "Children shouldn't be dancing for strikes and wars. The teacher is turning her into a little communist." And my mother said, "She's not even interested in Ruthie's Saturday night parties anymore. God knows what will become of her with all her dancing on the stage."

By January 1939 eight of us students had been in Miss Bea's dance class all four and a half years since it started. We presented a major new dance every year and were invited to perform our Dances of Protest at other settlement houses and even at the Hamilton Fish Library's basement theater, which I never even knew existed. We always got terrific applause and cheers and even screams, and Miss Bea taught us how to come out for bows and do one of our folk dances for an encore. I could now do good leaps and even twist in the air. I was lifting my arms into space, uncurling my bony spine, extending my bare feet out to the world. Unfurled! Unfurled like a flag in the wind! I always cried when a Dance of Protest was over, tears of both anguish as a character and joy at the applause of the audience. And after every concert I sat in my window and I pledged to the stars in the night sky, "I'm going to be a dancer when I grow up. And I'm going to be a teacher like Miss Baronofsky." And I reviewed every moment of the concert in my mind. One night, in a dream, I leaped across a vast stage filled with dancers, all leaping to thunderous drumrolls and thunderous applause. I woke up to the sound of a coal truck rolling over the cobblestones in the street outside. On the dawn of that day I woke up confident that my future would be a happy one. But there was always sadness too, for the victims of the wrongs we were protesting.

Three years after we first presented our protest dance on the bombing of Guernica, the government of Spain, sadly, was defeated by the insurgent generals and their Nazi allies. The returned veterans of the Abraham Lincoln Brigade, who had bravely helped in the attempt to save Spanish democracy, invited us to perform for a fund drive at their meeting house. At the end of our dance, which had now become much longer, they were so moved that there was a long pause before they applauded. Afterwards we were invited to join them for dinner at a restaurant, El Paisano, in the Spanish neighborhood of West 14th Street. I had wine and delicious Spanish food called paella. And I smoked a cigarette in public and nobody minded even though they knew I was only 12 years old.

Frozen Feet

One day after class Miss Bea told us that her own dance teacher, Hanya Holm, would be performing with her troupe at Washington Irving High School over on East 15th Street this coming Saturday night. I had never seen a professional modern dance troupe, especially Miss Bea's own teacher. She told us how to sneak in at intermission. "A big crowd will come out into the lobby around a quarter to nine, and some of them will go outside for a smoke. Just wait outside and when they start going back, go back in with them. Look confident. Trust me, no one will stop you."

Three of us, Sylvia, Esther, and I, were the only ones who said we could go to the concert. But Saturday turned out to be very cold and they both backed out. I walked by myself to the Avenue B bus that goes to 14th Street, proud of my devotion. I got there early. It was so cold standing there across the street waiting for intermission. I had on fancy patent leather shoes and my feet were freezing. Finally a big crowd poured out to the lobby, talking and laughing and lighting cigarettes. I opened my coat, put my gloves in my pockets, and sneaked inside. I took a seat on the last row of the balcony, took off my shoes, and warmed my toes.

The curtain lifted. Hanya Holm and her troupe exploded onto the stage to loud applause and live music. First came a suite of short dances, "Metropolitan Daily," about newspaper pages. My favorite was "Want Ad," a duet with Hanya Holm and a young dancer who took the part of her child. My next favorite was "Superman," where a male dancer in a cape came charging out on the shoulders of two striding females. And my next favorite was "Gossip Column," where all the dancers scurried into corners like mice, waggling their fingers like whiskers. Then came a long beautiful dance, my favorite, called "Trends," where the stage had all different levels and the dancers, in simple drapey costumes, composed themselves on the levels as if a painter was creating a large picture. The music fit in so well that it was just as if Miss Bea's lectures on the three united arts of dance, music, and painting had come to life. And Miss Holm herself! How alive she was! How her feet pushed down and sprang up with such ease whether she was striding or leaping, and how gracefully every movement flowed out of the movement that came before. Deep inside me I felt myself moving with her.

Afterwards, when the concert was over and the lights went up, I could hardly get my shoes back on. My feet had swelled up. Walking to the bus stop along 14th Street I had to keep sitting down from doorway to doorway and hold my feet. They hurt so much! I got to the bus stop just as people were getting out. I was inches away when it took off! I stood there and cried, I couldn't help it. A tiny old lady who had been on the bus came over to me and asked, so sweetly, what was the matter. I told her my feet were freezing and I just missed the bus. "Oh my dear girl, the next bus won't come for another half hour. I live right here. Do you see that big window? That's my apartment. Come in, come in, I'll fix you up. We have plenty of time." She led me inside and sat me down in a plush armchair near the window. "You sit right there and I'll have you fixed up in no time, don't you worry." Soon she had my shoes off and a blanket over my feet, then she rummaged around in a trunk by the kitchenette. "Ah, here we are." She brought out a pair of heavy socks and a man's leather slippers with flannel lining. She put the socks on my feet and tied the slippers on with string. She put my shoes in a shopping bag. "These slippers belonged to my late husband. You can return them tomorrow. If I'm not home just hang the bag on my door." Then she went back to the kitchenette and brought me a mug of hot tea. "Now you tell me what happened. What were you doing out alone so late?"

I told her how I froze my feet waiting for intermission to sneak into a dance concert. "How lucky you found me!" she said. "I'm a dancer, too, you know. My late husband and I were an acrobatic tap dance team in vaudeville. We danced all over the country." She went back to the trunk in the kitchenette and brought out a photo album full of newspaper clippings and advertisements, but I was nervous about missing the bus and kept turning to look out the window. She closed the album. I felt guilty. When it was time to go she walked me to the bus stop and waited with me to keep the drunken-bums away, and she kissed me goodbye.

It must have been close to midnight by the time I got home. I couldn't untie the strings and had to open the door with the men's slippers on my feet. My father was just getting ready to call the police. My mother was collapsed on the living room chair with a vinegar rag around her head. My sister Ruthie sat next to her. My father yelled "Where did you get those men's shoes?" I told them the whole story but only Ruthie believed me. Ma said if I go on with my dancing I'll end up a showgirl and will bring home a bastard for her to pretend it's her change-of-life baby. God knows where I was so late. Ruthie yelled at her for her dirty mind. Ma said, "Both of you drive me crazy. Why didn't I have four boys? This one wants to be a nurse bummika and wipe men's behinds and that one wants to be a showgirl bummika and sleep with who knows who."

Just then Sidney came home drunk, with lipstick smeared on his face, and headed straight for the bathroom. Ruthie ran out to the kitchen and came back with scissors to cut away the slippers and a wash basin of warm water for my feet, which had got frozen again walking home from the bus stop. While I sat bent over the wash basin the image of Hanya Holm's feet came to me, the walk she used in the "Want Ad" scene from her newspaper dance. The toes of her rear foot had clutched the floor for a split second on each step, and that made her look strong but weary. I decided to compose a dance using that step.

And then a second idea for a dance came to me. In the "Gossip Column" scene the dancers took scurrying steps to this corner and that, opened their mouths to look shocked, wiggled their hands and faces. I could make a dance out of my stupid mother and father who were carrying on about whether it was better for him or for her to go with me tomorrow to bring the slippers back and what to do if a man opened the door. I'll turn them into scurrying mice!

I decided to return the slippers very early next morning, before anyone was awake, and ask the sweet little lady to show me her album again. And that's just what I did after I left a note on the kitchen table so they wouldn't call the police to tell them I'd run away from home, which I felt very likely to do some day.

XXIII

Daisy

In October 1938, Japan invaded Canton, homeland of the thousand or so Chinese laundrymen in New York. The American Communists, Socialists, and labor unions demanded a boycott of Japanese goods. Shipments of scrap steel from the demolished Sixth Avenue elevated trains, bound for Japan, were held up at the San Francisco docks. The Longshoremen's Union refused to load the steel, warning that it would come back to us as bullets. Some young women in my neighborhood started wearing black cotton stockings to show support for the boycott of Japanese silk. Miss Bea Baronofsky, my modern dance teacher at Lavanburg Social Center, announced that we were going to work on a new dance, "The Rape of Canton," to add to our Dances of Protest concert, which, in addition to "Caliban in the Coal Mines," now included "Madrid Your Tears of Sorrow" for the Spanish Civil War, and an anti-lynching dance, "When Black Face is Lifted, Lord's Turnin' Away," for the Negroes of the South.

Next time I was in Frank Wing's Hand Laundry, I proudly told him about the steel boycott, the black stockings, and the plans for a dance to be called "The Rape of Canton." Frank Wing spoke many English words by now. He was surprised and pleased that my dance troupe cared about his country. He ducked into the back room and brought out a photograph of his wife and son. A skinny, shy-looking woman in a narrow dress, and a solemn boy in a school uniform and cap. Frank Wing said he sent them money every month. "Will you bring them to America?" I asked.

"Quota is one hundred five Chinese a year, no family, only men. Maybe law change, maybe I go back. Now, with

161

war, China in danger. Maybe wife not get money." He spoke rapidly, with little bows. He was smiling but his eyebrows slanted upwards in anguish.

"I tell my wife you dance for Chinese people," he said.

Frank Wing's building, like many other old buildings on the East Side, had a yard house in the back. You walked straight through the ground-floor hallway to the back, and there was a house, only one or two stories high, sometimes so old it even had a porch. Yard house rents were very low because the apartments were run down and had no heat or hot water, sometimes not even electricity. Mostly single old men lived in them, and hobos, and a few ragged families whose children didn't even go to school.

When Daisy started hanging around in Frank Wing's store next spring, she was so thin and shabby I thought she had come in through his back door from the yard house. I thought he was giving her food out of kindness. Soon I began to hear that she was his girlfriend, and the boys started making dirty jokes about how the Chinks did it. I said, "No, Frank Wing is married. She lives in the yard house."

Frank Wing's back door had frosted glass panes in a snowflake pattern but one pane had long ago been replaced with clear glass and we used to peek through it at night to watch him chop strange roots and vegetables with a cleaver and cook them in a steaming pan and eat with chopsticks on a pile of rice. Now all of us sneaked around to the back and tried to peek in but the clear glass had been covered with cardboard.

Daisy started appearing on the street. She was better dressed now, and wore bright makeup and high heels. She would sit in front of the store on a folding chair. People got used to seeing her around, but nobody spoke to her. She put out a dish of milk for the street cats and soon picked up a kitten of her own, so she made friends with the little children who came up to pat it. At times you could see that she looked woozy.

Customers began to complain that the shirt collars were coming back creased and had to be done over. It was now clear to me that Frank Wing and Daisy were living in sin in the back of his store and getting drunk together. I didn't want to talk about it, and unless I had to bring in the laundry I walked on the other side of the street.

Then, one afternoon, while the older boys were playing stickball down the block, Daisy came busting out of the Hand Laundry and ran like a streak right through the ballgame and around the corner. Frank Wing came running after her with the cleaver in his hand. The younger boys screamed "Chop-Chop" and "Go, Frankie, get her!" Danny Halpern tackled him from behind and brought him down. Others piled on and grabbed his arm. He bucked and twisted and held onto the cleaver, screeching "Catch her, catch her!" Some guys had already run after her, but they came back. She had disappeared. Frank Wing crumpled like a broken umbrella and, to everyone's relief, let go of the cleaver. "She take the money," he sobbed. "All the money. Find her. Please."

When my father heard the story that evening he shook his head and said, "Ah, the poor man. I know how he feels. The cashier in my delicatessen store, I was engaged to her, she was wearing my expensive diamond ring, she stole my money and ran away together with my waiter. They ruined the business. I lost everything. Everything. I lost my *life*."

My mother was putting supper on the table. She gave him a look, bitter as gall.

XXIV
Ruthie's Boyfriends

Ruthie is Sixteen!

As soon as my mother started getting extra money from her door-to-door consignment business she started saving for Ruthie's sweet sixteen. Sidney had become an adult at his Bar Mitzvah when he was thirteen. Ruthie became an adult at sixteen. I was nine. Ma sold the old-fashioned dining room furniture and got a brand-new three-piece living room set.

The Party

Ruthie had a lively party with balloons and streamers and colored light bulbs and dancing into the night. For a start, she borrowed a cocktail set from Rita Feder's sister, and Al, Ruthie's sort-of boyfriend, made everyone Manhattans, the most popular cocktail. At our house, beer was as unrestricted as soda. Children only began to drink beer when their desire to join with the grownups overcame the bitter taste. Ma thought beer or a shot-glass of whisky with meat was good for the digestion because alcohol dissolved the fat. It never occurred to her that anyone but a bum or a Christian could become an alcoholic. We had a song: *Shicker iz er, trinken mis er, vayl er iz a goy*—Drunk he is, drink he must, because he is a goy, that is, a person who is not a Jew. However, we never saw drunken Italian men on the street either, just Jewish high school boys who got stinking drunk and pukey on prom nights. What Ma hated most was cigarettes, but once boys were thirteen she didn't stop them. Girls should not smoke until they were sixteen. To her generation, once you were in high school she accepted that you were going to do what your friends did, with two great exceptions: girls must remain virgins and neither boys nor girls should have coffee before they were sixteen as it's bad for the nerves.

To ease everybody through the self-conscious period, Sidney and I brought out two large platters of hot pastrami sandwiches on rye. Pickles, mustard, soda, and small bottles of beer were already on the table, along with Camels and Chesterfield cigarettes, candy, potato chips, and shelled salted peanuts. There were also shallow silver cups with feet, filled with Turkish cigarettes rolled in lavender paper for girls and tan paper for boys. Whenever the guests stopped talking I'd pick up one of the bowls and circulate with it.

Then came the dance music. There was room for four dancing couples. Ruthie used Martin Block's "Milkman's Matinee." Each swing band got fifteen minutes of time. The overhead light fixture with three naked light bulbs was turned off. A peach light glowed from a lamp on the side table, a black-and-gold elephant bearing an orange silk shade. The light of the fish tank cast its mysterious glow. Glenn Miller's "Moonlight Sonata" was very popular. No words. Just the most romantic music. This was the first time that, in public and with a partner, I followed the actual music rather than the fixed ballroom dance steps. I only danced with Al, and he only danced with me. Al walked with a limp, but when he led me in dance he was like Fred Astaire swirling Ginger Rogers. I felt made of silk chiffon. Al was by far the handsomest boy there, but he was shy, maybe because of his limp.

After the success of her Sweet Sixteen party, Ruthie had monthly "gatherings" which were just the same but without the decorations and with a modest amount of snacks and soda.

Ruthie Dresses Up for Dates

Now that Ruthie was sixteen she was allowed to wear makeup, black dresses, jewelry, kid leather gloves, glamorous hats, to smoke in the street, and go out on double dates.

When she dressed for a date she let me search in her drawer and hand her each item of makeup as she called it out. That was the most fun. First the rouge, a small round gold compact. Inside, a little flat silk moire puff resting on a disk of pressed pink powder. Ruthie made a strong smile with her mouth closed, which pushed up her cheeks. She swirled the rouge onto the highest part. Next, sitting on the dresser, a big glass powder jar in the shape of a pagoda, filled with Coty's light beige face powder under a big pink powder puff with a little white satin ribbon. She slipped her fingers through the ribbon and made a cloud of powder as she dusted her face. She carried a compact in her purse to reapply powder during the evening. The face must never be shiny. Then she applied black mascara and brown eyebrow pencil. Only streetwalkers penciled their eyes and used eye shadow, I handed her one of her Flame-Glo lipsticks. Ruthie had three shades: pink, bright red, and plum. The colors had fanciful names that kept changing, like Sunset Splendor and Passion Rose. She was so pretty anyway, but with her makeup on she positively sparkled. Everyone said she looked just like Sonja Henie, the Norwegian ice-skating champion who became a top box-office movie star.

Ruthie's Dates

Ruthie started having double dates and then single dates. Ma and I would wait up for her, and when she came home we had a *knubl* party— garlic dipped into salt and rubbed onto the crust of rye bread, with beer on the side— while she told us all about her evening out.

Ruthie had nice boyfriends but she was holding out for a grown man who would look like the actor Warner Baxter. He would have black hair and a mustache and smoke a pipe and would be wearing a starched white shirt.

Tall Al

The Al I liked, the one with the limp, was called Short Al. Tall Al was clean-shaven and smoked Lucky Strike. He was an accountant, an esteemed profession in our family, signifying a smart and serious young man who looked to the future and would always make a living. She started going out with him. He was her first Saturday night date. He always showed up with a gardenia, took her to the movies or a dance, and even to Coney Island. But he didn't have a mustache and a pipe.

Milty

One of Ruthie's boyfriends did have a mustache and a pipe, but he was far from looking like Warner Baxter in a starched white shirt. Milty, a car mechanic who drove a motorcycle, came to Ruthie's parties in an aviator's leather jacket. He wore an aviator's helmet in the winter, glasses and all. His shirts had bold patterns. His pants were khaki work pants. When he wasn't driving his motorbike and wearing his helmet, he wore a felt slouch hat slightly tipped back on his head. Like Short Al at parties, he paid more attention to me, but unlike Short Al he didn't dance. Milty was the only boyfriend who hung around the house. He told jokes and showed us funny card tricks and posed riddles. He'd sometimes even be in the house when Ruthie went out with a date. Milty wouldn't call for her to take her on a date. They'd go to the movies together on a week-night, like friends.

Milty worked down the next block in the Italian part of Goerck street, between Stanton and Rivington. He worked in a little green shed in the blacksmith's yard at the end of the block, guarding the property and the tires and cars in the yard. He would repair cars, sell used cars for their owners, and park cars off the street in snowstorms. I loved to go visit Milty in his shed. I'd visit him in the evening while I pretended I was going to the settlement house. He had a radio with police and coastguard bands on it—I loved to hear the Morse code— and he drank beer and even whiskey. There wasn't room for a cot, but he squeezed in a big dumpy old stuffed chair and would sleep in it with his feet up on the office chair, which was on wheels. The two chairs took up all the space except for the ledge that held the radios and his cash box, and a slot of hooks where he hung his jackets. Under the ledge was a shelf where he kept a gun. I pretended not to notice it, but I decided he had to protect himself at night. Milty was thrilling, like a movie tough who goes straight and gets the girl who believed in him all along.

Blackie

Blackie came close to Ruthie's Warner Baxter ideal. She met him at a Friday night dance just after she graduated from high school in June. A lot of girls had brought their boyfriends to prom night and were already showing off their engagement rings. She caught his eye and smiled and that did it because she was so pretty and had on a beautiful black dress instead of the flouncy pastels all the other girls were wearing. Not too long after that they became engaged.

"We were sitting on a bench by the East River," she said. "He took my hand and held up this big diamond ring. Before he put it on my finger he made me promise never to bleach my hair. I never thought of bleaching my hair, so I promised. Then he told me he never again wanted to see me smoke in the street. So I promised that also. So we got engaged, without an engagement party because Blackie didn't want one.

Ma booked a very nice wedding hall for Ruthie in the Bronx, for October; nobody got married in the summer because of vacations. Then one day soon after her engagement Ruthie lit a cigarette in the street. "I wasn't thinking," she said. "It was just a habit. He slapped the cigarette out of my hand, right there in the street in front of everybody, and he gave me a look that could kill. I got scared that after we were married he would beat me up." So she ran upstairs and hid in the bedroom and made Mama go downstairs and give him back the ring.

The manager wouldn't give back my mother's deposit on the wedding hall, so she made a deal with him that if Ruthie married before the year was over he would use the deposit money for her new wedding.

Irwin

That summer Ruthie got a job as a bookkeeper in a Catskill hotel. A guest, Mrs. Calman, liked her a lot—who didn't?—and thought she'd be a great match for her son Irwin, so when her husband came up for the weekend he brought Irwin with him to meet her. As it happened, Ruthie quit her job after only two weeks because her bosses cooked the books to cheat on paying taxes and she was afraid to be a party to anything illegal, so when she got back to the city she started going out with Irwin. My parents were crazy about him because his parents had a dry-cleaning store on Park Avenue. We didn't know Park Avenue ended in the slums so we thought they were rich. Irwin told us he was going to dental school, and he drove a nice car. Ma started pressuring Ruthie to get married. She was already twenty. Irwin started pressuring her too. Belgium and Holland had fallen to Hitler in May, France surrendered in

June, England was barely holding out. Everyone knew that American boys would soon be drafted into the army, and all the young men were trying to get married to escape it.

They planned their engagement party. Then he told Ruthie that he was actually studying to be a dental mechanic and that the car belonged to his friend. She told us, "Well, I guess all's fair in love and war. It's like the Fred Astaire and Ginger Roger movies. They always lie to each other." I didn't like that, and I didn't think she liked it either. I thought she was sticking to the marriage plans because she didn't have the nerve to break a second engagement.

XXV
Thelonious Monk, One of Us

"Follow the form where it takes you."

—Cecil Taylor

When summer came, the Lavanburg Settlement House closed down its basement activities and moved to the roof. Some teachers could continue their regular clubs on the roof, others led sports or table games or found other work until September. Miss Baronofsky, our dance teacher, met us in the courtyard every Sunday morning and took us to one of the city's museums or parks and showed us inspiring works of art or nature.

One time Miss Bea took us on a hike across the Hudson River to the New Jersey side. We rode on the open top of the Fifth Avenue double-decker bus all the way to the George Washington Bridge, then we walked across the Bridge, then we climbed many many steps carved into the Palisades cliff until we reached the top. There we followed a trail to a grassy field where we had a picnic lunch while gazing at the beautiful Manhattan skyline from across the river. I was so enchanted by that day that I went on the trip again by myself next Saturday. But after climbing the steps to the Palisades cliff I took the wrong trail and got lost. I heard a piano and followed the sound, then I saw a sign that said Palisades Amusement Park, and then I came to an open pavilion where a skinny young man in a striped T-shirt was playing the piano while five or six other men were standing around with their instruments, swaying lightly to the music.

The pianist was playing bits of sound at a time, watching his hands as they moved and tilting his head to listen, as if the hands were improvising a duet. He'd play a little, turn his ear toward the keys, then play some more. The music was different but not difficult. It had an underbeat like the soft pulse of Miss Bea's wool mallet on her hand-drum: *tum, tum, tarum tum.* I joined in the swaying without even noticing. The man next to me, holding a clarinet, said, "You like this music?" I smiled and nodded. He said, "So, hey, you're one of us!" We both laughed and I swayed even more. "That's Thelonious Monk," he said. "You remember his name now, because he's gonna be famous." I was 12, so looking back I see that Monk must have been 22, but he looked much younger. When he paused for a bit I asked the clarinetist how to get back to the George Washington Bridge and the Fifth Avenue bus. He walked me to the Amusement Park bus stop, which took me to Fifth Avenue, so I had to spend two nickels to get home, which, fortunately, I had.

I did remember the name Thelonious Monk, and later, when I was grown up and he was famous, I watched him get up from his piano and dance-shuffle to the same soft underbeat that we had swayed to in Palisades Park.

XXVI
A Shower of Sequins

One May Day we had a celebration in the Lavanburg court featuring the Duncan dancers in a fluttery circle followed by our modern dance group with folk dances from Russia and Latvia. Some parents recognized the steps and joined in. Then the boys formed a chain dance and whipped around the dancers faster and faster. And then some goddess of a mother, that is, a woman who knew how to feed children indelible memories of joy, opened a bag at her window and poured down a shower of sequins containing all the sparkling colors of the world. They twirled slowly to the ground, some to be detained in our hair or in our supplicating palms. Other Lavanburg mothers left their windowsills and came back to fling out more bags of sequins, and still more. The sequins glittered in the sunlight, showering the dancers, the onlookers, the pavement, with silver, gold, ruby red, emerald green, sapphire blue, royal topaz. Everyone in the court twirled to catch them, the whole courtful of us turning and twirling in a dance of catching the sequins as they came twirling down. Where had they come from? The sequins had been imprisoned in their bags since the women stopped sewing them onto the bold evening dresses of the flapper age and turned to the lace trimmings of our own romantic age.

A Fiesta in the Courtyard. From *Practices and Experiences of the Lavanburg Homes, Third Edition* (Fred. L. Lavanburg Foundation, New York City, 1941). Used with permission.

XXVII

My Rooftop Romance

"Night and day, you are the one
Only you beneath the moon and under the sun"

—Cole Porter

Volleyball was a great game for a Lavanburg's summer roof activity. Anyone could play, grownups, boys and girls, children, beginners, just so long as the teams on opposite sides of the net were matched. The little ones and beginners only needed to hit the incoming ball underhand and keep it in play. I was just thirteen that summer and a pretty good player for my age. A boy of about fifteen or sixteen—I think his name was Arnold—sat on the bench where we waited to get into a game. He had been crippled by polio and had a twisted, labored walk with two canes. He was taught at home by a tutor, and I never saw him in the street. By sitting on the bench he always found someone to talk to, always a girl; now it was me. One day Arnold brought out a long poem he said he had written for me. He read it aloud. After a few lines it mentioned nubile breasts that will soon contain nectar for a god. He stopped and gave me a creepy smile. As the poem went on it named parts of my body that he wanted to feel up. I left the bench. I had to give up the volleyball games because of him.

I went to the quiet-activities section of the roof. When I passed by the sunbathers on their blankets, one of them called out, "Hey, here comes my gorgeous dance partner!" It was Phil. He used to come to the Social Center for the grown-up activities. We had talked for the first time last February, on Lincoln's birthday, when my dance troupe gave a performance of "Madrid Your Tears of Sorrow" at a fund-raiser for the brave boys of the Abraham Lincoln Brigade who had helped defend the Spanish Republic against the fascist insurrection. After the show we had been allowed to stay for the social dancing, and Phil was one of the adults who had danced with me. And afterwards we all went to a Spanish restaurant, El Paisano, where the Lincoln Brigaders hung out, and we had wine and sang Lincoln Brigade songs.

Phil asked to see the book I was carrying, George Bernard Shaw's *Intelligent Woman's Guide to Socialism and Capitalism*. I had wanted *Das Kapital* as a summer loan from the library because my brother Sidney teased me for not knowing who Karl Marx was, but the librarian said *Das Kapital* was very difficult and very boring and she advised me to read the Shaw book instead. I was so glad Phil saw me carrying it because he would think I was a serious person who read grownup books. He lay back on the blanket, shut his eyes, and asked me to read aloud. And that's how it began.

After reading awhile I lay down on the blanket alongside him, eyes closed and face up. The sun was so bright I felt its glare through my eyelids. The heat stung my cheeks and my thighs. He rolled over and asked me to spread cocoa butter on his back. My fingers tingled with pleasure as they moved from the fringe of his golden curls to the hollow of his spine where his bathing trunks began, feeling his muscles ripple under my touch. I inhaled the aroma of his anointed body next to mine, the cocoa butter obscuring the summertime rooftop odors of hot brick and tar.

I lay down alongside him again. I wondered how I looked in the glaring light. I was wearing my white sharkskin shorts and halter set, a thirteenth birthday present from my sister Ruthie. I tilted my chin up to make my nose look shorter. I had on Tangee Natural lipstick blotted until no more came off on the tissue, a matching rouge carefully blended at the edges, and a touch of brown mascara at the very ends of my lashes. Now I worried whether the makeup showed in the sunlight. A shade came over my eyelids and the whiff of cocoa butter got stronger. He was leaning over me.

"Roll over," he said. "It's your turn." His voice had a golden tone, like everything about him. Eyes still closed, I rolled over and rested my right cheek on my folded arms, showing the left side of my face, which made me look older. He spread the cocoa butter in slow, wide sweeps across the top of my back and into the corners of my neck and shoulders. I could hear the volleyball in the next court going thump thump. I felt a forbidden thrill.

We started meeting on the roof every afternoon. He brought up sunglasses, one pair for each of us. His skin turned bronze. The hair on his chest and arms and thighs became a shimmering gold. After a while we tired of Shaw and he brought up poems of Garcia Lorca, Walt Whitman, Unamuno. Then we read Edgar Allen Poe and Sherlock Holmes. When it rained we would go under the awning and Phil would teach me chess by replaying the master games.

Once he asked me what I wanted to be when I grow up. I said "What I already am. A modern dancer. What do you want to be, or are you already what you'll be?"

"Well, the Spanish Civil War made me think a lot about probabilities, so that's what I've been studying for a degree in mathematics." And that made me feel intensely flattered, to have him be my friend when he was so smart.

Two summer months passed, the most peaceful I have ever known, sunbathing, reading, watching the boats on the river. I put flowers in a metal card-file box and buried it in the sand of an empty lot by the river, with my initials and his, and Poe's poem "Annabelle Lee" and the date.

I had a plan. My sister Ruthie was about to become engaged to a boy I didn't like, and I had a feeling she didn't like him either. My plan was to get Phil and Ruthie together so she would fall in love with him and they would marry and then he would always be in my family. I convinced Phil and Ruthie to go out together on a blind date. Afterwards she said he was very nice but too quiet for her. He said they didn't have much in common and he couldn't find anything to talk about.

"I'm sorry," I said. "She's very popular. Everybody likes her. I just thought you would too."

"I do like her, I guess I just don't know how to behave on a date."

"Don't you date girls?"

"Look, what if I married your sister and then you found out you loved me?"

I blurted out "I do love you." He lowered his head and closed his eyes, as if in pain. He said, "I love you too." I felt a great shock. Suddenly it was real, and I was responsible. We knew we couldn't be just friends any more.

We had a last evening together at the closing dance of the season, under the roof's awning strung with colored lights. Arnold was in charge of the Victrola. He kept leering at me. Phil didn't notice.

The lights went out for the last dance of the night. It was Glenn Miller's "Moon Love," number one on the Hit Parade. Everyone sang along, and so did we, looking into each other's eyes by the distant lights of the city.

Can this be moon love,
Nothing but moon love
Will you be gone when the dawn comes stealing through?

Are these but moon dreams,
Grand while the moon beams
But when the moon fades away will my dreams come true?

Much as I love you,
Don't let me love you
If I must pay for your kiss with lonely tears.

Say it's not moon love,
Tell me it's true love
Say you'll be mine when the moon disappears.

The roof was dark. Everyone headed downstairs except the couples, who went off to separate benches and corners of the roof. We stood at the ledge and looked out over the rooftops. I asked him to pledge that we will both look at the full moon every month, so each will know the other is watching and know we'll be thinking of each other. He said no, I must take the time to grow up naturally, with friends my own age. I knew he was right. Being with him all summer had been a strain, dressing up every morning, keeping myself fresh and clean all day, staying away from my silly friends, pretending always to be the person I would like to be for him rather than the person I had been before I met him and the person I was when I was not with him. He said I had to finish high school and when we met again I would be an adult and then we would both see what had become of us and see if we would still fit together.

So we promised to meet on the roof again on my eighteenth birthday. He kissed my forehead but finally pressed me close. I clung to him. I closed all the space between us to keep the imprint of his body in my memory. I felt, even then when I was so young, I felt that so long as I lived, no matter what happened, he would always be the only one I could ever love. And so it was.

XXVIII
The Button Thief of East 14th Street

*"Some kill their love when they are young,
And some when they are old."*

—Oscar Wilde

Best Friends

I hadn't thought of becoming friends with Helen Boris, although I liked her. We were in the same eighth-grade class, 8A-1, the smartest. My eyes often came to rest on her long honey-colored hair, the way it draped over her starched white middy blouse, the way it spilled down her cheeks when she bent over her writing paper. She was a new girl, quiet, sort of a goody-goody. I sometimes wished I could be like her: straight hair, neat, never getting in trouble. My hair was frizzy and I had to keep it in braids when I didn't have a whole day to stay home and set it with my sister Ruthie's rollers. My middy blouses were a hand-me-down mess, and my stockings always wrinkled and slipped under my heels. And I didn't have good manners. My Civics teacher, Miss Chilton—we called her Miss Chilly—who was also my homeroom teacher and a reactionary, wouldn't call on me, so when I just *had* to make a point like we didn't drive Spain out of Cuba just to free the Cubans, I yelled out my answer. Then she would say "All right, Miss Kessler, that's enough of your bad manners. Let's hear from someone else. Miss Rosner?"

Lorna Rosner was my best friend in school ever since the lower grades when we were the same size and everybody had to stand, sit, and walk through the halls two by two in size places. We got used to always being next to each other unless the teacher separated us for talking. But we were really best friends because we had an agreement to be library partners and read the same books, not counting the political books I started reading last term to find out who was Karl Marx and whether I wanted to be a Communist like our volleyball coach Bernie Heinbach or a Trotskyite like my dance teacher Miss Baronofsky, or a New Deal Democrat like Eleanor Roosevelt, or a Fabian like the British author George Bernard Shaw, although we had no Fabians in America.

Lorna Rosner was the smartest girl in our class and the prettiest. She had a halo of black curls and the cutest little upturned nose. I tried sleeping on my stomach with my nose pressed up against a coat button but I only got a creased nose. I thought maybe I was almost as smart as Lorna sometimes, but aside from getting into arguments with teachers I was always reading ahead or thinking of something else or doodling, so I was never in the right place when my name was called and my grades were wobbly. I was best in English class, where I was the best reader. Miss Smith, from a New England Abolitionist family that had sheltered and taught runaway slaves—we called her Yankee Doodle—would call on someone to read and halfway through she would say "Sit down. Fay continue." She'd call on the next student, and soon she'd again say "Sit down. Fay continue."

It became a joke. My classmates called me Fay Continue, that is, when they weren't calling me Shell-Shock for walking past them on the street in a daze like those blank-eyed ex-soldiers. I couldn't help it. I was always holding a book and reading as I walked, or looking someplace far when I was expected to be seeing things near, or vice versa. Anyway, in a few weeks we would find out who was smartest in the whole eighth grade because we had just taken the IQ test and the student with the highest score would be called up in Assembly to be honored. We knew anyway: Karl Feldstein in 8B-1, the "one" class in the upper eighth grade. Karl was a refugee from Germany who knew the answer to everything and got a hundred percent on almost every test and played chess with grownup men after school. I secretly hoped Lorna would come out smartest of the girls because that would be an honor for me, too, as her best friend.

The Poetry Contest

I stopped being best friends with Lorna when we had the poetry recitation contest at the end of September. I didn't care how smart she was, I found out she was an opportunist. Once each term everyone in Junior High, meaning seventh, eighth, and ninth grades, read a favorite poem in homeroom class and the teacher picked the best one to represent the class in Assembly. The best recitation of the best poem in each of the three Assemblies got a Webster's Dictionary. Lorna and I practiced together for a whole week, arguing about one poem, testing out another. We said to each other, "If I'm not best I want you to be best," and we swore to share the dictionary if either of us won. To seal our pledge we linked right-hand pinkies and each blew a big pink bubble-gum bubble and we smashed our bubbles together in a bubble-gum kiss.

I chose "Abraham Lincoln Walks at Midnight" by Vachel Lindsay because it reminded me of the terrible war in Europe, with Hitler goose-stepping across the Continent and dropping bombs all over London.

> *His head is bowed. He thinks of men and kings.*
> *Yea, when the sick world cries, how can he sleep?*
> *Too many peasants fight, they know not why;*
> *Too many homesteads in black terror weep.*

Lorna couldn't make up her mind between "Ballade of a Ship" by Edward Arlington Robinson, with its grand refrain:

Where the bones of the brave in the wave are lying

or "The Tuft of Flowers" by Robert Frost, about a farmer whose heart is stirred when he sees that the mower in the meadow has left a patch of blooms for the butterflies. But that was just to fool me. When audition time came in our home-room class Miss Chilton said my Abraham Lincoln poem was too long and too gloomy. She didn't even let me finish.

Then Lorna got up and read an even longer poem that she hadn't told me about, "Little Orphant Annie" by James Whitcomb Riley, about a servant girl who tells witches' tales to the children at night by the stove. It's practically in baby talk.

It has the refrain:

An' the gobble-uns 'll git YOU ef you Don't Watch Out

Lorna swayed her shoulders as she recited the sing-song verses, and every time the refrain came around she pointed her finger at the audience on the word "YOU." She knew I couldn't stand stuff like that but she didn't care. She was chosen to represent our class, and on Wednesday in the eighth-grade Assembly she actually won the dictionary.

Helen Boris was different. She was dreamy and romantic. I didn't care for her poem too much, "Leisure," by W.H. Davies:

What is this life if, full of care,
We have no time to stand and stare

but she recited it with sincerity, even, I would say, with sorrow.

One stanza goes

No time to turn at Beauty's glance
And watch her feet, how they can dance

I had heard that Helen's mother was strict and didn't let her go to dances or even the movies. And you could tell she didn't know the Hit Parade songs when we sang them in recess. So her poem moved my heart. I decided to see if I could get Helen to be my best friend while I was being mad at Lorna. It took me less than two weeks to find out that it was the worst mistake I ever made in the entire thirteen years of my whole life.

At the Library

I started by asking Helen if she would like to go on the library line with me. Every Friday at three o'clock, as soon as the last bell rang and the teachers said "class dismissed," everybody ran to the Hamilton Fish Library. It was a block-and-a-half away, on Houston Street facing the park. Our school, P.S. 188 on the Lower East Side, had four thousand pupils, kindergarten through ninth grade. It was the largest public school in the whole world.

My class was on the top floor, the fourth, and by the time Helen and I clanked down the metal stairwell in our one-inch heels, the library line snaked all the way from the entrance in the middle of Houston Street, back to the police station next to our school, around the station house, and half-way up the next block, 1st Street. A long wait to get in.

The day was mild. We were having Indian summer. We spent the time on line discussing what kinds of books we should try to find. In the adult library on the main floor, where you got admitted in seventh grade, the most popular girls' books were *Green Mansions, Wuthering Heights, Jane Eyre,* and *Gone with the Wind.* The girls would love to take out any of these books again if we could get hold of them except that I wouldn't read *Gone with the Wind* because the Communist boys on my block said it was pro-slavery and they had picketed the movie when it showed on Broadway. Library books were due back in two weeks. Helen and I agreed to take out one book each and exchange at the end of one week. That's how I used to do it with Lorna, but I didn't tell Helen that because I didn't want her to feel like Lorna's substitute.

When we finally got in, Helen ran to the shelves with everybody else while I checked at the Reserves desk. Students were not allowed to reserve books but one of the librarians, Miss Adler, made an exception for me and always left me a book on the Reserve shelf ever since I asked her who's Karl Marx. Some of the books she saved for me were political, like my favorite, *The Intelligent Woman's Guide to Socialism and Capitalism* by George Bernard Shaw, and some were about capitalist exploitation, like *The Jungle* by Upton Sinclair about the horrible working conditions of the meat-packers in Chicago. This time Miss Adler had saved me *The Grapes of Wrath,* about a family that lost their farm in a Dust Bowl famine, and *The Good Earth,* about a Chinese family that lost their farm in a locust famine. I took the books to the library tables and got two seats together. Helen soon found me. She had managed to grab *Ramona* from the Returns cart. A good catch, hard to get hold of, and neither of us had read it.

It was about the forbidden love between the adopted daughter of a wealthy Spanish-Mexican widow and an American Indian who was doing the sheep-shearing on her large estate. I held Helen's place while she went back to the shelves to see what else she could find.

Our table was all girls. Boys took their books to separate tables. They read mostly detective stories, exploration, and biographies of famous men. The boys piled up high stacks of books between their elbows and traded them like they were Wheaties baseball cards. Each boy would try to trade one book for two or three even if he didn't have time to read them. At the girls' tables it was the opposite. We yelled out our titles and traded one-for-one and changed our minds and shoved books this way and that like a drunken shuffleboard game. The librarians knew they couldn't shush us on Friday afternoons and they didn't try. Helen brought more books back from the shelves and sat down beside me and we started looking over our pile. The noise around us stopped. I looked up. The girls in our class were staring at us. Big Charlotte Shorr, who wore a big bow in her hair, spoke up first.

"Lorna's right behind you, Fay. Aren't you gonna sit with her?"

"Not right now." Her stooge Gertrude Bernstein said, "Are you mad at her?"

"Ask me no questions and I'll tell you no lies."

Lillian Adler, my nosy upstairs neighbor, pitched in: "So why aren't you sitting with Lorna?"

"Oh, hello Lillian. Have you met Helen Boris? She's only been in your class since the first day."

Helen blushed. Actually, it was hard for new girls to get into a clique without first having a friend, though once in, girls were always getting mad or glad and changing friends except for a few who always stayed together, like me and Lorna. But how could I tell those dopes that I was mad at Lorna because of a poem that won her the Assembly prize?

I got busy looking over our pile. Helen too. I could see she wasn't enthusiastic about *Grapes of Wrath*. I didn't like hillbilly stories myself. She had read *The Good Earth* and said it was very

189

good and she would read it again if I wanted. I said, "Let's see what we can trade it for."

I called out, "Who wants *The Good Earth*?" and we quickly made a trade for a book of short stories by Dorothy Parker called *Here Lies*. We left the rest of the pile on the table and got out of there. I had to pass by Lorna on the way to the take-out desk. She stuck a book up in front of her face. It was *Savage Symphony: A Personal History of the Third Reich*, about an anthropologist who was ruined by Hitler for refusing to fake evidence of a white Aryan master race. It was my cousin Pearlie's favorite book. Lorna knew Miss Adler was on the lookout to reserve it for me. She only held it up to spite me.

Helen Comes to My House

Next morning, Saturday, Helen came to my house to read together. It was the first time I saw her dressed up. She had on a brown chesterfield coat with a velvet collar, a pink silk dress of pale autumn flowers, and brown baby-jane shoes. She looked so pretty, like a rich girl from uptown. My mother greeted her like an honored guest and right away asked her to sit down and eat. Helen said "No thank you, I've had breakfast," but my mother went right on without a stop.

"I can give you pickled herring, Rice Krispies, scrambled eggs, whatever you want."

"*Ma*," I said. "She doesn't *want* to eat."

I hurried Helen along to the girls' bedroom, which we had to ourselves. My sister Ruthie had a bookkeeping job with a wallpaper firm next to Bloomingdale's department store and she had to work half a day Saturday, then she always went shopping on East 14th Street before she came home. I had to drape Helen's coat over the sewing machine—the closet was jam-packed. To distract her from my crude manners I made a show of plumping up our two enormous pillows and arranging them at the headboard of the bed.

"These cushions were custom-made on Allen Street from one of my grandmother's two featherbeds from Russia. They're great for reading on."

We had hardly settled ourselves against the pillows when my mother burst in holding a platter heaped with tangerines, *rugelakh* buns, and paper-wrapped fruit candies. I gave her a dirty look. She said, "It's for later." She was so embarrassing.

Ma had never liked Lorna. She used to say Lorna bossed me around and was my friend just to get help with her homework. That was completely wrong. The real reason was that Ma was jealous of girls who were prettier than me and smarter in school. But she was all-over-the-place groveling to any of her children's friends who were rich. Now my mother was dancing around Helen as if she needed to bribe her to be my friend. "Take a rugela," she nagged, "home made." To be polite, Helen tasted one. "It's delicious." I couldn't stand it. As soon as my mother started to leave I followed her to the door and slammed it shut.

We began with *Ramona*, taking turns reading aloud. After a few chapters my mother's platter was empty without our even noticing. I was the one reading when Ramona and Allesandro, the Indian hired hand, were discovered in their first kiss, in the dark by a stream. He was banished and Ramona was locked in her room. Plans were started to send Ramona to a convent. She pined away and was about to die when Allesandro sneaked in through the woods at dark of night to elope with her. When I came to their tender reunion scene my voice quivered and my eyes filled up. I had to put the book down. Helen was reaching in her coat pocket for a handkerchief, her face flooded with tears. We looked at each other and got the giggles. We collapsed on the bed laughing but we couldn't stop crying either. My mother knocked on the door. At least she didn't barge in this time so we had a minute to put ourselves in order. She needed the bedroom. She had to get dressed to meet Ruthie on 14th Street. Ruthie was getting married soon and they were going shopping for a honeymoon outfit, and also my mother needed earrings to go with her gown.

While Helen and I were waiting at the kitchen table for Ma to change clothes, my brother Sidney came home with Butchie, our little tan-and-white terrier mutt. As soon as Sidney took her off the leash she jumped around and wriggled and put her paws up on me and on Helen too. Helen looked uneasy, so naturally Sidney picked Butchie up and pushed her in Helen's face: "Give her a kiss, go on, give her a kiss." Butchie started licking and pawing the air and Helen kept backing off.

Sidney kept shoving until Helen was leaning back against the stove and Butchie was all over her face but she couldn't get up the courage to push the dog away. Sidney's way of being friendly. I had to grab Butchie away from him.

After my mother left the house I took Butchie back in the bedroom with us and laid her down beside me out of Helen's way. Helen picked up *Ramona*. I liked the way she read, subdued and yet expressive. Ramona found out that her real mother had been an Indian. She was ecstatic. She had known all her life something was missing, something was wrong. No wonder she was drawn to Allesandro! She galloped off with him on horseback to join her own people.

At about four o'clock we had reached the part where Ramona and Allesandro were on a dangerous journey into the Sierra Mountains when my mother, my sister, and my sister's best friend Rosie Shuster burst into the bedroom with armloads of packages, laughing and sparkling like Christmas. They dumped the packages on the bed and threw their coats on top of Helen's on the sewing machine and their hats and pocket-books on the top edge of the folding bed behind the door.

"Wait till you see what we got," Ruthie said. She opened one box after another, spreading tissue paper all over the bed, including all over Butchie, who twirled about happily tearing at the paper and messing up the boxes until my mother picked her up and put her out of the room. I saw glimpses of gray wool, white satin, a swirl of black taffeta.

"Try on for Feygie with her friend," Ma said. "Feygie" was what my family called me. I hated it but I could never get them to call me Fay.

"Yes, we want a preview, a fashion show," I chimed in. "Ma, did you get earrings?"

"Ay, what earrings! Wait till you see."

Rosie, Helen, and I sat down in a row on the edge of the bed, leaving Ruthie to make a fashion runway out of the narrow aisle between the bed and the wall with the closet. Ma stood by the door, opposite the sewing machine, with her arms folded like a proud impresario. I wondered whether Helen minded the invasion, whether she felt trapped and would rather go home. I tried to catch her eye, but she was watching Ruthie.

Ruthie pulled off her dress and threw it over the pile on the sewing machine. She kicked off her shoes and stood in her slip. She reached past us to pull out one item after another from the mess on the bed. First she held up a black taffeta slip with fitted seams and darts at the bust, no lace trim. "A dollar seventy-five, Orbach's." Rosie said, "That's the best thing under a dress, a plain tailored slip."

I said, "Very nice. Next!"

Next Ruthie held up an ivory satin blouse with a wide set-in bow at the collar and with pirate sleeves and pearl buttons. "Three dollars, Orbach's."

"Ooh, that's so pretty," I said.

I wondered if she would let me borrow it and then I remembered she wouldn't be living here anymore.

All her clothes and scarves and makeup and hair rollers would be leaving with her.

Next Ruthie put on the most adorable two-piece dress, really a light-weight suit. The material was a worsted wool sharkskin in tiny black and white houndstooth checks. First the skirt, straight and slim with a kick-pleat at the back and a matching scotch cap. Then the top, cut like a coachman's jacket, with a double row of black velvet buttons down the front to the waist and a peplum that curved all the way around from the waist to the hips. The lines brought out her round, high-bosomed figure and small waist. Holding her arms straight down at her sides, she bent her hands back at the wrists and pirouetted in place with tiny steps, like Betty Boop. "Eleven dollars, as is, at Lerner's." Ma, Rosie, and I cheered in chorus: "Isn't that gorgeous? It fits perfectly! It looks so expensive!" Ma said, "The customers in the store couldn't get over it. Everybody went in the back to find the same suit."

Ruthie pulled three small boxes out of the pile. She put on black patent leather pumps with spike heels. Pearl button earrings. "Nineteen cents, Woolworth's." A square black velvet bag with a silver clasp. "Two forty-five, Hearn's." She pointed a toe, put the bag against her left cheek, and wiggled her fingers to flash her diamond engagement ring. "Show over."

We clapped and cheered. Helen clapped too.

"Kanahora ptu-ptu-ptu," Ma pretend-spit to make Ruthie seem worthless and protect her from the evil eye of envy. "Like a doll," she said.

"Like a movie star!" Rosie cheered.

"Isn't she adorable?" I yelled. "That's my sister! Adorable."

Hand on hip, Ruthie strutted back and forth along her bedroom runway. The many buttons on her jacket reminded me of the chant where you count buttons to see who you would marry. I jumped up and began counting, backwards for good luck.

For the two buttons in the back, I counted "Soldier, sailor." Then the double row of front buttons from the bottom up: "Indian chief. Rich man, poor man, beggar man, thief. Soldier, sailor, Indian chief, rich man . . . Oh!" Only nine buttons up the front. One button was missing, at the top right near the lapel.

"I know," Ruthie said. "This suit was the only size eleven and we couldn't sneak a button off another jacket because the salesgirl didn't leave us alone for a minute."

"Do you have to find a whole new set of buttons?" I asked.

"I hope not. We're going back to Lerner's next Saturday. They had a lot of these suits in the rack."

Ma said, "You know what we forgot? Next Saturday we have to go for a wedding gown fitting, and we still have to look for a bedspread on Grand Street."

"I'll go," I said. "You know I'm good at sneaking off buttons."

"All right, get two buttons," Ma said, "so she'll have an extra."

I invited Helen to come with me. She said yes, she would like to. I told her she would have to dress up to look older. I said Lerner's only sells ladies wear. "Wear your heels. I'll bring lipstick."

"Hey, Ruthie," Rosie said, "You know what? As soon as you sew that button on, you're gonna marry a poor man instead of a rich man. Ha!"

"It's too late. Thanks for the warning but I already know he's not a rich man. At least he's not a beggar or a thief." Actually, Irwin was still in dental mechanic school but he had to get married right away to avoid being drafted in the army. They would have to go stay with his parents and live on Ruthie's seven dollars a week while they looked for a cheap apartment and he looked for a part-time job.

We left Ruthie to put her new things away and shooed ourselves into the kitchen. Ma brought out salami, mustard, rye bread with caraway seeds on the crust, sour pickles, and a quart bottle of beer. We made sandwiches. Butchie was already waiting under my chair. I always snuck food to her.

As soon as Helen sat down my mother started pestering her with questions: Where was her family from? Minsky-Gebernya, in Russia. What did her father do for a living? He passed away; he was a diamond merchant on the Canal Street Exchange. "May he rest in peace and what do you do after school?"

"Ma, stop!" I said. "Listen to you. You're giving her the third degree!"

"What's the matter with you? I'm interested to know your friend, what's the matter with that?"

"It's rude, that's what's the matter. It's not your business!"

Rosie laughed. "Don't mind them," she said. "They're always at it."

Helen blushed. She said, "It's all right, I don't mind. I just graduated from the Downtown Talmud Torah on 8th Street. Hebrew schools are until five o'clock so after school I went home."

"You went to the Talmud Torah?" said Rosie. "Me, too, I went there." So they started talking about the teachers they had, and so on and so on, so Helen was spared from more of Ma's questioning.

Ruthie came in the kitchen with a small white box. "Here, Ma, put on your earrings." Ma screwed them on. She had pierced ears but she never used the holes because they were a mark of the foreign-born women. "*Nu*, you like it?" She stood by the sink, chin up, arms stiff at her sides. They were sparkling rhinestone chandeliers, almost down to her shoulders. "A dollar seventy-five, from Hearn's, from under the glass."

"They're beautiful Ma!" I said. "A knockout! Wait till Dora sees them." Dora was my mother's kid sister. They were jealous of each other.

"Oh, they're gorgeous," Helen said, "they really are!"

"Ma, let Helen try them on. Go ahead Helen."

My mother poured the cascade of flashing stones into Helen's eager hands.

Ma asked me, "How much did we spend all together?"

"All together? Twenty fourteen. Plus Ruthie's shoes. Ruthie, how much were the shoes?"

"Three-fifty."

"Okay, twenty-three sixty-four."

Ruthie said, "Oh my God, Ma, you spent a fortune!"

Ma said, "Never mind, never mind, you only get married once *Alev Ha Sholem,* with God's help."

Helen turned to me. "How did you figure the total so fast?"

"She always asks me how much money we spent," I said. "I keep the count going in my head."

Ma said proudly, "I taught both my girls arithmetic from the prices on the paper bags when we go shopping. Not like in school where you break up every number in two columns and count one column at a time."

"It's really easier," I said. "You just keep adding to the nearest round number, then you take off or add the leftover numbers. I'll show you later."

Rosie said, "Don't let them kid you, these Kesslers here are sharp, including Butchie. C'mere Butchie, show Helen your tricks."

Butchie jumped out from her place under the table. "Sit up and beg." Butchie begged. "Gimme your right paw. Your left paw." Butchie did. "See? A Kessler." She gave Butchie a slice of salami. "C'mon, Ruthie, grab your sandwich before I give all the salami to your cute mutt."

Ruthie sat down to the salami and beer. Helen screwed on the earrings and looked at them in the mirror of Rosie's powder compact. Ma went to change into her housedress. I gave Butchie more salami. Once we were all settled, four at the table by the window and Ma standing with her sandwich by the sink, Sidney came into the kitchen to help us demolish the rest of the salami. He must have smelled it from his bedroom. He squeezed the step-stool in next to Helen and told her his English-accent jokes and leered at her the whole time. Ma put another bottle of beer on the table and made some tea.

Ruthie and Rosie took out cigarettes and Sidney went to get his cherry-wood pipe, a Bar Mitzva present from our older brother Maxie. I sneaked puffs of Ruthie's cigarette when my mother wasn't looking. She hated cigarettes. She said to everyone who smoked, even strangers, "I can't understand, the air is so thick with poison fumes as it is, tell me, what satisfaction is it to take into your lungs more poison fumes?"

Sidney came back with his pipe, took his place next to Helen, and blew little clouds of smoke in her face.

"Rum and maple," he said. "How do you like the a-*rom-a*?" He leaned in and wiggled his eyebrows. She gave him a big glowing smile. She still had on the chandelier earrings. I hoped to God he wouldn't turn her into another one of his girlfriends. At fourteen years old he was already a lady-killer.

Sharing Secrets

I walked Helen back to her house, on East 5th Street between Avenues D and C. The streets along the way were almost empty. Most of the neighborhood stores were closed on Saturday for Shabbas. Everybody dressed up and went shopping uptown or to the movies or to visit relatives. When Helen and I came to her building we spread out our handkerchiefs on the stoop and sat enjoying the silence. Across the street, behind a broken fence, was an empty lot where the toilet sheds of P.S. 15 used to be. Among the mounds of coal ash and old lumber were stands of feathery autumn weeds.

The afternoon sun over Avenue C to the west sent pink-gold rays into the lot, lighting up bits of tin and glass, masses of goldenrod, and a row of corn stalks and sunflowers someone had planted against the red-brick building on the east side of the lot.

The scene made me think of the old run-down Indian village where Ramona found beauty and happiness with Allesandro. She had never felt at home where she grew up. She never fit in with the formal gardens and gilt-framed paintings and bustling servants. Sitting there on the stoop next to Helen, I wanted her to know that I was a serious person, like Ramona, that I wasn't really a shallow materialist inside even though I had made all that commotion in my house about fashions and money. I began by telling her I had always felt different from everyone else in my family, even though I acted like them when I was at home. I told her I used to dream that I was adopted and that my true mother would find me some day. Helen said the same thing happened to her, that she would dream her real mother was walking in a garden sighing for her lost child. In her dream she would call "Look here Mother, I'm over here," and she would wake up crying. I told Helen my father and mother had an arranged marriage and they hated each other and fought all the time.

I said my mother used dirty words and didn't know how to dress, and she was always embarrassing me because she was so loud and ignorant and superstitious.

"I thought your mother was nice," Helen said. "I had a good time at your house," she said, "It's so lively."

"Look, in my house if you don't make a lot of noise everyone thinks you're sick. But inside I'm really very different. I can't wait to grow up and leave home." Then I told Helen my deepest secret. First I made her kiss her right pinky and raise it to heaven and swear to God she would never tell. "I have a secret boyfriend," I said. He's twenty-three years old. We spent all last summer together on the roof of my building. We love each other so much we had to stop seeing each other because I'm too young but on my eighteenth birthday we're going to meet on my roof and if we're still in love we'll get married." Then I couldn't resist making my story more glamorous. "To say goodbye I had a real date with him at a Spanish restaurant and I smoked in public and drank wine and nobody knew I was only thirteen." What really happened, my whole dance company went to the restaurant with a lot of boys after a fundraiser for the Lincoln Brigade volunteers who had come back from the war in Spain. But our love was true.

Then Helen told me her deepest secret. I also kissed my pinky and swore to God I would never tell. Her mother only pretended she was a widow; she was really an *aguna*, a deserted wife.

"She tried to kill herself while I was in school. She stuffed rags under the door and turned on the gas. The rabbi's wife was coming up the stairs to visit someone sick and she smelled gas and saw the rags peeking out.

"They took her to the hospital. They called me out of school and brought me to the rabbi's house to wait. I knew what happened from the way he looked at me and questioned me.

"I prayed to God please let her live, I'll do anything you ask I promise, just let her live." Helen looked down at the step beside her. She rubbed the side of her thumbnail back and forth along its gravely surface. "The rabbi found work for my mother taking care of men who were sick in bed. Sometimes they would grab at her while she was washing them. She used to come home with scratches on her arms. So then the rabbi made her the caretaker of the women's section in his synagogue. She put on a wig like the religious women and she started wearing dark dresses with long sleeves, and now everything is all right." She stopped filing her thumbnail and looked out over the empty lot. So Helen wasn't rich after all.

"Who took care of you when your mother went to work?"

"Oh, I was nine by then. After school I did the shopping on Avenue C on my way home. I got supper ready too.

"I still do except Shabbas, and Sundays my mother cooks." She smiled at me ruefully. "So now you know why I don't know how to dance or anything."

"I'll teach you," I said. "It's easy. Can you get out at night?"

"I don't know. Now that I finished Talmud Torah I can ask my mother."

"Tell her I live in a supervised settlement house and the parents help run it. We have social dancing every Friday night and there are clubs and other activities. I go every night from seven to ten. It's called the Lavanburg Homes Social Center. It's in the basement of my building. She can ask anyone, it has a good reputation."

Helen's life was so much worse than mine. I remembered her poem "What is this life if full of care" and I was determined to help her. I said, "I know you'll have a good time and lots of friends. Some day the nicest boy will fall in love with you.

"I can feel it. You have such beautiful honey-blonde hair, and so many girls at school think you're prettier than Lorna. I do, too."

She looked down at her shoes. Her hair spilled down her cheeks in that way that I loved. "I don't know," she said. "I'm so confused."

"Is it your mother? Or the girls?"

"It's silly, but I don't know what I'm supposed to do or not do. What bothers me is, I spent seven years in Talmud Torah, seven years studying Hebrew and learning the prayers. I said Blessed be the Lord a hundred times a day, blessed be for this, blessed be for that, but I don't know who God is. Does he care about us? Is he really watching us to see if we're obeying his laws? I'm supposed to be finished studying but I don't know any more about God than when I started, and I promised to worship him if he saved my mother but I don't really know how. It's so confusing." She covered her face with her hands. I was alarmed.

"I don't believe God is watching us," I said. "I believe God shows himself in nature and in everything that lives.

"I believe he wants us to appreciate everything he made— you, me, the goldenrods across the street, the cats in the alley." I listened to myself babbling. It was so corny when you weren't reading poetry.

"I believe that too," Helen said, "but when you're Jewish and you don't obey God's religious laws, what's the difference between you and everybody else?"

"I know I'll always be Jewish even if I'm not religious. I don't believe God made all those laws, and I believe that if he were watching us he would stop Hitler from killing the Jews."

"My mother keeps all the laws," Helen said. "She believes they all come from God and that he *is* watching every Jew because he chose us to be his people. She thinks the *Meshiakh* won't come until all the Jews are pious. She thinks Hitler is a punishment and a warning to us."

Up in Helen's House

The afternoon sun was sinking, and a chill came into the air. Helen invited me upstairs. Inside, the hallway gave off the familiar odor of old East Side buildings: stale tobacco smoke mixed with mold, cockroach spray, and cat's pee. We climbed four dark flights to a rear apartment.

The hall door opened onto an unlit dining room. Mrs. Boris was sitting at a table at the far end, with her back to the window. Some light still came in from the yard, and she was reading from a prayer book. She looked at me over the rim of her eyeglasses and asked Helen in Yiddish if I was Jewish. Then she asked me if I kept kosher. I lied yes, and she went back to her reading.

The room was surprisingly bare. Aside from the table and two chairs near the window, there were only a bureau along one wall and an end table and chair against the opposite wall. No photographs or candy plates or china figures, no rug or even linoleum on the floor, just bare planks of wood. Helen hung my coat in a small dark bedroom to the left of the dining room. Then she led me in silence into the kitchen on the right, where she put out two glasses of milk and biscuits.

The kitchen was dimmer than the dining room—its window faced an air shaft—but she couldn't turn on any lights until Shabbas was over at sundown. The silence hung over us. The ironing board was out, and to make conversation I told Helen I wished we had one in my house. My mother did the ironing on folded sheets at the kitchen table, and my middy blouses came out terrible. Helen said she could teach me how to iron them and I could come and use her ironing board whenever I liked.

It was dark in the dining room when I left. I could only see Mrs. Boris's silhouette against the window. Her head was drooped. She had fallen asleep.

Wardrobes

In school Monday I kept my eyes turned away from Lorna, and between classes I walked along the halls with Helen. The girls made a point of giggling and whispering when they saw us but we didn't care.

After school I went home to get *Ramona* and two creased-up middy blouses and brought them to Helen's house.

She showed me how to mix the starch and dampen the middy blouses and iron them through a thin cloth to prevent scorch. Her iron wasn't electric; you had to keep reheating it on the stove. While I ironed, Helen read *Ramona* from where we had left off, stopping now and then to help me with the seams and corners. It was so peaceful in her kitchen, listening to her calm voice above the hiss of the steam, watching the fabric smooth out, inhaling the clean odor of the starch. Not even traffic noises could reach us, only the faint sounds of a radio through the air shaft and the occasional yowling of cats in the yard.

I finished at about five and sat listening to Helen until the end of the chapter where Ramona had a baby girl, then I followed her to the bedroom to get my coat.

All Helen's clothes were in one side of a double chifferobe. She showed me her wardrobe: a tan pinwale-corduroy dress with a thin leather belt, the autumn dress she had worn on Shabbas, a tailored pink blouse, a brown jumper, and a pink tweed coat next to her brown chesterfield. So few clothes, but everything matched: brown, pink, and tan with touches of green.

"Oh, you have *two* coats!" I said. "They're both beautiful. So is *everything*!"

"My brown coat is from last year; it still fits. I get a new outfit every year, plus shoes and a skirt for school. The rabbi's wife brings them and takes away my old clothes for charity. Her sister is a buyer uptown at Best and Company. I only have to buy the middy blouses."

Below the wardrobe compartment of the chifferobe Helen had two drawers to herself. The top drawer held middy blouses, a pink sweater set, everyday sweaters, and scarves.

The bottom drawer had mostly underwear. Panties, slips, handkerchiefs, and even her brassiere, were in plain white cotton. I picked up a strange-looking girdle. It was so short it couldn't have covered the private parts, and it had very long garters. "That's a garter belt," she said, "for my stockings."

"Is *that* how you keep your stockings straight! Nobody told me. My sister said you need a girdle so I tried hers on but I couldn't walk in it."

"They don't show garter belts in the windows, maybe because they look like burlesque." The word "burlesque" got to me. I held the garter belt over my hips and did the hoochy-koochy. The straps flew around like tassels. Helen started laughing, so I hooked the garter belt around my waist, picked up one of her scarves, and I made up a wild snake dance while singing a Russian *kazatska*. She picked up another scarf and joined in, and we landed on the bed in a fit of laughing.

I went home carrying my nicely pressed middy blouses over my arm. I was all excited. I made new plans for myself.

I'll buy my own middy blouses in my own size and do my own ironing, and I'll buy a garter belt to keep my stockings straight. And I'll cut off my braids and do something with my hair even if Ma gets mad at me. And I planned how I would buy an ironing board and keep it against the wall by the folding bed and after Ruthie got married I would organize the two big dresser drawers so that instead of all the stuff being jumbled together I would put my things in one drawer and my mother's things in the other drawer and I would keep everything in my drawer neat and ironed and folded and sell the rag man all the stuff I don't wear any more. Then all I had to do was control myself and be polite. I would be quiet, gentle, a little sad, like Helen. She was like a Cinderella in a story, with a fairy godmother to bring her beautiful clothes. Pretty, polite, lady-like Helen. That's what I loved so much about her. She was lady-like! It had been my dream, and I was going to make it come true.

When I reached eighteen I would have fine clothes and fine manners, and Phil would fall in love with me all over again, and we would get married.

Tuesday after school Helen went with me to Clinton Street where I bought a white garter belt and three middy blouses and three pairs of Dawn Mist sheer stockings.

I didn't want to count the money I spent, probably half my savings till next spring and it wasn't even October. When I got back home I kept out a dollar to buy an ironing board and another fifty cents for spending money and put the rest back in my tin treasure-box that I kept hidden behind all the underwear.

The top left dresser drawer had a big jewelry box, letters and postcards, and a messy pile of handkerchiefs, collars, dickies, and who knows what. The top right drawer had all Ruthie's makeup, curlers, hair things, and a private locked box. That drawer would be mine, a whole empty drawer to myself.

Next day, Wednesday, I felt like a new person, with a fresh new middy blouse and neat stockings, but only Helen noticed. After school I walked her to her house and we did our history assignment together and read a little more of *Ramona*. It rained hard Thursday. We went home separately.

After my homework I read the Dorothy Parker stories. I loved them. "Big Blonde" was my favorite. It was about an aging drunken floozy who tries to kill herself because she's tired of having to be a good sport. We exchanged books on Friday. I now had *Ramona* to myself for a whole week. I planned to start it again from the beginning. It was still raining so we said goodbye till next morning, when we had to dress up and go to 14th Street for Ruthie's black velvet button, rain or shine.

Partners in Crime

Saturday was sunny and cool, a perfect day for shopping. I got to Helen's house early. I had combed Ruthie's setting goo into my hair and crossed my braids over the top of my head like a Russian-Spanish style coronet. It looked good. I wore my purple silk blouse, and my one-inch black leather pumps, and I dangled the straps of Ruthie's black leather pocketbook in the crook of my elbow. I had on my Ruby Red Flame-Glo lipstick that I used on stage for folk dances. With the new garter belt on, my stockings were smooth and the seams were straight. I figured I looked at least sixteen. I leaned against the banister post at the bottom of the steps and waited. I didn't want to sit on the stoop by myself with lipstick on, in case a fresh boy or a drunken bum would try to sit next to me.

The morning sun lit up the north side of Helen's street. The goldenrods in the empty lot, still in the shade, just looked like old scruffy weeds. I called to the pigeons pecking in the gutter—*cooROO cooROO cut cut*—until Helen came out. She stood in the sunlight at the top of the landing. While I watched from below, she raised her hands from the wrists and made a pirouette with tiny steps, the way Ruthie had done

207

while we looked at her clothes. Helen had on a tan angora beret, almost the same color as her hair.

She wore her pink tweed coat, her tan pinwale dress, a pink-and-ivory silk scarf, and pigskin oxford shoes. She had that glowing smile and looked prettier than ever. She could easily have passed for sixteen.

I yelled "*Kanahora ptu ptu!*" She came down the steps, still posing, one pointed toe at a time. Then we hugged as if we hadn't seen each other all week, except keeping our heads apart not to muss our hair. I took out the lipstick and said, "Stretch your lips across your teeth," and I put some on her. She said, "You're the best friend I ever had." I said, "Me too, you're my best friend also."

I blotted her lipstick with my handkerchief and we kissed. Then we linked arms and set off to get my darling Ruthie the black velvet button. Two buttons.

"Remind me," I said, as we walked along. "Two buttons, I keep thinking one."

"How will you steal them? Aren't you afraid of getting caught?"

"It's not really stealing. The salesgirl might even give them to me if I asked, because it's only an as-is dress. They're always missing something. The problem is, the dress has a lot of buttons and if she decided to say no Ruthie would be stuck. She would have to find ten matching black buttons that fit in the buttonholes and two more of the same buttons in the back but smaller."

We passed by Avenue C. It looked forlorn and filthy with the pushcarts gone on Shabbas and all the stores closed. There were only the cats and some nervous pigeons poking through the remains in the gutter, and a flock of sparrows in the middle of the street pecking at the oats in the dried horse manure.

We turned uptown on Avenue B, which was clean and had nice open stores and dressed-up people strolling along. At the corner of B and 6th we paused at the window of the photography store to choose the prettiest gowns in the wedding pictures and the handsomest boys in the graduation pictures. Then we crossed the street to Loews Avenue B to see the movie stills of Bette Davis in "All This and Heaven Too." Then at the corner of Avenue B and 7th Street we turned into Tompkins Square Park to take the shortcut to Avenue A and 10th Street. We had to pass by a gang of grown-up Polish boys sprawled on the benches, smoking and drinking beer. They wolf-whistled at us. We looked straight ahead and kept a straight face, but when we got a safe distance from them we broke out laughing.

Along 14th Street between Third and Fourth avenues, just after the Academy of Music movie house, I showed Helen the entrance to Julian's famous pool parlor up a double flight of white marble stairs. I was going there soon with some boys from my block to watch Willie Mosconi, the best pool player in the world. I told Helen I could teach her the game because we had pool tables in our Social Center. She was surprised that girls played.

"Girls don't. I have to play with boys."

"You're so funny," she said, and drew closer and hugged my arm.

Next we came to my favorite place, Fox Furs, an upstairs store on the corner of 14th Street and 4th Avenue, where three live models paraded furs from a corner display window.

We joined a small crowd watching from across Fourth Avenue. The models wore different-colored satin gowns: scarlet, jade, and fuchsia. They had on pancake makeup and false eyelashes and they wore their hair in upsweep styles to show the fur collars. Their expressions were aloof. As they sauntered from the 14th to the Fourth Avenue side, they placed heel in front of toe, heel in front of toe, to make their hips swing with every step. One model paused in each window to do two opposite half-turns and one full turn, then moved to the next window while the third model quick-changed her fur behind the drapes at the back. First we watched a belted gray Persian lamb coat and matching Cossack hat, next a sheared beaver sports coat.

Then a model I knew in person came out in a hip-length lynx jacket. I jumped up and down and waved to her. She gave me a smile and a subtle wave of her fingers. "That's Dotty," I told Helen. "She lives in Lavanburg's and we're sort of friends because we both love dancing." Next we watched a mink coat, a leopard-skin sports coat, and then Dotty came out again.

This time she wore a floor-length black Persian lamb with an ermine collar and muff. I waved again and showed her how I could do the heel-to-toe walk but I accidentally bumped into a man. He pushed me back so hard I almost fell over. I yelled after him, "I pity your wife, you jerk."

The gray Persian lamb started again. While we watched another round of modeling, I got an idea for a modern-dance composition. I'd call it "Dance of the Midnight Mannequins" and make it spooky, with lots of ghostly sheer curtain fabric in place of the furs, maybe starting out with the fabric over their heads as if they'd been covered for the night.

"I'd love to be a model," Helen said. "I love the lynx jacket best."

"Oh, it would look gorgeous against your blonde hair," I said. "You know, you look like a lynx." She punched my arm. "No, I mean it. Lynxes have the same hazel-green eyes. They're beautiful." She punched my arm again. I staggered sideways, just to kid around, and I bumped into a rich lady. She yelled "Watch where you're going." I said "I can't, I'm cockeyed," and I crossed my eyes in her face. I was having such a good time

I kept forgetting to act like a lady. That's how I was that day, one minute grown up, the next minute goofy. Sometimes I felt older than Helen because I had been out in the world and knew about so many more goings-on, and sometimes I felt younger because I couldn't help showing off and clowning around in front of her.

The crowds were thick around Orbach's, the most fashionable of the 14th Street department stores. It was like the stores uptown, where I only went at Christmas time for the window displays and to see Macy's Santa Claus. The Orbach's display window showed three mannequins in a preview of winter fashions. One wore a magenta wool coat with black skunk collar and muff, the next had on a black silk opera gown with diamond shoulder straps and tiara. The third was a male mannequin in tuxedo and top hat, leaning against a lamp-post. The scene glistened with display snow. As we walked on, the crowds thinned and I showed Helen the game of counting out-of-town girls by their stockings. New York girls wore their stockings inside out, with the seams on the outside, to make the stockings lie flat against the skin. If you counted ten out-of-town girls—or sometimes ten taxis—the next boy who spoke to you was the boy you were going to marry. Then came some little stores selling fabrics and shoes and things, and then we reached Lerner's, where Ruthie had bought her honeymoon outfit.

Lerner's was a small old-fashioned bargain store. It had two show windows facing each other and an entrance door set way back from the building line. The show windows were cluttered with signs. Every dress, hat, pocketbook, and pair of gloves had a sign on it with a hand-lettered price. Before we went in I said, "Just stay next to me and look interested." The store had only two salesladies. The one at the front right, behind the cash register and display counter, looked like a pig. The one roaming the floor looked like a vampire. There weren't many customers. I went up to the counter, Helen beside me. I asked Miss Pig if they carried cocktail gloves. I needed elbow-length silk gloves in size six as a present for my sister. I could tell in advance it was unlikely. "Sorry, we don't carry that item." I thanked her and said to Helen, "Let's look around while we're here." We looked at the two-for-seven-dollar bargain dresses a couple of minutes, skipped the better dresses, and moved to the back where they had hats and the as-is racks. Miss Vampire came over. I said, "We're just looking," and she went up front. I spotted my sister's houndstooth check suits in a recessed rack along the right wall, on the same side as Miss Pig at the cash register. They were mixed with other dresses and suits, and the sizes were in disarray. I said to Helen, loud enough for Miss Pig to hear, "Oh, I like this one. Start at that end and look for size nine." I went to the near end and worked my way along the rack. Helen looked nervous; she kept peeking over at me. I figured I'd better hurry. I leaned into the rack while holding onto one of the houndstooth jackets with both hands, only the outside hand showing. While I pretended to read the label I was twisting off a button with my inside fingers. In less than a minute I had a black velvet button in my pocket and went on casually ruffling through the suits. Miss Vampire was helping a customer. I moved along the rack until I got to Helen and while facing her I twisted the second button off. Then I saw that some of the matching scotch caps had a pretty medallion pinned on. Ruthie's cap didn't have one. It must have been stolen. So I also got a medallion off a cap and into my pocket also. "These clothes are all for older girls," I said. "Let's try Hearn's." As we passed by the better dresses I said out loud, "Look at these prints, the patterns don't match up at the seams. My father is in the business and he says if you have to buy cheap get a dark solid color." It was true. He did say that.

Outside, I said, "Got 'em. Two buttons. And a trimming that was missing from Ruthie's cap. I'll show you later."

"I was scared," said Helen. "I didn't think you did it, you acted so natural."

"That's the whole secret. You have to act natural." I explained the art of stealing to her as we went along. "Everything you do, from the minute you get in the store to the end, no, even before you go into the store, it has to be what you would naturally do anyway. No peeking around to see if anyone is watching you. And don't decide in advance when to make your move. Keep looking through the merchandise until you're absolutely sure no one is paying any attention to you."

We stopped at a little nut store called Chock Full O'Nuts for a quarter pound of roasted cashews. A handsome counter-boy in a white uniform and cap poured the nuts into a white paper bag and weighed it on the scale. He gave us extra weight, with a wink at Helen, and said "Thank you" when I handed him my nickel. Afterwards Helen said, "He spoke to you. That means you're going to marry him." I said, "He winked at you. I think he'll marry both of us." That set us off on another laughing fit.

Just for fun we crossed 6th Avenue and went on to Hearn's, the last of the three big department stores, after S. Klein and Orbach's. It was the quietest, good for school and office outfits. Junior Girls was on the first floor up. We stepped side by side onto the moving escalator steps, Helen holding onto the banister and my arm because it was her first time. She was definitely getting braver. At Junior Girls we picked out skirts and blouses to mismatch. I found a pleated plaid skirt in green, orange, and khaki, matched it with a fluffy pink blouse. Then I made a cross-eyed fish face at myself in the mirror. That got Helen going. We hunted out more wild combinations and made goofy faces in the mirror until we were laughing so hard the salesgirl came over and told us not to handle the merchandise unless we were buying. We ran back down the up-escalator steps and leaped off at the bottom. I wished the girls from class could see Helen now! Next to the exit doors we stopped at a jewelry counter. A tray on the countertop held a stack of dainty lockets and pendants on cards, ten to twenty-nine cents each. Helen picked up a gold Jewish star with tiny set-in fake diamonds on a slender gold chain. She held it in her hand, staring, then she stared at me, then back to the star. She put it back in the tray but didn't let go. Her eyes darted everywhere. She was going to steal it! And she was screamingly conspicuous! I moved along the counter and called the salesgirl over to some pearl necklaces draped on a stand. I placed myself so that she had to turn her back to Helen.

I got her into a discussion of the right length for a pearl necklace to go with my shirtwaist blouse, holding up one after another with big gestures to take attention away from Helen. I bought a single-strand necklace of pea-size pearls for ten cents.

As soon as we got outside Helen uncurled her hand. Nestled in her palm was the card with the Jewish star.

The price was twenty-five cents. She lifted it to me like a cat showing a mouse. "Was I good?" she asked. I had to say, "Yes, you were good." I didn't have the heart to make remarks while she was so proud of herself.

On the way back we stopped in at Orbach's. Inside the plate-glass entrances were brilliant crystal chandeliers and mirrors. The glass counters displayed jewelry, evening bags, and aisles of cosmetics. The air was scented with a fall fragrance, something with moss and citrus in it. I looked around for Helen. She had stopped at the jewelry section near the main entrance and was staring at a display bin on the counter again, with that catlike look as if she were fixing prey. I got over there as fast as I dared without attracting attention. I put my face in front of hers and my elbow on the counter, and smiling as if we were having an ordinary conversation, I said, "I think we're being watched. Let's go." Outside, she showed me a large rhinestone lapel pin shaped as a swishy italic *H*. She was triumphant! I said, "Gee, that's pretty!" The tag said eighty-nine cents. It made my knees weak. "But you know," I said, "we had a close call. I don't think we should take anything actually for sale, with a price tag on it. It could get us in serious trouble."

"Then can we look for more dress trimmings?"

"Okay, we'll go to Klein's and get one trimming and then I have to go home, okay?"

"Okay," she said, but her lynx eyes still looked a bit wild.

At Klein's Ladies Formal the as-is racks were a mess. Some of the gowns were torn, some had fallen off their hangers. Helen pulled out a purple crepe gown with a necklace of multicolored celluloid bellflowers on a rhinestone chain.

The chain was tacked on under the collar with thin thread. It looked easy to detach. I grabbed a bouffant gown and we went to the try-on room. There half-naked ladies of all ages, sizes, shapes, and social standing jostled for space in front of a mirrored wall, each standing by her pile of clothes on the carpeted floor. I found a spot at the back wall, threw down my pocketbook and topper, and put Helen's purple gown on them. Then I stood in front of Helen, spread out the skirt of the bouffant gown to hide her, and looked in the mirror as if trying to decide whether I wanted to try it on. Under cover of the gown, Helen cut the threads of the necklace with her teeth and slipped it into her coat pocket. That done, thank God, the stealing spree was over.

We celebrated at a 2nd Avenue delicatessen with two frankfurters and one root beer. Each item cost five cents. I would personally rather have gone to the 14th Street Automat for their luscious lemon meringue pie but Helen would only eat someplace kosher.

At the next candy store I bought a cigarette and wood match for a penny. I had to take the brand of whatever pack was open. Luckily, it was a nice mild Chesterfield. We stopped off at Rosie Shuster's building on 4th Street across from P.S. 15 to look at our loot in her hall toilet. If someone asked what we were doing there, which they never did anyway, we could say we were visiting Rosie. The toilet smelled of iodine and pine tar from CN disinfectant; it got up my nose. We put all our things on the toilet lid. I had four items: the two buttons, the medallion, and the ten-cent strand of pearls I had bought to cover up for Helen's first theft at Hearn's. Helen had the Jewish star, the swishy H rhinestone pin, and the bellflower necklace. She stared down at them for a long time. She said, "When my father left he took every piece of jewelry, even the pile of imperfect stones I used to play with. My mother said he had gone to open a store someplace and that he would send for us when he started making a profit. I knew she was lying."

She fell silent, almost crying, Then she said, "I don't know how to bring these things home. I'm not allowed to shop on Saturday."

"Hide them in your coat pockets till after school on Monday, then when your mother gets home from work you can tell her you bought them off a pushcart."

"I don't know if she'll believe me."

"Well, you can say I gave them to you."

"What if she says give them back?"

"So then you can leave them with me and I'll bring them to school whenever you want to wear them." She looked doubtful.

We put away our loot and took turns sitting on the toilet lid while I smoked my Chesterfield. She didn't want to try a puff.

"I wish I were like you," she said. "You're not afraid of anything."

"I wish that were true. Remind me to tell you about the million things I'm afraid of. Rats. Spiders. Deep water. I'm terrified of fire." I didn't mention her stealing spree that got me so scared.

We rehearsed both of Helen's alibis all the way to her front stoop. She still wasn't sure what to do. We were both tired and I wanted to get home. Before she went upstairs I took out my handkerchief and had her spit on it, then I wiped off the traces of lipstick. She told me she'd had a wonderful time, and I said I had also, and we kissed goodbye till Monday.

My mother was the only one home besides Butchie. I put the two black velvet buttons on the kitchen table and added the medallion, which she immediately recognized. She said, *"Ay, a kliga kup,"* a clever head, and nuzzled her fist into my forehead in her deepest show of approval.

I said, "I got you a present," and I gave her the strand of pearls. Near the clasp was the little white tag that said "Hearn's 10¢." She said it was beautiful, such a bargain. Then she took my head between her hands and gave me a kiss on the forehead and put a big dollop of home-made strawberry jam in my tea.

Deep Trouble

Helen wasn't in class Monday morning. I missed her. I wanted to show her I was still wearing my braids in a coronet—my new hairstyle. I wondered if she'd caught a cold from all that running around Saturday. She'd looked so tired at the end.

At about eleven o'clock, in the middle of our Civics period in home room, a monitor came up to Miss Chilton's desk with a note. Miss Chilton called out my name and said the principal wants to see me. "Take your coat and books," she said, in her malicious way. "You won't be coming back."

What did she mean? Was I being transferred? Why? A policeman was waiting in the hall. I was startled. "Oh please, what happened?"

"The principal wants to see you. She'll explain."

It must be an accident. Maybe Sidney got run over. Or Ma was in the hospital. *Oh please God don't let it be Ruthie.* The policeman was big and had a long stride but I kept up with him. I flew down the stairwell to the second floor. We came out to the left of the Assembly platform. Miss Waller's office was on the other side. As we crossed in front of the platform I noticed another policeman. He was sitting up on the banquette. Helen sat beside him, her head lowered. What was she doing there? In my confusion, I tried to think whether her misfortune could be connected with mine.

My cop brought me into the vice-principal's office and left me standing there in the middle of the room. Miss Waller sat calmly behind her huge oak desk. Her wavy brown hair, creamy complexion, and soft chin gave her a mild appearance but everyone knew she was mean. We called her Miss Wallop. But now I couldn't see her clearly. The drapes behind her didn't meet in the middle and they let in a shaft of glaring light just behind her head. She pointed to a chair in front of the desk. "Put your coat and books down and remain standing." Was someone coming to break the bad news?

"Well. I have been waiting to see who is this Fay Kessler, in our own school, in an advanced class, who took Helen Boris on a crime spree two days ago."

My face and hair tingled. The air around me tingled. I heard a sea-shell roar in my ears. Her lips went on moving but I couldn't hear her. I couldn't rearrange my mind in time. Gradually the sounds came back but the meaning of her words lagged behind. ". . . came to her senses . . . confessed to her mother . . . from four department stores." She reached for a notebook on her desk. "I have been learning more about you this morning. I am dismayed. You not only steal, you—" she read from the notebook with a show of pained regret— "smoke, drink, play pool, go out dancing at night, have dates with grown men."

The strip of light blurred and dimmed. Helen told! She swore to God, right in front of me, and she told! Why? I could barely follow the words, barely keep standing.

". . . persistent inattention. . . poor conduct. . ."

Miss Waller was far away, across a darkening chasm. I stared at the edge of her desk. Maybe if I reached out I could hang onto it.

". . . pattern of a juvenile delinquent."

I had to concentrate. I had to answer her, defend myself. She spoke on and on with such confidence while she got everything twisted around.

"We asked the police captain to consider your youth and the deprived circumstances of your family, and I am relieved to say he agreed to keep these crimes off your record. But there must be no further incidents or we might not be able to save you from reform school. I spoke with your mother this morning and she promised to keep you under close supervision and see that you learn the Ten Commandments."

219

My mother! I was so unnerved by this time that I couldn't stop tears from rising up. I didn't sob or anything but I had to wipe my eyes in front of her. I was so angry and ashamed. But she still wasn't finished. She said I had to get the stolen goods and give them back. I opened my mouth to explain about the as-is buttons and pin and that I paid ten cents for the pearls but she stopped me.

"Do not interrupt! There is nothing more for you to say. The officers are waiting outside. You and Helen Boris will return everything to the store managers with an apology. We will also see to it that you two are separated. You will be removed from Helen's class and will not try to communicate with her in any way. Tomorrow morning, report to Class 8A-4 in Room 511. Placing you in advanced classes was an error on our part. In 8A-4 you will benefit from the slower pace and will have a chance to improve your grades. You are a lucky girl to get off so easily."

We Return the Stolen Goods

I sat in the back of the patrol car with the big cop. Helen sat in front, head down, slumped against the corner of the passenger door. The cop who was driving looked as big as mine.

When we got to the front of my building, I begged to go up to my house alone. My cop said he had to come with me but he would stand in the stairwell while I went inside. He said, "Take your time." I was afraid to open the door and walk in. Now my mother knew I smoked and went to Julian's pool parlor. She knew about Phil. She had been told that I stole the pearls. Worst of all, she had been summoned to school for a lecture from Miss Waller that had to have left her humiliated. The few times my mother got hysterically mad at me, when I had made her worry herself sick by staying out too late, she had grabbed my hair in her fists and yanked my scalp back and forth. It was horrible. Oh! My coronet! I braced myself and rang the bell.

Ma flung the door open, eyes blazing, nostrils flared. Her voice shook. "What kind of . . ." I ducked into my neck like a turtle. "What kind of a *bestia* should snitch on her own flesh and blood, should rat to the police! A mother she calls herself? A *bestia! Ptu!*" She stamped her foot.

Oh, my little Mama. Those were the sweetest words I ever heard.

"Come," she said, and led me to the kitchen table, where she had the two buttons, the medallion, and the strand of pearls ready for me to take downstairs. "Ma, I didn't steal the pearls I swear to God. I paid for them with my own money." I covered my face, put my head on her shoulder, and bawled my heart out. She patted and stroked me. "*Sha, sha,* I believe you. Don't worry. Just take everything back and don't argue with them. Don't say nothing to them. *Sha.* Just you be quiet and let them talk. Here, we'll keep one button for Ruthie. Tell them you lost the other one. Don't be afraid, they won't send you to jail for a button those *bestias!*"

Oh, Ma. Why did I wait till you were dead in your coffin before I could tell you. You were the best mother in the world!

The patrol car drove off just as all the school kids were coming home for lunch. Helen was still slumped in her corner up front. I slid back in my seat to make sure they wouldn't see me through the windows. I chanted to myself, over and over, *Just be quiet and let them talk. Don't be afraid.*

The first stop was S. Klein. Helen's cop walked in front with his big hand wrapped around her arm, a pistol in his holster, a billy club swinging from a loop on his belt. My cop walked half a pace behind me, the keys on his belt chunking with every step. All eyes were on us as we proceeded down the long main aisle to the service elevator at the back of the store. On the way up the elevator I had my first good look at Helen. She was so changed! Red puffy eyes and sore nose in a splotchy face, her mouth half-open, her hair hanging in strings. She looked like an old doll left out on the fire escape. I had to remind myself not to feel sorry for her.

The S. Klein manager sat hunched over his desk like a frog, with his elbows out and a cigar in his thick wet lips. Helen's cop walked her up to the desk. She put the bellflower necklace on it. The manager took the cigar out of his mouth with his thumb and forefinger.

"What can you do with these people," he said. "They're animals. They steal anything, they don't care. They're killing the business." He rolled his tongue around the cigar and stuck it back in his mouth.

The Orbach's manager couldn't be found. The assistant secretary brought us to the head buyer. He rose from a glass coffee table strewn with fashion photos. He shook hands with the policemen. He took the rhinestone *H* pin from Helen and sighed. "I hope you've learned your lesson," he said. "A striped uniform would not look becoming on a pretty girl like you."

At Lerner's, as soon the cops opened the front door Miss Vampire rushed to the front and blocked our way in.

She looked at the police with panicked eyes. My cop told her I came to return a button and a pin I had stolen.

"What? What button? What pin? I don't sell buttons and pins."

I spoke up. "My sister bought a dress here and a button was missing so I came back to get one and I saw that the medallion was missing from her cap also. It was the as-is checked suit in the back."

She stared at me as if I were speaking Chinese. She took the button and medallion, gave the policemen a contemptuous look, and turned her back on us.

The Hearn's manager was a stern thin-lipped Christian with silver-rimmed glasses. He held up Helen's Jewish star necklace. "The Star of David," he said with fake awe. "You stole the emblem of the Hebrew people on the day of the Sabbath." Helen buckled in a fit of crying. Her cop had to hold her up by her armpit.

I put my necklace on the desk. I told myself, *Don't argue with them. Just be quiet.* That was it. The last return.

My Punishment

The gossip got all over school, Sidney's ninth-grade class included. He waited till supper was on the table, then he said, "So I hear you turned Helen into a crook."

"It wasn't my fault."

"Oh yeah, she just went for a walk with you and decided to steal a load of jew-lery."

For once Ma stood up for me. "Be quiet, Sidney, you don't know the whole story."

"I know I'm not gonna eat with no crook."

He got up and piled a lot of stuff on his plate and headed for his bedroom. I yelled after him, "You're mad because you had your goo-goo eyes on her." He turned back, banged his plate on the table, and reached out to hit me with his fist, but Ruthie bent over and covered me. He stormed out. Ma followed him with the plate of food, "Sidney, here, I made just for you!"

Next morning when I reported to class 8A-4 with my transfer slip, I was surprised to find that the homeroom teacher was Seymour Barrett, the teacher for my science class, who used to like me. He said, "Okay, everybody, pipe down now. This is Fay Kessler. She's joining our class. Nice to see you, Fay." What a sweet soul!

There were far more boys than girls. Their ties were loose and they sprawled in their seats. The girls had elaborate hair-dos and looked dressed up even in their middy blouses. Mr. Barrett said, "There have been some wild rumors about why you were transferred here. Would you like to tell us about it?"

I faced the class and said loudly and bitterly, "I'm sent here for punishment. I only took a button and trimming off a dress. My sister bought the same dress in another size but the button and trimming were missing. It was only an as-is dress so I don't consider that stealing, and then because of that they decided I stole a ten-cent strand of pearls that I really bought with my own money. But this isn't punishment anyway.

"I have Mister Barrett for science so I know he's a good teacher and very fair."

The class exploded with laughter. Mr. Barrett smiled also. He said, "Thank you, Fay. Take any empty seat." I went straight to the back and sat in the last row. I was hoping to be inconspicuous but everyone turned around to look at me, only with big friendly smiles.

My New Friend

When three o'clock came I decided to walk home with my nose in a book and pretend not to see anybody from my old life. But as soon as class was dismissed, three of my new class-mates came up to walk me home: the two boys who sat next to me in the back row, Irving Goldfine and Joseph Georgioff, and a sweet-faced girl who had been sitting nearby, Jenny Adorno. Jenny was also new in class. She was a transfer from a Catholic school that had kicked her out for playing hooky.

We walked side by side to my house with Jenny and me in the middle and the boys on either side of us. I didn't have to care about bumping into any of my old friends. Joseph was small and skinny, hardly taller than me, and dark. He had thick black hair and deep-set eyes. He talked without a stop, waving his arms like an opera singer. "My name isn't Joseph, that's my school name. My real name is Asa, Ace. I'm the Ace of Hearts. I fall in love all the time. I love to be in school with all the girls so pretty in their white sailor shirts and sailor ties. I sing to myself red tie is grade 7, blue tie is grade 8, black tie is grade 9. I'm almost sixteen but I'm only in eighth grade because we move around a lot picking crops and sometimes I get back to the city too late. We just got finished bringing in the grapes, we got grapes for sale all over Attorney Street. Come with me and see tomorrow? It's like a parade."

So Joseph, Asa, was a Gypsy. I knew the Gypsy grape market. They had it every autumn. Dozens of Gypsies all selling the same round blue Concord grapes from overflowing baskets on both sides of the street, Jews from all over buying them for putting up the Passover wine, the Gypsy women dressed in long colorful skirts and loose drapey blouses, the Gypsy men in vests and jaunty felt hats, the Jews in their Sabbath best, all babbling in Russian, Romanian, and Gypsy Romany.

Jenny and Irving had never seen the grape market, so we said okay. But Asa didn't show up in class next day or the day after. On Thursday, when he was still absent, we set out to look for him in the Gypsy district. It was mainly on Sheriff Street. They lived in stores with bright-colored curtains over the front windows. On the way it dawned on us that Sheriff Street was in another school district and Asa must have been using someone else's name and address. The stores were empty, the curtains gone. We went to the grape market but it too was gone.

Jenny said a private goodbye to me on Friday. She was pregnant, it turned out, and her father was making her boyfriend marry her. She said he was a grown-up, actually

225

her father's friend, and they were in love anyway. He worked at night and made a good living in wholesale produce. Jenny would have a nice apartment and wouldn't have to go to school anymore, and she liked babies, so she was happy.

On Monday I took the same seat in the back row, next to Irving, but I hardly looked at him I was so embarrassed. I didn't know if he would ask to walk me home, just the two of us.

At three o'clock he asked, looking embarrassed also, and I said sure in the most casual way, like it was very ordinary to walk alone with a boy who was not your regular boyfriend. I hoped the girls in my old class, including Helen, including Lorna, would see me with him so they wouldn't pity me for being in the dumb class. He was a catch, tall and slim and blond and shy and squinty-eyed, like a cowboy in the movies.

Irving told me he hung out at the candy store on Houston Street in case I wanted to go over there on the way home. He said "I have money. You want an egg cream?" I said yes, and that meant I was willing to be his girlfriend. Neither of us said another word until we got to the store. I was sad. I thought of the person I used to be last summer, when I swore my love to Phil, so long ago. In the candy store Irving brought the egg creams over to a small square table. He asked me how I got into trouble. From the minute I started he thought it was funny and kept laughing until the part where the police came. Then he turned so sympathetic and even pained that I almost cried again but I didn't. And I was glad to have him for a new friend. Irving' house was on Houston and Goerck Streets, an old three-story building next to the corner pool parlor. He told me he had a job there. Every morning before school he emptied the ashtrays, took out the garbage, and swept the poolroom and sidewalk. He asked me if I'd like to leave my books there and go for a walk along the river. I did.

At the bottom of Houston Street was the new Franklin D. Roosevelt Drive for cars only. To get to the East River you had to get across the Drive by an overpass or wait a long time for the red light to change. Then you had to go past baseball fields and a cement walkway with benches before you reached the river itself. At the river's edge they had put up an iron guard rail where the seagulls now roosted all in a row. East Street was gone. Our dock was gone. Irving walked me all the way along the river to the South Street docks in the warehouse district, where girls didn't go.

We stood at the front of a wood-plank pier, surrounded by water on three sides, and watched the boats. Irving knew where each freighter had come from and what cargo it was unloading. He told me the words for the parts of a ship and words for the sails on the fishing boats as they passed on their way to the Fulton Fish Market. He lit a Camel from a pack. I took a few puffs. They were too strong for me. He smoked like a sailor in the movies, with the cigarette cupped in the palm of his hand.

Every day after school Irving and I stopped at the Houston Street candy store for an egg cream. He paid. Then if the weather was okay we left our books in the pool parlor and went to the South Street docks. I always brought a penny Chesterfield with me and we smoked on the pier and threw our cigarettes in the water at the same time and watched them bob on the waves. One day he asked how my hair would look if I let it go free in the wind. I said terrible, I wouldn't think of doing that. Another day it turned freezing cold on the open pier. He had on only a light green jacket made of cotton flannel fluffed out to look like wool. He stood with his shoulders hunched and his hands deep in his pockets. He tried not to show it when he shivered. I wished I could put my arms around him and help him get warm.

Ramona was a week overdue! I had forgotten all about it. I brought the book to school with me, and after our egg cream Irving walked me to the library. He didn't want to come inside even though it started to rain hard.

Instead of going to the docks we went to the movies. We saw a cowboy picture and then James Cagney in "City for Conquest," about a boxer who is blinded in a fight and ends up selling newspapers at a newsstand. I could tell Irving didn't read books but we still had a lot in common. We both liked hanging out in the candy store and we both liked the river and James Cagney movies and we were not goody-goodies and not mean to anybody either. And we had no other friends.

What Is the Truth of You

At home I was silent. Ruthie was away, having supper with each of her friends in turn to say goodbye because her wedding was for relatives only. Extra guests were too expensive. My father would come home, wolf down his food while he read the paper, and rush out as usual without noticing what was going on. Maxie ate at his secretary desk in the living room while he listened to the radio shows. No one was allowed to talk in the living room while he was there. I wasn't speaking to Sidney. I waited on the couch by the radio till Sidney finished supper. When he got up and went to his bedroom I sat down at the kitchen table alone. Ma never stop nagging. "Why don't you talk to Sidney?" she would say. "It's not nice you should be angry with your own brother."

After supper I did my homework on my bed then I went back to the living room couch until seven o'clock, when Lavanburg Social Center opened. I went straight to the Senior Lounge to play pool. On Wednesdays I went to my dance class. We did leaps across the floor while Miss Bea called out "Next-two, begin. Next-two, begin."

For dance improvisation I worked on the Midnight Mannequins dance. I imagined myself inside the Fox Fur windows, imagined mannequins whirling around me and strange faces staring through the windows. A dance of coming and going and turning and circling, of swirling sheer curtains with ghostly dance partners. I made up words I would recite to a pulsing, shimmering tambourine.

Let two begin.
Who are you? Who are you?
What is the truth of you?
Which have the others decided is you?
What have the others decided is true?
Show them the truth of you!
Next two begin.
Who are you? Who are you?

Miss Bea liked it. She said my movements and variations were nicely consistent and she said to keep working on the dance. She said to repeat the same words through the entire dance, that it would have a fine pulsating effect.

Eighth Grade Assembly

I felt self-conscious waiting outside the double doors for the Wednesday afternoon Assembly to start. It was my second Assembly since I was thrown out of the 8A-1 class and I hadn't made friends with any of the girls since Jenny left, so I was afraid they would think I was stuck up.

Mrs. Berkowitz struck three chords at the piano and started the march music. The double doors were opened by monitors. My 8A-4 class marched in first and stood at our seats in the back rows, girls to the right and boys to the left. Then came 8B-4, the other dumbest class. Then came the 3s and 2s. The 8A-1 and 8B-1 classes, the smartest, marched in last and took all the front rows. Assembly had about 350 pupils. We sang the Star Spangled Banner, we recited the Pledge of Allegiance, then we sat down and sang from a Christian hymn book:

> *Holy Holy Holy, Lord God Almighty,*
> *Early in the evening our song shall rise to Thee.*
> *Holy Holy Holy, Merciful and Mighty,*
> *Perfect in power, in love and purity.*

I sang extra loud to show I didn't care. At the last line, instead of singing "purity" I shouted "liberty."

There was a rustle and turning of heads all around me. The girl at my right punched my arm and grinned and pushed me over to the girl on my left who pushed into me with her shoulder and also grinned. I sat up straight, glanced right and left, and smiled back.

After the hymn the Speech teacher read a passage from the Bible and then Mrs. Berkowitz played a classical piano piece. Then Miss Waller went up to the podium and said that today's theme for the Assembly was our potential. She said that today when we went back to our homeroom classes we would find our IQ test results and she wanted to stress that the tests were strictly to evaluate our potential. She counseled those eighth-grade students with the most potential for college to take a foreign language and advanced mathematics in the ninth grade and to register for the all-boys Stuyvesant High School for science, or the all-girls Washington Irving High School, which taught various subjects. Those boys who showed potential for manual achievement—we all knew she meant the dumb boys—were counseled to transfer to a vocational school at the end of the eighth grade to prepare for a trade. The rest, she advised, should apply to the coeducational

Seward Park High School, which emphasized secretarial skills and accounting for girls and the liberal arts and competitive sports for boys. Then Miss Waller announced the student with the highest IQ, Karl Feldstein, as expected. He had 168. Not only that, it was the highest score in the whole school. We applauded while he stepped up to the platform and shook Miss Waller's extended hand. Karl's class applauded the loudest, and there were yays and foot-stomping.

Then Miss Waller made a speech about how Mister Feldstein had been in America only two years and what an example he set for other refugees and how he had a promising future in this land of opportunity etcetera etcetera, and we applauded again when she shook his hand again. Then she raised her hand for silence and announced that there had been a tie, that a girl had also got a score of 168.

Heads turned to Lorna and a girl in 8B-1, Alice somebody. For the moment I forgot I was mad at Lorna and I half-rose in my seat to get a look at her. Miss Waller said, "By contrast, this girl has a long way to go to fulfill her potential. We on our part are ready to give her whatever help she needs. Will Fay Kessler please come to the podium?" Out of shock I plunked down in my seat. The girls at my side practically lifted me up as my class shrieked and clapped and stomped their feet, all out of proportion, because one of their own had been singled out for such an unlikely honor.

The other dumb class in the back, 8B-4, picked up the commotion as soon as they saw me rising up from their midst. I had to walk all the way down the aisle while Miss Waller banged the gavel to quiet the riotous noise from the rear.

When I reached the platform all went silent but she didn't shake my hand, so I turned and shook Karl's hand, which brought on more yelling and stomping. Miss Waller shouted

"Assembly dismissed." With both hands and a toss of her head she signaled Mrs. Berkowitz to play the exit march.

I ran back up the aisle and tried to get to my place on line but my classmates reached out at me from all directions with slaps on my back and head, and punches on my arms, and even kisses. What a crazy surprise!

"You're Not My Type"

Irving left homeroom class while I was still getting my coat out of the coat closet. I ran down Houston Street and caught up with him at the corner of Goerck. He said with a crooked smile, "You don't want to hang out with me anymore. You'll soon be back in your old class with your friends."

"I don't have any friends," I said. "You're my friend. The class doesn't make any difference."

"It makes a difference to me. Let's face it, you're not my type."

"Irving that's not fair! I'm just the same type as I was yesterday. And I can't go back to my old class anyway because I'm not allowed to associate with Helen Boris, like I told you."

"Look, I don't want to talk about it." He walked off. He turned back. "I just want to know one thing. When I was telling you the parts of a ship, did you already know them?"

"Of course not! How could I know them? The IQ doesn't mean I know everything. It's just that I can read fast and I can do arithmetic fast, that's all. I'm not really smarter."

He interrupted me. "Okay, that's all I wanted to know." I watched him go down the street and disappear into his building.

At home, my mother said, "I'm glad you're so smart, I'm not surprised, it's only to your credit. But you have to have common sense also. You get too smart a boy would not want to marry you. The boy always has to feel he's smarter. You can end up an old maid like Aunt Minnie don't forget. She went to college and look what she got, a boyfriend in the show business to leave her with a nervous breakdown."

I screamed, "Ma *stop*! Stop comparing me to *Minnie*! I don't want to *hear* it any more! Can't you ever let me enjoy my achievements without giving me a lecture?"

She lowered her voice. "Don't mention in front of Sidney. He got a 128, also a very high mark don't forget, normal is a hundred, and I want he should be proud of himself without comparing to you."

But my mother's low voice was still too loud. Sidney was in the living room reading the newspapers. He came rushing in and yelled at her, "I told you, stupid, I had interference." He turned to me. "You're a crook. Everybody knows you cheated on the test." I yelled back, "If everybody got a lower score than me, so who was I gonna to cheat from? Karl Feldstein isn't in my class, you know."

When Sidney had no comeback his temper took over. He started to pummel me right on my tender bust. I tried to fight back but Ma got in the way.

"I told you not to bother him. Why do you always have to answer back?"

I couldn't stand it any more. "I hate you," I screamed. "I hate you both! Both of you!" I ran out of the house crying, without my coat.

I had nowhere to go. No friends. I went back for my coat and took Butchie with me to a bench by the river. I let her off the leash and let her run back and forth chasing seagulls off the railing. When she dashed along the railing they rose in the air, when she had passed by they settled down again. She ran back and forth, stirring up wave after wave of gulls. When she got out of breath she flopped on her belly and panted for ten seconds then started again. I didn't go home till it got too cold. Butchie was so knocked out I had to carry her back.

Remorse

Next morning Mister Barrett greeted me with a big smile and a transfer slip back to my old class. I said, "It's a mistake. Helen Boris's mother doesn't want me to be in the same class with her."

"Helen moved away," he said. "She transferred to a Hebrew high school for girls in Williamsburg."

Moved away! Williamsburg! I was afraid I would cry again. I had to make myself turn and say goodbye to the dumb class, and in my heart to Irving.

"I have to go back to my old class so I just want to say goodbye and I'll miss you, and thank all of you for being so nice to me." And then I went to the girls' bathroom and I did cry.

Miss Chilly was her old self. She said, "It's a mystery to me where you got your brains, you certainly haven't been using them." The class bust up laughing at my expense. She said it was time I stopped being lazy and that I would be getting extra homework assignments to help me reach my potential. She asked my fellow students to cooperate by not distracting me; she meant by not talking to me.

I was so despondent about Helen, about Irving, about being without a friend or a place to fit in with other people, that I didn't care what she said, it didn't bother me any more.

After class, big Charlotte Schorr with the big bow in her hair came up to me in the hall. "Lorna wants to know if you're still mad at her. She's having an all-girls dance party in her house after school and she wants you to come." Lorna lived on Cannon Street, two blocks away from Goerck, in a nice second-floor front apartment. Her mother was a milliner's trimmer in a good line of hats that sold to Macy's. I rang the bell instead of walking right in.

I had left on my school skirt and just changed to the purple silk blouse and my black one-inch pumps. Lorna came to the door. She was wearing a green silk party dress with gold sandals. She said, "Do you want to be friends?" I said, "Yes. I'm glad at you again." She said, "I missed you." I said, "I missed you too." She said I never gave her a chance to explain. She found the Orphant Annie poem at the last minute. She wouldn't have read it if she knew it would make me mad at her.

I said it didn't matter, I shouldn't have got mad at her, and I said she was right because after all she won the prize. She said, "It's yours as well as mine, remember? But it's only a children's dictionary. It doesn't have menstruation or masturbation in it." I said, "A children's dictionary is your just reward for reading a children's poem." I said it with a smile, she laughed, and that broke the ice. I added my coat to the pile on the dining room chairs. The party was in the girls' bedroom, the front room facing the street. You went in from the dining room through double doors that were left open.

Lorna took my hand and we went in together. Her big sister had got rid of the bed, put a divan against the wall, and turned the bedroom into a living room. All our friends were there, holding paper cups of soda and eating potato chips. Like me, they had changed to silk blouses and dressy shoes but kept on their skirts.

Lorna announced that the party was to practice dancing with boys. Each time we danced, one partner had to pretend to be a boyfriend and then we could switch.

Bernice Levitson was in charge of the records. She put on Frances Langford singing "I Didn't Know What Time It Was" with the Benny Goodman band, a big Rodgers and Hart hit.

Lorna took the boy's part. We held hands and she put her other hand around my waist. We all sang along as we danced.

I didn't know what time it was, then I met you.
Oh what a lovely time it was, how sublime it was too!
I didn't know what day it was, you held my hand.
Warm as the month of May it was and I'll say it was grand.
Grand to be alive, to be young, to be mad, to be yours alone!
Grand to see your face, feel your touch, hear your voice, say
      I'm all your own!
I didn't know what year it was, life was no prize.
I wanted love and here it was, shining out of your eyes.
I'm wise, and I know what time it is now.

Lorna didn't let me go after the song but continued to hold me close, cheek to cheek, then put her arms around me. I hadn't realized until now that I hurt her by getting mad at her. I hadn't thought that she truly liked me as much as I liked her, that she would miss me, that I was good enough for her. I felt a new tenderness toward her. I also felt old and sad. Lorna and I never changed partners. She remained in the lead.

There were six or seven couples, dancing close together, singing along with the romantic hit tunes of the year—"Blue Moon," "Stairway to the Stars," "All the Things You Are." No one else changed partners either.

At the end of each record the girl taking the boy's part would practice-kiss her partner. After awhile, the kisses got longer, and eyes closed. Then, while the music came to a prolonged ending with drum rolls and clashing cymbals, one pretend-boy bent her partner backwards and practiced an ardent kiss like a Latin lover, and another pretend-boy cupped her hand over the budding breast of her partner. Bernice stopped the record abruptly. We looked up.

There was Lorna's father standing in the doorway like a statue, staring into the living room with blurred gray eyes, a long gray beard, and a religious Jew's skullcap on his head. Tears were streaming down his face into his beard. How long had he been standing there? Lorna rushed over. "Don't mind him. He has the sleeping sickness. He's walking in his sleep."

We heard a strangled sob from deep in his throat, and one arm, bent at the elbow, started flapping. "Come, Papa, let's go back to your room." She called out over her shoulder, "Party's over. 'Bye everybody. Thanks for coming."

We grabbed our coats and fled. We couldn't get out of there fast enough. We scattered like cockroaches when the lights get turned on, never to mention the party again.

I went to the river and walked along the railing in the darkening sky. The face of Lorna's father haunted me, his stricken, tear-streaked face. And Helen's tear-streaked face haunted me, her face in the elevator at S. Klein, it had never gone away, I saw it every night when I closed my eyes, I saw it now. So long as I was the one being punished I had been able to suppress my guilty conscience. But now everything was different. Helen's punishment was so much worse than mine. And I had started it, all the trouble. I had taught Helen to steal. I had not given her a chance to settle in her heart those questions she had about God. I had not talked with her seriously, meaningfully—about religion, socialism, capitalism, the war in Europe, about a better world to come, all the things I had talked about with Phil. Instead I had flaunted my materialist side and had made her giddy with desire for superficial things. Now she was shut away in stupid dull Williamsburg, in an all-day all-girls Hebrew school, for years and years, never to dance, while I was here scot-free, back in the "one" class with my best friend Lorna, dancing whenever I pleased.

I needed to tell Helen I forgive her for ratting on me, and I needed to ask her to forgive me too, for showing off like a juvenile delinquent and for teaching her to steal.

The walkway by the river crossed under the Williamsburg Bridge. I stopped and watched the wavelets lapping against its stone base. I listened to their sound:

whis-per swish whis-per swish whis-per swish

I made a plan. Every Saturday I would walk across the bridge and search up and down the streets of Williamsburg until I found the Hebrew high school for girls. Then three o'clock next Monday, as soon as my class was dismissed I would cross the bridge and get to Helen's school before five o'clock when her school let out. I would stand across the street until she came out. And then I would be waving a white handkerchief to symbolize a white flag of peace and surrender, and when she saw me I would place it over my heart to symbolize forgiveness and love. I prayed to God she would understand.

The next Monday it snowed. Then all winter it was too cold and deserted on the bridge. Then in spring I lost my way on the crooked and dead-end streets of the Brooklyn side. And I didn't see any girls. And no one had heard of the religious girls' high school. And creepy men leered at me.

I stopped trying. I never found Helen again.

Fay at sixteen

XXIX

On the Delancey Street Bus

It was raining hard and I was late for school. I had no time to put on makeup. I threw an old kerchief over my hair but left my bangs out to drip down my forehead and hide my pimples. I looked a mess. I prayed I wouldn't run into any of my friends until after I'd fixed myself up in the girls' bathroom.

I jumped on the Delancey Street bus and Oh! There was Phil sitting at the back! We had been so in love on the roof one summer when I was too young and he had pledged to come back on my eighteenth birthday and if we were still in love he would marry me. I had dreamed for years of how I would be leaning against the roof ledge wearing white chiffon in the evening breeze and how he would come up to me and say how beautiful you are and how I would say I've loved you every moment since we parted.

Heart racing, I quickly turned my head to face front and I sat down in the first seat. I wasn't fast enough. Our eyes had met in the split second it took me to turn my head away. I thought, Oh I made a mistake! He'll think I turned away because I don't love him any more! It's not too late to turn around and face him. But I couldn't bear to have him see me looking so ugly. The bus was coming to a stop. I jumped off without turning around.

On my eighteenth birthday I went up on the roof, just as I had dreamed, looking beautiful in a white chiffon dress. I waited at the ledge in the evening breeze, and in the chill night air, and stared out at the stars until they faded into dawn. And also on my nineteenth birthday. And also on my twentieth, six weeks before my wedding. Phil never came back.

There was a song. By Don Rave and Gene de Paul. I couldn't get it out of my life. Not to this day.

You don't know
What love is
Until you've learned the meaning of the blues
Until you've lost a love you had to lose

You don't know
What love is
You don't know
How hearts yearn
For love that cannot live yet never dies
Until you've faced each dawn with sleepless eyes

You don't know
What love is
Do you know
How a lost heart fears
The very thought of reminiscing
How lips with the taste of tears
Lose their taste for kissing
You don't know, you can't know, what love is.

XXX

Why Did She Have to Go and Kill Herself?

Rosie Shuster's mother threw herself out the kitchen window down the airshaft onto a heap of garbage. Just an ordinary housewife, always at the sink and stove with a dirty apron on and stockings rolled down, never even lifting her eyes to say hello when you came in the door. This happened just after I finished the best book I ever read in my life, *Anna Karenina* by Leo Tolstoy. How I cried when Anna threw herself under the oncoming train, all for a ruined love. It desecrated the tragic act of suicide to have such a dull stupid woman as Rosie's mother kill herself and in such a disgusting way.

Rosie Shuster and my sister Ruthie were best friends. Rosie lived in an old three-room railroad flat on East 4th Street just across from P.S. 15 where Ruthie went to school before we moved to Lavanburg Homes. So when Mrs. Shuster killed herself Rosie ran to our house to hide from the commotion around her building. She sat on a kitchen chair and squirmed and bawled and tossed her head as if she wanted to shake it off her neck. Ruthie hugged her from behind the chair while my mother wiped her face with a clean wet dishtowel. Rosie took the towel and blew her nose in it. That was the last time I saw her. The whole family moved away: the father, Rosie, and her three younger brothers, all four children born in the first seven years of marriage. They disappeared like Gypsies in the night.

My uncle Alya-Leyb and Aunt Pulla lived on the same block as Rosie. Aunt Pulla came over next day and told my mother the whole story. She said Manny, the oldest boy, came home from basketball around four o'clock and he noticed that the airshaft window was wide open so he went to shut it and he

243

saw that the clothesline was dangling from a loose hook with socks and underwear flapping against the bricks so he reached down to pull up the line and that's when he saw a housedress at the bottom of the airshaft, and then an arm. He flew down the stairs and got the janitor to open the hall door to the airshaft and there she was, face down in the garbage. The boy was right behind him and saw the whole thing. "Believe me," Mrs. Shuster said, "he'll never forget it."

My mother said Mrs. Shuster couldn't have fallen out, the window sill was too high. "She was a small thing, she must have climbed out poor thing, may her soul find peace in Heaven." They couldn't think why she did it, there was no reason, four healthy children who never got in trouble and a respectable husband with a steady job.

This was just before Ruthie's wedding, where Rosie was supposed to be the Maid of Honor and had already bought an expensive rose-colored gown. What bad luck.

Twenty years later I went to see my friend Cecil Taylor, the avant-garde free-jazz musician, who had moved into Rosie's old building on East 4th Street. It turned out to be the very same apartment except that now the walls were painted white and Cecil's grand piano filled up almost all the space in the kitchen. He was playing when I came in. I begged him to go on. As I listened to Cecil's turbulent, heart-wrenching music my eyes kept wandering to the window as if the piano were calling to Mrs. Shuster's gray ghost and it was struggling to raise itself up the airshaft, struggling to reach the window sill and rebuke me.

XXXI
The Mikva on East 5th Street

"*Gut farshteyt.* God understands. You don't have to be religious to be a good Jew, and you don't have to be Christian to be a good American."

—Mama

Finally, after months of shopping and planning and fighting and turning the house upside down, Ruthie's wedding was this coming Saturday, only two days away. And here I was, not even grown up yet and Ruthie's chosen maid of honor, about to escort her to the mikva after sundown. Also coming along was our mother, Irwin's mother Mrs. Calman, and Irwin's sister Peppy, the matron of honor. The men in the wedding party were at the synagogue getting drunk with their friends.

Mikva! A word even more secret than "menstruation," whispered in the street by the girls—("I bet you don't know what mikva means." "No, what?" "I'm not telling")—finally explained to me. A secret pool in a bath house, or in a yard house behind the synagogue, where brides and married women are made pure by a religious ceremony.

Just as we were finishing our wine and cake in the living room and were getting ready for the mikva, Mrs. Calman, in a sweetly innocent voice, slipped in a little request that Ruthie follow a bridal custom from her side of the family out of respect for her mother in Romania. She asked that Ruthie spend the wedding night at her house so that she could cut out a blood-stained square from the marital sheet to mail to her mother.

Ruthie turned red as a beet. "What? Certainly not! I never heard of such a thing!"

Ma leaped in. "I am so insulted. I never thought this from you, Mrs. Calman. If you don't trust my daughter, I am happy to call off the wedding right here and now."

Mrs. Calman said, "You don't need to feel offended, Mrs. Kessler. I don't mean any disrespect. I did this with my own daughter, ask her." Peppy, bored as usual, was holding up her pearlized compact and freshening her lipstick.

My mother said without a glance at Peppy, "I don't want to know what you did with your daughter, that's not my business. I don't know what kind of a small village you come from in Romania but you will have to tell your mother we're in America now."

Ruthie was by now in the bedroom, trying to control herself. I ran in to her, about to cry, but she sent me back to get Mama. We left Mrs. Calman and Peppy standing in the living room.

Ruthie said to Ma, "I'm not going if the mikva woman examines me."

"No, no, believe me, she won't do that. That was a hundred years ago. Even in my time they stopped doing that."

"What about my hair?"

"I asked a religious friend and she told me, she promised, that now they only cut the hair of the very religious who ask for it. They don't even bother with taking a lock. I should live so, if she just mentions your hair, I'll walk right out with you, I swear."

So we tried to calm down and make the best of it.

We walked the six blocks to the bath house, from Goerck and Houston to Fifth Street and Avenue D, in two groups: Ma and I on either side of Ruthie, and Mrs. Calman and Peppy behind us. Thank God the sidewalks were narrow because we didn't want to walk side by side with them after hearing about

246

their bloody sheets. On Fifth Street we turned the corner toward Avenue C.

I knew this block very well. Helen Boris, who used to be my best friend, lived here. I used to meet her in front of her building. We both went to P.S. 188 on Houston and D. But I wasn't allowed to see her any more. We had gone to Lerner's on 14th Street to steal a velvet button my sister needed for her honeymoon suit—she had bought it "as is" with a button missing—and, well, while we were at it we stole a few stupid dress trimmings. Stupid Helen went and confessed to her mother, and her mother went to the cops and got me in deep trouble.

But I'd never noticed the bath house. It was across the street on the uptown side of 5th in an old two-story gray building wedged in between two tall apartment houses, with faint Hebrew lettering in the stone slab over the entrance.

The vestibule, on street level, had green brick tiles halfway up; the rest of the walls were rough plaster of a vague dirty yellow. Its old wooden hallway door opened onto a dim corridor with a flooring of tiny hexagonal bathroom tiles, deeply cracked, and walls of yellowed pressed tin, bulging and peeling here and there. Plumbing pipes and valves ran all along the low ceiling. A cardboard arrow, marked with the Hebrew letter M, pointed to the rear. A damp, stale odor of mold mixed with something like rotting garbage became more intense as we walked past two double doors and got to the back, where an arrow pointed down some steps to the basement. Here the odor was even moldier and definitely putrid. A dead rat somewhere?

Ruthie took my hand. Ma said to Mrs. Calman, right behind us, "Is this the place?" Mrs. Calman said, "My friend told me that here they do it the right way. You can't always tell by looks."

At the bottom of the basement steps a creaky door let to a small room of unpainted cement. Here, in the middle of the room, was the mikva, a murky green pool, only seven feet square. Along the wall next to us as we crowded into the room were three changing booths, each with an identical skimpy curtain pulled back to show one small bench and nothing more. Ma called out, "Missus. Missus. Anybody here?"

From the back door of the room, out came—Helen Boris's mother! Oh Jesus. I sidled behind my mother, but I was sure she saw me, I was right in front. Did she recognize me? Would she call me a thief in front of my mother? In front of *Irwin's* mother?! I was only in her house once, on a Saturday. She was sitting in an upright black chair when Helen brought me home, reading from her prayer-book with a shawl over her head, and all she did when Helen introduced me was give me a look and ask me if I kept kosher. I lied yes.

Mrs. Boris took Ruthie by the shoulders, like she was in charge of her life, and led her into a booth. I waited in misery and terror, wondering what she was doing to my sister and how long she would be in there with her. I tried to get behind Mrs. Calman and Peppy and stand near the front door. But then I decided to hide in a booth, so I went into the one nearest the door and slumped at the back of the bench. I didn't dare draw the curtain lest Mrs. Boris notice and fling it open.

Ages passed. Ruthie came out barefoot, without clothes on, wrapped in a sheet. Mrs. Boris positioned her at the wall facing the pool. She called out, "Let the matron of honor stand here," pointing to Ruthie's right, and "Let the maid of honor stand here," pointing to Ruthie's left. She kept her eyes on me as I came out of the booth and crossed over, my heart thumping. "Take off the sheet," Mrs. Boris said to Ruth.

We never exposed ourselves in my family. In my entire life, living and sleeping in the same room with Ruthie, I had never seen her naked. I didn't look. Mrs. Boris talked on just as if Ruthie were standing there with clothes on.

"Missus, the bride tells me she has bathed and has on her body no make-up or hairpins or other foreign matter. Now, according to law, I make sure she has no dirt under her nails."

She picked up Ruthie's hands, showing us Ruthie's long, carefully groomed fingernails. She held out the ring finger of the left hand. Her eyes fixed on me as I stood alongside Ruthie. Very, very deliberately, eyes still on me, she pulled a pair of scissors out of her pocket. With a sudden hard strike she snipped the nail at the quick. "Wait," Mama said. "Wait! Just the tips! You just need to cut the tips!" But she had a grip on Ruthie's fingers. Nothing would stop her. Snip snip. Down to the quick. The second finger. Snip snip. The fifth, third, the thumb. The nails dropped onto the sheet. The other hand. Snip snip. Snip snip. I wanted her to look at me again so I could show her my hate, my rage. Ruthie's eyes were squeezed shut. Her fingernails were stumps. It was over.

Mrs. Boris never looked at me again. She led my naked sister to the steps of the pool. The water was filthy, slimy—you couldn't see bottom. Ruthie drew back. "This is natural rainwater from heaven," Mrs. Boris snapped. "The mikvas that use water from the pipes are *treyf*." Not kosher. Then, in a prayer-voice, "When the Meshiakh comes he will throw pure water on the obedient."

Ruthie had to dunk in over her head, three times, and say the same prayer as for wine but with a different ending:

Barukh ataw adonoy elohaynu melekh ha-olem
asher kidishanu bamitzvotuv vitzivanu al hatvila.

Blessed art thou, Lord our God, King of the Universe,
Who hath commanded us concerning the immersion.

Outside again, Irwin's mother said, "When I took Peppy to the mikva they cut her hair." Ma pretended not to hear her. Peppy studied her rhinestone watch. We said a quick "goodbye we'll-see-you-at-the-wedding" and rushed home.

Ruthie ran to the bathroom to shower. I brought the wine and cake into the kitchen and Ma put up some tea. We sat down at the table and waited.

After forever, Ruthie appeared in her royal-blue crepe dress, a blue silk turban around her wet hair, and smelling like heaven in her Evening-in-Paris perfume. Soon the three of us were making plans to get elbow-length white kid gloves, like a debutante's, to cover her nails at the wedding. Thank God she had picked out a *treyfa* wedding gown, one with forbidden short sleeves.

XXXII

Remembering Ruthie's Wedding

Ruthie got married at the age of twenty. Sixty years later, I asked her to write me what she remembered about her wedding. She was a widow, and lived alone. I was divorced, and also lived alone. We read the letter together in her living room and had a good many laughs.

"Getting ready for the wedding was like preparing for a war. First came the wedding attire of both men and women. It was unbelievable, all the stores we went to and the discussions that went on!

"We finally went to the Bronx, where I hired my wedding dress, veil, shoes, and fur wrap, for seven dollars. I don't remember your outfit and much of the ceremony. Mom went all over the department store basements looking for a bargain until she got a very nice gown back here at Klein's, teal velvet top and taffeta skirt, with cheap earrings to match. The men rented tuxedos and Irwin rented tails. The day of the wedding I went to the beauty parlor and had a hair-set, nails, and eyebrows, all three for one dollar. You came with me, remember?

"Peppy [Irwin's older sister] *by coincidence bought the same dress Mama had, but in rust. She felt terrible about it. There was no color coordination. I don't remember if I had bridesmaids or all ushers. Were you my bridesmaid? I think Peppy was my matron of honor.*

"When we got there at a temple in the Bronx—I don't remember the name, it was near Crotona Park—I was ushered into a small Bridal Room where I remained until the ceremony so I saw nothing of the smorgasbord or the dancing or music. When it came to the ceremony, nobody told us which finger the ring went on— so after trying on a few, Irwin finally put it on the right-hand

251

pointer and it was the right one, so he turned to the audience and said, 'It doesn't fit.' Well everyone laughed, including me—I laugh when I'm nervous. At the end of the ceremony I went to the Rabbi and apologized for laughing and explained why I had laughed. He was very angry and said he was never so insulted before!

"The wedding continued in true Jewish fashion. Almost at the end, one of my mother-in-law's cousins fell and broke her arm. She sued the caterers or the hall and got two hundred fifty dollars and bought a new living room suite of furniture. Rhea [Peppy's daughter] *was the flower girl. She had a screaming fit and ran under a table. Ruby* [Peppy's husband] *had to pull her out and take her home.*

"At the end of the wedding when pay-up time came, my father-in-law had changed the menu from pot roast to chicken for a dollar more per person. It might not seem like a lot, but it was a lot since we had two hundred people. Don't forget it was 1940, and we were still recovering from the Depression. Papa looked sick at the extra expense."

That night when we came home from the wedding without Ruthie, I took out *This Singing World*, my poetry book from second grade, and I looked for a poem that could help me live within my body, which was filling up with grief at losing my sister. Nothing. I found it in my other poetry book, *Leaves of Grass* by Walt Whitman.

> *Tears! tears! tears!*
> *In the night, in solitude, tears.*

When all were asleep I took the book to the kitchen table and read the poem in the dim light of the night bulb over the sink, over and over until I knew all the lines by heart and had unloosed my ocean of tears.

Ruthie told me she had cried all that night, too, in silence, after Irwin was asleep. Peppy and Peppy's husband Ruby had

252

given her a "surprise present" at the wedding. They had been living with Irwin and Peppy's parents since their marriage, and now they were moving out with their little Rhea so that Ruth and Irwin could have their bedroom and save on rent money. Ruthie wasn't given a chance to say whether she would like to live with her in-laws.

That night, in a midtown hotel room before going off to Niagara Falls for their honeymoon, Ruthie made Irwin promise that he would not make her pregnant until they had an apartment of their own. Then they got into bed in the dark because Ruth was so modest she wouldn't let him see her undressed. And she was too shy to speak when Irwin started making love to her. She thought he was breaking his promise. She didn't know he was using a condom—a scumbag, we used to call it. She didn't know respectable people used them. She had thought that when the time came she could pretend to be asleep.

All this Ruthie told me in her living room after we finished reading her wedding letter. Of course we laughed our heads off.

XXXIII
Blackout

On the Sunday afternoon of December 7th, 1941, I was strolling along Houston Street with my girlfriend Theodora, Teddy, on our way to go window shopping on Clinton Street. The sky was a bright clear blue. Only twenty or so people were out and about. The loudest sound was the click-click of high heels. All of a sudden a young man in a flapping dark coat came tearing down the street yelling, "War! War! Turn on the radio! The Japs are bombing us." All heads shot up to look at the sky. It was empty, clear blue. Radios were turned on, windows opened, and we heard the news while we walked on. Pearl Harbor. Where is Pearl Harbor? Our fleet was destroyed there. Why?

On Monday, December 8th at 12 noon, before going home for lunch we sat in our classrooms and listened to President Franklin Delano Roosevelt over our new public address system. No one will ever forget how he said that this is "a day that shall live in infamy." He asked Congress to join the Allies and declare war on the Axis Powers. That meant joining England, Russia, and China to fight Germany, Italy, and Japan. What will happen now?

On Tuesday, December 9th, New York City's Mayor Fiorello LaGuardia called for "air raid wardens," volunteers for civil defense against air raids. Against bombs from the sky! I asked Teddy, "Do you think we'll be sent away like the children of London? Or will they let us stay and volunteer?" Her eyes filled with tears.

Only two years before most of the Jews in Alsace including Teddy's family fled across the border to France just before the German army invaded, and then her family barely escaped to England in a little fishing boat when the Germans took over France and rounded up all the French Jews for the death camps. "England sent us to America to be safe," she said, "but now we're not safe here either."

Three months later we heard air-raid sirens in New York City. Between the newspapers and the radio and the schools, everyone knew it was only a test except some Jewish refugees who ran around screaming or folded themselves up in the space under the stoops of their buildings. Teddy's mother, who didn't speak a word of English and was too timid to even go out in the street, crouched against the back wall of her kitchen, the farthest she could get from the front-room windows, and accompanied the sirens with a hair-raising wail. We heard her moaning the prayer for the dead, *yis-kedal vi yis-kedash.* "Who shall live and who shall die, who in his appointed time and who before his time." She was sure that the Nazis were coming and that we were lying when we said it was a just a test.

Then came our first real blackout. Street lights out, sirens wailing, air-raid wardens on patrol. Teddy's mother climbed out onto the fire escape to jump off and kill herself before the Nazis reached her. A warden spotted her with his flashlight and ran up the fire escape steps, calling out in Yiddish, "I'm a Jew also. Come with me, I'll bring you to a safe place." He brought her down to the ground while everybody stuck their heads out the windows to laugh and cheer, though it was forbidden.

But soon enough we had to take the blackout very seriously because German U-boats were prowling along the New Jersey shoreline and sinking our merchant marine boats carrying military equipment. They could see our boats in silhouette when the night lights of New York were on.

The Nazis never did bomb us, of course. Why not? In England the cryptologist and computer genius Alan Turing cracked the secret code that the Nazi bombers were using in order to find their way to London and the other targets. Then so many of their planes got shot down that Germany couldn't replace them fast enough to reach New York.

XXXIV

World War 2 Comes to the Lower East Side

Lavanburg Homes, our model housing project down near the docks, was close to its fourteenth birthday when World War 2 broke out. Everyone on our street turned instantly patriotic, from the isolationist Republicans to the revolutionary Communists. My mother became a Red Cross volunteer. She packed first-aid kits every morning five days a week. We have a picture of her standing proudly in a white uniform, with a red cross on her white head-scarf. A Jew wearing a cross was unthinkable before the war. My father, in his tenth year as a part-time janitor at Lavanburg's, was put in charge of a canvas honor roll bearing the names of our boys in the service. It hung on the front of the building between the two courts. When a group of our boys was called up, their mothers gave them a block party. Tables loaded with delicatessen sandwiches, pickles, honey cake, and soda appeared on the street. Fathers brought down beer and whiskey, and we danced the Lindy and foxtrot to loudspeakers hooked up on the lampposts. At the end we gathered round the honor roll to toast each departing recruit, making sure he got good and drunk, and we sang "For He's a Jolly Good Fellow" while the art teacher painted his name on the honor roll and his mother cried her eyes out. By 1944 the honor roll was almost full, and gold stars started appearing next to the names of the dead—a shower of stars after D-Day in June when the Allies landed in France. My family was lucky. My big brother Maxie, who was an amateur photographer, spent the entire war at the Hotel Breslin on Broadway and 29th Street, handling V-mail, letters that were reduced to tiny film negatives for transport overseas so as to save space on the ships. My mother cried with the other mothers anyway, assuring them he was about to be called to the front. "It could be any minute."

At our Social Center in the basement of Lavanburg Homes, the clubs and activities we grew up with had been in decline. The youngest of the Lavanburg kids were now in high school and had gone farther afield for new friends. The once-thriving art and theater programs had lost their teachers when the government withdrew its Federal Works Projects funds; we had to make do with advanced students and adult volunteers. I was the only member of my old performing troupe who was still interested in modern dance. I had to continue my studies at the Henry Street Settlement where the teacher had a whole different kind of approach. She had modern dance training but a show-business background. Her dancers were long-stemmed American Beauty roses with natural or bleached blonde hair and the latest fashions in leotards. They were hoping to find work in Broadway musicals. I didn't even know where to buy a leotard. I figured they were too expensive anyway.

One night, it was at the end of April, while we were doing warm-ups on the floor in my new class, lifting and stretching one leg at a time with a hand at the inside heel, the teacher came up to me. "You can do better than that," she said, and turned my left leg out, viciously, as if she were taking off a chicken thigh. I felt an electric shock at my tailbone and then a spreading needlelike pain. I had to face it. I was out of place, a slum kid, no release at the hip, no training in high kicks, the wrong hair, the wrong looks.

I sneaked out of class unnoticed, crawling backwards on my behind while everyone was lining up for leaps across the floor. I never went back.

It had taken more than a month for me to recover enough to start practicing again, but my left leg had strangely lost its spring, its power. In mourning for myself I stopped wearing dresses, stopped putting on makeup, kept my hair short and frizzy, read Dostoyevsky all day long while I brooded and chain-smoked and developed a cough. I never went downstairs to the Social Center anymore except to play pool once in awhile in the Senior Lounge. I was surprised, the last to know, that our once-beloved administrator Abraham Goldfeld was gone, gone to East London, the birthplace of the settlement house movement for uplifting the poor while settling among them. He had said his work here was done. In fact, the Lavanburg fathers had grown tired of having him direct their lives. And the mothers were furious at him for defending a gang of Lavanburg boys who had been accused of attempted rape of a girl who was on the roof taking laundry off the clothesline. He said the boys were normal adolescents who must only have been curious to know what a girl's private parts look like. And, he said, was she really just taking down the laundry when everybody knew that boys hang out on the roof? It was all supposed to be hushed up but it wasn't, and the girl and her family moved away.

The war brought the clubs back to life. It started when President Roosevelt told the nation that canned food had to be rationed because metal was needed for the War Effort. He asked us to grow our own food on every bit of available land and do our own canning in glass jars for the duration. Our Fathers Club and the former boys clubs got together to start victory gardens in the empty lots along Goerck Street. They pulled up the overgrown weeds, hauled away the gravel and rotted lumber and rusted trash, broke up the hard ground, and brought in government-issued soil and seeds. The Mothers Club and the former girls clubs portioned out the vegetable plots and did the planting. Then our clubs moved on to other streets and helped other tenants start more victory gardens.

Henry Street Settlement, Madison House, the Educational Alliance, and dozens more settlement houses did the same. Soon the whole Lower East Side had thriving victory gardens and was abloom with flowers as well: marigolds and petunias in the borders of the vegetable plots; sunflowers, rose bushes, and climbing vines against the old brick walls. While we worked we sang a new song on the Hit Parade:

> *There'll be bluebirds over*
> *The White Cliffs of Dover*
> *Tomorrow just you wait and see*
> *There'll be love and laughter*
> *And peace ever after*
> *Tomorrow when the world is free.*

Chairs and folding tables appeared. The men played cards and dominoes, sporting all sorts of hats, caps, and eyeshades to keep off the sun. The women sat on makeshift benches and knit. The former knitting club got together to give out shopping bags full of government-issued khaki wool with instructions for making Army sweaters, socks, and scarves. On weekends I joined my old girlfriends in the victory garden across the street from Lavanburg's, next to Elya Schwartz's shoe repair shop, to knit long thick scarves for the soldiers. The older women knit socks. They knew how to shape the heel, an art none of us tried to learn because we would have had to follow instructions and count stitches, and we wanted to talk while we knit. We had all signed up in high school to correspond with Jewish soldiers for their morale, and while we knit we read passages of letters to each other and laughed over the torrid paper romances some of us were getting ourselves into.

When summer was over, some of the victory garden groups decided to continue meeting indoors, and that's how our Lavanburg Social Center got going again. The Activities

Director, Miss Sparks, who used to be Mr. Goldfeld's secretary, renewed the theater program. Our little stage in South Hall, once a showcase for left-wing one-act plays and musical reviews, was now given over to Flag Day pageants and presidents' birthday celebrations.

In February 1944, when I was sixteen, Miss Miller remembered the anti-lynching dance "Sistern and Brethren" from our Dances of Protest concerts and asked me to revive it as a solo for Lincoln's Birthday. I jumped at the chance. I had been a leading dancer in the Lavanburg dance troupe, proud and confident and highly praised. Someone had even come to my house with an invitation to study with the great Hanya Holm at the famous Bennington College summer dance school in Vermont. I needed my parents' permission, but they wouldn't give it. I begged them to let me go. I fought with them, I stopped eating, I stopped speaking to them. It was hopeless. So when I was asked to dance solo in South Hall I put my heart and soul into choreographing an original version of "Sistern and Brethren." I had only a week to prepare. I borrowed a rehearsal drum from my former dance teacher, Miss Bea Baronofsky, and I enlisted my old dance partner Esther Mandelker to beat it for me. Miss Bea promised to come to the performance and bring her own Alan Lomax folk-song record which included the song I needed. I dug out my old costume from a laundry sack in the back of my bedroom closet, my austere brown cotton-sateen shift. It used to come down to mid-thigh, now it barely covered my torso and I had to wear a black bathing suit underneath. I cut my hair short, up to my earlobes, and left it naturally frizzy to suggest a Negro man.

On Lincoln's Birthday I was ready for my solo dance, eager to show my old friends and neighbors that I had grown up to be a serious dancer with a big talent. But when I came out onstage in my short brown shift, the boys in the audience acted as rowdy as if they were at a burlesque show. They wolf-whistled and chanted "take it off, take it off" until Miss Sparks from the sidelines threatened to turn on the lights and throw out anyone who made a sound.

The boys may have been imitating the soldiers in the movies and USO shows, or maybe it was my age, or theirs. Anyway, that was only the beginning. Miss Bea had sent a telephone message less than two hours before the performance that she couldn't come. She left no provision for me to get the record. I wrote down the words and enlisted my Aunt Minnie, a Greenwich Village bohemian who read poetry at recitals, to read the song through the microphone at the side of the stage while Esther beat the hand drum. The first stanza went:

> *Sistern and brethren, stop foolin' with pray*
> *Sistern and brethren, stop foolin' with pray*
> *When black face is lifted, Lord's turnin' away*

I could never have imagined that any living soul would recite those lines the way my Aunt Minnie did. While I trudged across the stage with the heavy steps of a convict in chains, she stood benevolently at the side chirping out the lyrics in a strange, high-pitched elocutionary voice like an imitation of Eleanor Roosevelt. At "black face is lifted" I rose in a high arched stretch, head flung back, arms hanging limp behind. At "Lord's turnin' away" I threw my head forward and dropped to the floor as if cut down from a rope. The suddenness of this fall at the front of a line of ten dancers had always made audiences gasp. Now, laughter and more wolf-whistles. More threats from Miss Sparks. In the next stanza it got worse:

> *We're buryin' a brother they kill for a crime*
> *We're buryin' a brother they kill for a crime*
> *Tryin' to keep what was his all the time*

Here I swooped and twirled, swooped and twirled, like a manic vulture, while the wolf-whistles gave way to howls. Someone yelled out to the tune of "Ol' Black Joe": "I'm comin', I'm comin', for my dick is hangin' low." I wanted to stop the performance but I had too much discipline and pride. In the pause before the next stanza, which was supposed to be "When you tucked him on under what you gonna do," I swooped myself over to Aunt Minnie and whispered "Last stanza, go to the end." This was:

Stand on your feet, club gripped 'tween your han'
Stand on your feet, club gripped 'tween your han'
Spill their blood too, show them you're a man!

While Aunt Minnie rattled the pages and in some confusion recited "spill their blood too," I stepped up to the front of the stage and glared out at the audience in fury, and when she recited "show them you're a man" I raised my fist high to sarcastic cheers from the house. It was my last performance at Lavanburg's. I was through with those idiots.

Backstage, Esther thrust the hand drum at me and ran up front to catch the next act. I reminded Aunt Minnie that my family was expecting her for tea upstairs and said I would be up in a few minutes. Thank God they never came to my performances. I dressed haphazardly and sneaked out of the theater in the dark, holding back tears.

In the dim corridor on my way out, someone stood leaning against the door under the red light of the exit sign, someone in a snap-brim hat and open raccoon coat, hands thrust deep in the coat pockets. When I came closer, I saw that it was the art teacher, Norma Cannon, grinning at me. I would bump into her once in awhile in the senior lounge, or when I watched her painting a name on Lavanburg's honor roll when a boy got drafted, but we had never spoken to each other.

"I waited for you," she said. "Good show."

"Oh, no. It was terrible!"

"Well, the boys were cretins and the narrator was odd, but your dance was really good. Look, would you like to go for an ice cream soda?"

I didn't understand. You got ice cream soda on a date or maybe a birthday. Was she trying to console me with a treat? I couldn't bear that. I told her I had to go home, my aunt was waiting for me. The truth sounded stupid. I felt embarrassed the moment I said it and didn't even remember to explain that my aunt had been the narrator.

After the Lincoln's Birthday fiasco, Norma would stop to greet me when we passed by and ask how the dancing was going. She was always dressed the same: a hat with a brim shading her eyes, a big tan scarf and raccoon coat—in the spring, a dark blue smock over a workshirt and khaki skirt. She had a way of standing close and looking straight into my eyes expectantly. It was intimidating. I told her I was still in dance class at Henry Street and no we weren't planning a concert yet. I didn't tell her I wasn't going back, wasn't taking lessons anymore.

One June evening Norma came in after art class and joined us at the pool table. She was sensational! She played doubles with me against the boys, and we won four games in a row before we were beaten. The lounge chairs were all taken, so we picked up cigarettes and soda at the candy store across the street and went to sit on a bench in the deserted victory garden. The night air smelled of roses and corn shoots and fresh-turned soil and sounded of crickets and peepers. I asked her where she had learned to play pool.

"In my father's basement game room in Brooklyn. I like taking on the boys."

"I do too."

She clinked her soda bottle with mine. "Cheers," she said, and took a swig. "Today's a big day for me. I just signed a lease on an apartment around the corner on Stanton Street. I got it 'as is' for only twelve dollars a month, three rooms with steam heat and an inside toilet. I'm going to turn it into a studio and live there too."

"By yourself?"

"Sure."

"You want to move to the East Side? Everybody wants to move out."

"Oh, I love it here. It's not just the cheap rent. It's a great neighborhood."

I had never heard anyone say that. We'd all grown up with the aim of leaving the Lower East Side as soon as we got married. I didn't know anyone who stayed, not even in Lavanburg's. I knew that artists were different, but it was still hard to believe that if they had money they'd actually want to live in these ugly old rat-traps instead of in the charming little houses on the tree-lined Greenwich Village streets with their crooked lanes and outdoor cafés and exotic shops. And Norma must be rich enough to pay good rent if she could afford a raccoon coat and a game room in the basement.

"Do your parents mind?" I asked.

She laughed. "We settled that a long time ago. I've been living with some other girls in a private house near Brooklyn College, but I study in Manhattan at the Art Students League and all the classes I teach are around here in the settlement houses, so it's time for me to move. Look, when the studio is finished I'd like to do a portrait of you. Would you pose for me? I also need an assistant to help me set things up. Would you like to work with me on Saturdays this summer? We could agree on a rate of pay after you've seen the place."

I was stunned. My mind raced in all directions as I thought what to say. I thought of my ruined dance classes. I thought of how everything I had been doing with my life up to this moment had come to nothing, and I said to myself, yes, why not say yes? And I did.

XXXV
Norma's Studio

I came up to Norma's studio on a bright Saturday morning in June. It was in the old seven-story building on the corner of Stanton Street, next to Goerck, the tallest building in the neighborhood. When I reached her apartment on the top floor, I saw that she had taken off the inside doors between the front room and kitchen and put them out on the landing.

The Top Floor

The big advantages of living on the top floor: You and your neighbor on the landing are the only ones there; the other tenants don't go past on their way up to their apartments, so you have privacy and extra space out in the hall. You can keep your seltzer box outside your apartment, for instance, and your umbrellas and galoshes and beach chairs. The other advantages are the better light and fresher air, the cheapest rent, and you're right next to the roof. You just go about ten cement steps up the stairwell under a skylight ceiling, push open an iron door, and step out onto the roof. There you can hang your wash, look out over the city, sunbathe in your beach chair in the summertime, be alone with your boyfriend at night. And on the roof of this particular building was something special: Anthony Fanelli's pigeon loft, now being tended by his little brother Nicky until he got home from the Army.

Inside the Apartment

I knocked at the open hall door. Norma was in the living room on her knees, ripping out the old linoleum with a knife and scraper. "Come on in," she called out, "and look around." I entered through the windowless kitchen, about ten feet square. Its once-glossy ivory walls were smudged to brown by smoke and grease. Opposite the hall door were a deep porcelain sink and bathtub. On the tub's enameled tin cover were neatly stacked paint cans, buckets, cleaning stuff, an open toolbox, and a spare workshirt. Big wooden cupboards loomed over the tub and sink, almost to the ceiling. Against the right wall a gas stove sat up on high tin legs. Next to it was a deep cruddy square on the floor where the icebox had been taken out. Years of water overflowing the icepan had broken down the linoleum and some of the flooring beneath.

The Front Room

The room on the left, which we called the front room, where Norma was working, was going to be her studio. It was bare except for a ladder, an old metal folding chair, and strips of linoleum all over the floor. All the front-room's walls were painted lavender speckled with silver swirls. Norma swept aside some linoleum strips and exposed the original wooden floor. "Look at these wide planks," she said. "They're pine. They'll be beautiful when they're sanded and stained. And look at these nice long windows. They face north." I shuffled up to the windows and looked out. From this high up I could see way over the Lavanburg's rooftop to the roof of my old school, P.S. 188, on Houston and Lewis Streets, and when I looked downwards into Goerck Street I could see the honor roll hanging in the middle of Lavanburg's between the two courts. "Oh," I said, "you have a wonderful view."

The Little Room

"Go and look at the next room," Norma said. Another window, in the room on the right, faced east toward the river. It would have been the bedroom. When I leaned out I could see all the way along Goerck Street from Gelman's drug store on the corner to nearly the end of the next block, Rivington Street. At the far end of the little room, behind two doors, were a small clothes closet and a private toilet that used to be the hall toilet. Norma joined me in the little room. "In here I've decided to take down all the plaster from the outer wall and expose the brick. The rest of the room I'll paint a lively green; it'll set off the bricks nicely."

"Is the landlord letting you do that?" I asked.

"Well, I took the apartment as is. That means I have to fix it up myself, right? He won't mind. He shouldn't. I'm getting the leaky roof-drain fixed for him."

Then she told me my first job would be hacking out the plaster in the little room. "We'll each carry out two buckets of plaster every time we go downstairs. After that we'll clean up the kitchen, patch and repair. Then we'll paint. The rest of the walls will be white. Last we'll do the windows and floors. So, let's get you started. After you see if you like this sort of work we can talk about rates, okay?"

My Brothers Should See Me Now

Norma set up the ladder in the bedroom and handed me a painter's cap and the extra workshirt to put over my clothes. I was already wearing old jeans and a faded plaid shirt but she said the plaster would get into everything. She gave me a hammer and a wide-edged chisel, the first time I ever held men's tools in my hands. I didn't know if I was strong enough to make them work. I went up to the wall and started pounding.

Norma rushed over. She laughed. "You don't want to make a hole to the outside and fall through." She showed me how to set the chisel at an angle and swing the hammer rather than drive it. "You provide the aim and momentum, let the hammer do the work." It worked beautifully! The chisel chipped the plaster away so easily! My entire life I had believed that only men had the strength to use men's tools. I could have laughed and cried at the same time.

Norma said it would be best to start at the top of the ladder and work my way halfway down, then start again standing, then do the bottom half while sitting on the metal chair. I had an awful fear of heights. I was scared of going up ladders and even more scared to come down. At first I was dizzy and thought I would faint, but with the plaster giving way to my chisel and the bricks emerging in such a variety of shades, and having to go down only one step at a time, I forgot to be afraid until I found myself near the floor. A few more times up and down the ladder and just like that my lifelong fear was gone! Soon I was leaning out sideways this way and that, indifferent to all the chunks of plaster falling all around me, and even climbing up and down the ladder single-handed. I wished my family could see me, especially my two brothers who always treated me as no good at anything but cooking and cleaning. When I caught glimpses of Norma stripping out piles of linoleum and liberating planks of pine, I felt as if we belonged in the new home-front army of skilled women workers.

At twelve-thirty Norma took off her workshirt and said, "Let's get lunch." We washed our hands at the kitchen sink and wiped them with paper towels. There was no mirror. Norma dampened a paper towel and wiped the plaster off my face, off my eyebrows and lashes, slowly, as if she were applying makeup. I felt her gaze.

It made me feel awkward. But I thought she must be studying me for the portrait she wants me to model for.

We each picked up two buckets of plaster and started single file, Norma first, down the seven flights of stairs. The buckets were way too heavy and my left leg kept buckling but I forced myself to pretend I was carrying coal on stage in our troupe's dance for the striking miners. I chanted to myself, *"down in the dark and the damp, down in the dark and the damp,"* and I just barely made it to the bottom. We dumped the plaster in the garbage cans in front of the building, parked the buckets behind the ground-floor stairwell, and went off to an Italian grocery store on Grand Street.

The Hero Sandwich

I had always admired Italian grocery store windows with their display of fancy wedding cakes and cookie tins and had loved to peek in at the many kinds of cheeses, sausages, and hams hanging from the ceiling on ropes. Being a Jew I had never eaten ham, the meat of pigs, even though I didn't obey the kosher laws. If Norma ordered ham I wouldn't tell her it was my first time.

A skinny woman stood behind the marbletop counter, a white butcher's apron over her black dress, her thick gray hair caught up in a net. Norma said, "One hero regular please." The woman took a long loaf of crusty Italian bread from a glass bin behind her and placed it on the counter. With a huge knife she cut off the ends and sliced lengthwise through the middle. She stripped out the soft dough and threw it to the cat—every grocery had to have a cat to keep out the rats. Then she poured a thin stream of olive oil into the bottom part of the loaf and put in layers of a smooth pink ham, a dark pebbly salami, a soft white cheese, and bright red roasted peppers.

Then she added another few layers of a purple ham that was outlined in pepper and streaked with fat. She closed up the sandwich and pressed down the top. She asked, "One or two?" Norma said "Two." She cut the loaf in half and wrapped each half in heavy waxed grocery paper. The whole thing took about a minute.

The sandwich cost fifty cents. We got two root-beer sodas, each a nickel plus two cents deposit. My share came out to thirty-two cents. I didn't have nearly enough money. I had to let Norma pay. Would she allow me to owe her my share? I had an idea: Volunteer my labor and then she would probably offer to pay for lunches. On the way back I told her that I loved fixing up the apartment, that I was learning so much, and that I wanted to help as a neighbor—I was too shy with her to say as a friend—and that I didn't want to be paid. She wouldn't hear of it. She said she would keep track of the hours and pay me a fair sum when the work was done. She smiled. "And lunches are on me." She was so nice.

I came to the studio every Saturday morning at ten and left at five. The summer wore on and the heat settled in. Norma brought up a second-hand floor fan for the studio and two table fans, one for the kitchen and one for the little room. We worked until about twelve or one and then went for lunch, always the same sandwich and root-beer soda. I liked the Italian crusty bread better than the Jewish rye, and compared to ham our Jewish pastrami was too fatty and salty, especially in summertime.

At the Front-Room Window

Norma and I ate lunch at the wide-open fire-escape window in the front room. I settled in sideways onto the broad old-fashioned window sill with my knees up and my back against the side. Norma pulled the ladder over and sat on it facing the street, one hand around her sandwich and the other around her soda bottle, gazing out from below her hat brim. She said the brim kept the glare out of her eyes so she could see the light and color better. She explained, "Artists need windows facing north because the north light is steady. With south windows, the sun moves from east to west and keeps changing the colors." I felt the thrill of learning about something so important to artists. Sometimes Anthony's pigeons would swoop past us from the rooftop to merge with flocks from other rooftops here and there while the pigeon keepers swung long poles to keep them in flight. The keepers were playing their Saturday game. When the birds came back to their lofts the keepers would see if pigeons from other flocks had been enticed to settle with their own, or if any of their own pigeons were missing. Every so often the pigeon keepers would visit each other's lofts and swap birds to get their own back. While I tried to memorize which birds always came back to Anthony's I sometimes noticed that Norma was watching me instead of the pigeons or the sky. But I was getting used to it and even made little adjustments in my posture and the angle of my head to show myself to advantage for the portrait.

We began to talk more during lunch break, that is, I did. Norma wanted to hear about my family and about the early years of Lavanburg Homes and about my dance training. She said little about herself but once in awhile she would tell me about one or another of her five roommates, all of them painters or writers.

They shared a car as well as a house, and on Sundays they drove to a house on a private Long Island beach that they rented by the week, or to a lean-to along the Appalachian Trail. I wanted to know so much more about her, especially how she had become an artist, how she had gained the freedom to leave her family without being married, whether she had a boyfriend, but as I was so much younger and we were not really friends, it would be rude to question her on such personal matters.

By the first Saturday in August the old apartment had been turned into a bright new studio with smooth white walls and ceiling, gleaming pine floors, sparkling clean windows, and a charming green brick-walled sitting room. With the inner doors between the kitchen and front room gone, the studio was amazingly spacious. The doors had been a leftover from the old days when everyone sat around the kitchen coal stove in winter and shut off the other rooms to save money. Now most Lower East Side buildings had steam heat that came up from basement coal furnaces and warmed the apartments with silver-painted pipes and radiators, but no one I knew of had ever thought of taking down those two inside doors.

I Pose for the Portrait

Norma was ready to start my portrait. She gave me a twenty-dollar bill for my studio help. It was enough for a dressy winter coat with a fur collar and muff. She said she had figured it at the going rate of fifty cents an hour for a handyman, and that now she would start paying me a dollar an hour to pose for three-hour sessions, the same rate the Art Students League models got. I was to have a private five-minute break every twenty-five minutes and a fifteen-minute break halfway through, also like the Art Students League.

Norma positioned her easel sideways between the two front-room windows. At her right hand was the palette, which was the utility cart that had been in the kitchen. I sat on the metal folding chair in front of the wide door frame that led to the kitchen. I wore a white cotton short-sleeved shirt with a lapel collar and a light-blue chintz circle skirt that I had made for our folk dances. It fell about mid-calf. Norma posed me sitting upright with my knees spread and my hands folded in my lap, looking straight ahead and leaning forward a little.

I loved posing. I had always liked being still and silent, and a pose was like a frozen dance movement. And I loved watching Norma. She was big, big bosomed. She wore a man's oversized workshirt. She had blunt-cut hair and used no makeup. She seemed so comfortable within herself, as if she never needed to look in a mirror. I tried guessing which part of me Norma was painting by where her eyes rested. I was dying to see the painting emerge while she worked but she kept a black cloth draped over the easel post and when our first twenty-five minutes were up she dropped it over the painting. "You're not supposed to see your portrait until it's done," she said with a grin. "It's a tradition." I tried not to wonder whether she thought me beautiful, or whether I was going to come out looking beautiful in the portrait. I knew well enough it was amateurish to think that way about art, but I couldn't help it when I was the subject.

Before I got up from my first twenty-five minutes Norma marked the chair legs and outlined my feet with chalk lines while I spotted the angle of my knees against the lines of the floorboards.

To spot the position of my head I closed one eye at a time and sighted the edge of my nose against each wall, then I sighted my shoulders and arms and memorized the position of my hands. Each time I finished a break I got back into the exact same pose I had before. Norma said she'd never known a model who didn't need adjusting. "It's my dance training," I said, although no one had trained me in spotting.

Norma worked in a world of her own, in deep concentration. Her eyes fixed on the easel, the palette, me, and back again, sometimes taking long pauses, sometimes dashing from one to another. She smoked while she worked, sometimes with the cigarette in her left hand, sometimes between her lips while squinting to keep the smoke out of her eyes. She kept an ashtray on the window sill but often missed it when she flicked her ashes. I watched her hands. Her fingernails were blunt, her fingers tobacco-stained. Sometimes she would tell me to look at her. It felt odd to be looking into her eyes while she was studying mine. It felt like a children's staring game and I was afraid I might giggle, but I didn't. She smoked Camels. She was always running out of cigarettes or matches, and I soon started coming up to the studio with extras for her, which she always accepted with grateful surprise.

Norma rinsed her brushes frequently in a jar of turpentine, making a jingling sound. She would squeeze a mound of paint onto the palette from one of her large tubes and add some linseed oil from another jar. The odor of oil paint, turpentine, and linseed oil mixed with cigarette smoke and the sun-softened roof tar came to me in waves as the rotating head of the floor fan carried the air around the room, sickening at first but I got used to it.

I posed for Norma every Saturday afternoon through August. No more lunches. I left my costume in the closet between sittings. In September, when I went back to school, I brought reading assignments to the studio and held the book in my lap so that I could study when she wasn't working on my head or hands. That made the time go by faster—too fast, as I found that all week long I lived for the Saturday to come.

Hurricane!

One Saturday afternoon, while Norma was concentrating on her work, I watched the sky turn leaden and saw the dust of the street rise in a gathering wind. Suddenly the sky became dark gray-green and as we rushed to shut the windows a heavy rain broke out. It beat against the window panes, sounding like nails against the glass. The wind hummed and moaned through every crack. We heard garbage can covers rattling and clanging along the sidewalks. Objects flew up from below and pigeons flapped in the air like so much paper. The building itself started swaying and creaking in the wind! We were in the midst of a hurricane!

Norma drew the cloth over the painting and we watched, elbows on the window sills. I wanted to run away but there was no place to go. Peering through gushes of water, we saw people running through the streets with their clothes pasted to their skin. We saw them ducking into hallways. We saw umbrellas torn from clutching hands and sent flying. We watched a cornice being torn from a rooftop and crashing into a window, shattering the glass, then landing with a thud in the street below. Now there was not a soul to be seen, only newspapers flying and an ashcan rolling toward our building, spilling its garbage to be picked up and carried in the wind.

Just then I saw my father down on Goerck Street! He was sailing our way, horizontally, accompanied by bits of paper and trash, hanging onto the canvas honor roll of our Lavanburg boys in service as the wind carried it along, his feet sticking out behind like a duck's. He sailed and ran on his toes and sailed again and ran on his toes again to the corner of Stanton, just below my window, and was still sailing when the side of the building blocked my view. I ran to the sitting room and looked for him through the east window. There was my mother! Solid on the ground, bending with the wind as she trudged toward Delancey Street in her worn-down Minnie Mouse shoes. She was picking up discarded umbrellas to repair and sell later. I didn't see my father again, and soon I lost sight of her, too.

I came back to the front room and didn't say a word to Norma. I prayed she hadn't seen anything. It was too outlandish, ridiculous, cartoonish. Pa risking his life for a piece of canvas, Ma risking her life for a few pennies, no one else crazy enough to be outside.

The hurricane turned out to be the worst that had ever happened in New York City, and it was officially written down as the Hurricane of September 13, 1944.

Opening Night of the Portrait

On the last Saturday in September Norma told me the portrait was done. This was to be its opening night. "Of course you'll come, won't you?" she said. "Everyone will want to see you." She placed the easel flat against the wall next to the window and set the painting up on it, still wet and smelling of linseed oil. There I was.

The features were striking: diamond-shaped eyes staring straight out at the viewer, a triangular nose with flaring nostrils, lips tensed at the corners, high chiseled cheeks, square jaw, muscular neck, muscular arms. I had always thought of myself as on the wispy side.

"Do I look like that?"

"You will." She laughed. "That's a famous reply Picasso gave to Gertrude Stein about her portrait, and he was right. Go and see it at the Modern, it's wonderful."

"I look so defiant," I said.

"Right! If this were nineteenth-century Paris, I'd title it Spirit of Defiance."

And then it came back to me, that moment when I had lifted my fist at the boys in the audience at the Lavanburg dance concert. Norma must have conceived the portrait then and there. The background had a sort of theatrical look. It was in three color areas, red, lavender-pink, and lime green, somewhat curved and suggestive of curtains. The planes of the white blouse and blue skirt were as sharply defined as the face but the brushstrokes were broad. The entire figure was edged with slashes of blue and black. The hair was the same blue and black as the outline but painted in brushy swirls with white highlights, like roiling ocean waves. I had such a tangle of thoughts and reactions. It reminded me of portraits by Van Gogh, Picasso, Cezanne, and Matisse that I had seen on posters and in reprints that Miss Bea used to bring to dance class. I got a lump in my throat. My heart raced. I sensed that she had understood me, deeply, in that terrible moment on stage, and had rendered it forever in this harshly beautiful painting. I felt somehow restored to myself. The only words I could muster were, "I like it very much." And I kept on looking and looking at it, and I smoked a whole Camel cigarette while I looked, hoping she would understand from my close attention how very much it affected me, how much it meant to me. She came and stood beside me, also silent, and we looked at it together. She took a long drag on her cigarette and said, "No one will like it. They'll remind me I'm an American and should be painting in an American style. Regionalism, folk, ash-can, neoimpressionism, even abstract, anything but Paris School. But that's what the portrait called for, so I don't give a damn."

Norma asked me to help her get ready for the party, to start in a couple of hours, after her friends had finished their Saturday gallery and museum rounds. She had been picking up old milkboxes since June. Some were stacked up to make a bookcase, some were set under the window sills as seats with padded cushions, some were set open-end up to serve as bins for paint supplies and work clothes. She had tossed a few large pillows on the floor and had brought up from the street a big comfortable chintz-covered chair that someone had most likely thrown out as too old-fashioned. A long table against the side wall was actually just planks of plywood on sawhorses. We covered it with sheets of unprinted newspaper; artists bought it by the roll for sketching. We set out the food. A big Italian ham on a breadboard, three kinds of cheese on another board, Italian bread slices in a large flat basket, bunches of red grapes in a large round basket, a heaping bowl of black olives, four bottles of Chianti wine in their straw cages. All but the grapes and wine came from the Italian grocery store on Grand Street.

Then Norma dragged over a Salvation Army carton from a corner of the kitchen and took out unmatched glasses, plates, and cutlery. She gave me a boxful of votive candles and some jar tops. "Put them anywhere you want."

I placed some candles on the table, some in the window sills of the studio, and moved on to the sitting room. There Norma had shaded the window with a heavy green burlap curtain and had fashioned a daybed from milkboxes, plywood, and a spring mattress. I recognized the daybed cover from the display window of a Polish folk-art shop on East Sixth Street: a red woven-wool throw and matching embroidered pillows. In front of the daybed was a round coffee table made of a cable spool from the warehouse district. A pile of blue velvet couch pillows were propped up against the opposite wall. I put three votive candles on the spool table and lit them in the darkened room. I called Norma to come and see how beautiful the little sitting room looked by candlelight. She said it reminded her of her favorite Greenwich Village restaurant, Seventeen Barrow Street, and that she would take me there sometime for *shashlik*. She seemed to glow with pleasure in the soft light. I was thrilled at this first signal that she planned to go on seeing me.

By three o'clock we were all finished. I looked around at every single detail of Norma's studio, to fix it in my memory as it was at this moment. My heart filled with longing for a place of my own just like this, and to entertain just like this. The rent was low, you could furnish it for almost nothing, the food was simple but delicious, and you didn't have to shop for days and cook for hours over a hot stove and be all flustered when people arrived. And they could help themselves without anybody running in and out of the kitchen with endless plates and bowls.

I thought with shame of my own apartment, crammed with ugly useless things: the oversized expensive living room set that hardly left enough floor space to turn around in, the double beds and dressers and vanities in the bedrooms that left only narrow aisles to move in sideways, the useless doodads on every surface in every room. How could I have lived there all my life without realizing how different things could be? How could I go on living there now without room to dance or invite friends over or breathe freely?

I lost courage for the party. I felt too self-conscious. I didn't know how to behave with people like Norma and her friends. I wouldn't know how to disguise my feelings, or express them in a whole roomful of writers and painters years older than me who lived beautiful and interesting lives. What did I know about art, about writing? Nothing. Even though I knew modern dance, I wouldn't know how to talk about it at a party, and even if I did, they still wouldn't treat me like one of them. They would ask me a few questions, make a few condescending remarks, and then they would all turn to each other with their latest doings and ignore me. And I guessed that though they wouldn't be dressed up, they wouldn't be dressed in blue jeans either, and I didn't know what kind of clothes I could put together to fit in. Why hadn't I thought to take my modeling outfit home and wash it? The girl in the Norma's portrait glared at me. I was desperate to get away.

Norma appeared in the doorway of the little room in a deep red shift down to the floor, tied at the waist with an embroidered Polish sash, looking radiant and expectant. I should have remarked on how good she looked. Instead I mumbled that I couldn't come to the party, that I forgot we were having company at home, my brother in the army was on leave. I could hardly hear my own voice it was so weak. I was instantly sorry. She came up to me and stood very still, her eyes probing mine. Of course it was clear to her that I was lying. Should I take it back? Should I try to explain myself to her? "How disappointing," she said quietly. "Well, I understand." She went to the kitchen, as if there was nothing more to be said. I retreated to the closet at the back of the sitting room and packed up my modeling clothes. When I came out again Norma was standing where the icebox stain had been, near the front door, holding out my pay. I forced myself to meet her eyes. They were kind. "You were a good worker and a fine model," she said, "and I enjoyed your company very much. Come by any time. I'll be here."

"Thank you," I said, "Thank you for everything." I put the money in my jeans pocket and left.

Spirit of Defiance

I made my way down the seven flights of stairs concentrating on the rhythm of my feet, step after step: *Left* foot-and *Right* foot-and *Left* foot-and *Right* foot. A ditty formed in my mind and stayed with me all the way to the bottom landing and beyond:

> *Spir*-it of De-*Fi*-ance, *What* you gonna *Do*?
> *Spir*-it of De-*Fi*-ance, *What* you gonna *Do*?
> *Spir*-it of De-*Fi*-ance, *What* you gonna *Do*?

I Never Stopped Thinking of Norma

I never stopped thinking of Norma, of wishing I could be like her, live the way she lived, independent and proud and creating beauty all around her without any fuss. She revealed a truth that the urban utopians who wanted to build us big modern houses had never thought of, that you could turn a cruddy old East Side slum into a clean, elegant space with a few dollars and a few tools and your own bare hands, even if yours were female hands.

Norma never showed up anywhere. Just about all the women painters were squeezed out, brushed aside, unless they were useful to the men who were returning from the war, so bent on proving that art was a masculine act of courage, not something done by females and sissies. She must have gone to California, or Mexico. Or Paris.

XXXVI

A Breach of Promise

All through the war I corresponded with a soldier in the Pacific named Harold Bresman, Hal, to keep up his morale. I was assigned to him in high school from a list of Jewish soldiers who wanted pen-pals. I wrote once a week, mainly about the plots of movies. He wrote about his buddies and about how lonely he was for back home in Rutherford, New Jersey. After two years, we were writing about being boyfriend and girlfriend, and I wrote about all the places we could go to on dates after the war.

When Hal was discharged in 1946 he invited me to his homecoming party. I took the Grand Central Railroad train. He and his father met me at the Rutherford station and took me straight to the party. It was like a wedding, more than a hundred people in a catered hall. His parents sat in front with me while he made a little "glad to be back" speech, then he took my hand and got me to stand up beside him and he introduced me as his girlfriend and all of a sudden put a big engagement ring on my finger. Everyone screamed and stood up and applauded while I had to stand there with my mouth open like a dope I was so shocked. I had never even seen him until that night and he had not made a great impression on me. He just seemed very young and kind of clumsy for his age, and the picture he sent me in his uniform made him much better looking than he really was. But I couldn't do anything on his homecoming day except try to smile and wait for another time to take the ring off and give it back.

I slept overnight in the family's six-room private house, and Hal and his father drove me home Sunday morning. Only my mother was home. Hal's father took out a nice lunch festively wrapped and introduced himself and the ring while Hal and I both stood there looking nervous. Then when the lunch was ready and we all had sat down, his father said he had a candy store right at the station when you come off the train. "Ay, the best location," Ma said. And then he told us that as a wedding present he was giving Hal and me a house of our own, a partnership in the candy store, and ten thousand dollars. She shook hands with him and kissed and hugged Hal. I was quiet.

As soon as they left I said "I don't like him. I'm giving the ring back." She turned beet red and yelled, "What, you think you're a princess? What more could you expect? This is the best match from our whole family." I yelled back, "You want to sell me!" And I was so disgusted I stopped speaking to her. I went in my bedroom and didn't come out until my father got home. Then I came out while he was feeding his fish in the living room and I asked him to meet me later at the Garden Cafeteria on East Broadway so we could talk, it was very important. I was sure he would understand me and be on my side.

In the cafeterias you came in through a turnstile and took a ticket and every time you ordered something the waiter punched the ticket to show the price. Then when you were ready to leave you took the ticket and paid the cashier and she let you out through the turnstile.

Ma had already told him about the surprise engagement. "Pa, you have to help me get out of this. I'll give you the ring. Please take it back to Mister Bresman in his candy store."

He said, "This is a wonderful marriage, better than anyone could expect. You have to realize not to be foolish. Give him a chance. He seems very nice. They seem like very refined people."

"But he didn't ask me," I said, "and I don't love him a bit."

"Love is not so important as you think. What you need for a good marriage is enough money and for both partners to be reasonable. The trouble with my marriage is your mother was never reasonable."

"So why did you marry her?"

I knew—I thought I knew—the whole story, but I asked him anyway. We had never had a real conversation about anything, just the two of us, in my whole life.

"Your Aunt Dora is younger. She was engaged to your Uncle Philip for four years waiting for your mother to marry first. Your mother was already twenty-four and she would be like an old maid if Dora married first. But then your Uncle Max, the baby in the family, eloped with Eva when they were both eighteen. So a marriage broker made an arrangement for your mother to get married right away. Naturally her father was willing to pay. So the marriage broker came to my father in the synagogue to see if he knew anyone waiting for a match, and my father recommended me. You see, I needed money to save my delicatessen store on Allen Street. I had the idea we modern young friends could have discussions and read poems in a delicatessen as good as in a cafeteria. I did good business, and I got engaged to the cashier, she had on my ring, but she and the waiter stole money from the cash register little by little and I couldn't meet my expenses. I tried to figure it out with a friend who was a bookkeeper and the truth came out that income was missing. Just on the dot the cashier and the waiter ran away. So I had to get married to save my business and my father knew her father and he said it was a good honest Jewish family and I couldn't do better so we got engaged. But then I found out that I was over my head with bad credit and the money I got from the matchmaker came too late to save the business so I decided to call off the marriage and give back the money on an installment plan. So then your mother's father wouldn't listen and he made them throw me in jail for breach of promise. Can you imagine? No discussion, no negotiation, just throw in jail the son of a respected poet and scholar. You have to understand, he was the *shammis* of the Willett street synagogue. He was the one who arranged all the holidays and entertainments and all the right prayers according to the Jewish calendar. So my father got me out on bail and told me I must go through with the wedding for the family's reputation. So the marriage was not only arranged but it was forced. It was bad from the beginning."

I asked the question I never dared ask before. "If you had such a bad marriage, how come you had four children?"

He started with Maxie. "After two years her family spread it around that I wasn't capable so I had to show there was nothing wrong with me, otherwise I would have to live in shame."

"And Ruthie?"

"Your mother pestered me. She didn't want to raise an only child."

"And Sidney?"

"That was because she needed either a baby or a scraping to get rid of some woman trouble, and the scraping was dangerous."

. "And me? And what about me?" I was fighting an inner hysteria. I supposed he would say Mama didn't want Sidney to be an only child either, because Maxie and Ruthie were already so much older.

But he said, "You're old enough now we can talk about such things. A man is not like a woman. He needs to relieve himself."

Those words! Those words! The many times she told me never be a mattress for your husband. The many times I found her nodding off on the living room chair. The many times she sneaked into my bed when she thought I was asleep. I needed to scream. I needed to get away. I grabbed one of the cafeteria tickets so I could pay and get through the turnstile. He reached for my arm and tried to hold me back. The coffee spilled. He hissed, "What's the matter with you? Come back. You don't understand." I ran to the front with everyone staring. I threw down a dollar bill and got through the turnstile and ran down the subway, panting, heart pounding, people staring at me all the way to my stop.

I couldn't stand the two of them any more. I had to get away from them. I still had the ring. I made a decision. I would marry Hal as quickly as possible, to get out of my house. Then I'd refuse to sleep with him. Then we'd get a divorce and I'd be free. All I had to do was stay calm. Stay calm. Don't get crazy.

Hal's parents came to visit us the next Sunday. We met them at the Delancey-Essex Street subway station to escort them the ten blocks to Lavanburg's. His mother walked with Ma and me, his father walked behind with my father. Hal hadn't come. It was a Jewish custom that the groom doesn't take part in wedding discussions. His mother looked at our streets with disgust. Her condemning eyes sought out every drunken bum, every wash line of drying laundry, every bit of garbage in the gutter. And all the while she clutched her handbag as if any minute someone would come up and grab it away from her. When we reached Lavanburg's she was so relieved. She congratulated us that it looked so nice. She had been afraid that we lived in the slums. They started planning the wedding. I felt poisoned. I felt venomous.

I went everywhere with Hal. His money was endless. We went to the theater, jazz spots, expensive restaurants. I brought my friends along and he paid for them too. He was having a marvelous time and thought my bad temper was a mark of city sophistication. He was an only child. He had been a fat boy until the army slimmed him down. I was his first girlfriend. He wanted to make love but I told him I can't do that and wear a white wedding gown, it would make me a hypocrite. He believed me and respected me for it. When I was drunk enough I tolerated his kisses. I drank heavily. I smoked heavily.

I lost weight and developed a deep cough. I started coughing with blood. I was whisked off to the Workmen's Circle tuberculosis sanatorium in Liberty, New York, high up in the Catskill Mountains. His father came up and begged for my understanding. His son is too young to take on the responsibility of a sick wife. The scene out of Camille! I played the role of the noble mistress. I gave him the ring.

The doctor couldn't find the TB germ but all the other symptoms of TB were so pronounced that he made me stay three months to see if the germ developed. Then he dismissed me, almost with disgust, as just a bad case of bronchitis. Ma came for me and we went home on my eighteenth birthday.

Back home Ma started fussing over me as if I were an invalid. To push her away I said I'd be leaving home as soon as possible. I said I'm going to be a model at the Art Students League. She got hysterical. She said, "How can you live by yourself not married? Everybody will say you're a prostitute." I screamed, "You want to *make* me a prostitute! You couldn't *wait* to sell me off to the Bresmans for money. Money! Money! Money! Money!" I screamed in her face. She ran out of the kitchen. I ran screaming after her. She escaped to the bathroom. Time passed. Silence. The door was partly open.

"Ma. Are you all right?" No answer. I opened the door. She was slumped on the toilet lid, barely conscious. I panicked. "Ma, did you take anything?" I shook her. She was a rag doll. I fell to my knees and cried and I promised I wouldn't leave her. She recovered. God knows if she really took anything, or was just exhausted, or was just acting. Finally, finally, I felt sorry for her.

Morris Kantor views Bill Chaiken's painting at the Art Students League.

XXXVII
Artists in Residence

After the war our ex-soldiers were rewarded with a Government Issue Bill that gave them a free college education. Many art students poured into the city, jammed the classes at the Art Students League to overflowing, and set up studios on the top floors of the abandoned sweat-shop buildings all over the Lower East Side. They established a couple of cooperative galleries and worked for each other's respect, very much like the jazz musicians of the time, with whom they were allied in friendship and understanding.

I went to the League myself as a model, hoping I might become a part-time student and learn to dance with brushes and paint, and I was suddenly popular as an authentic native girl of the Lower East Side, the neighborhood that was more real than Greenwich Village, a native female who knew how to get things cheap and throw good parties at the co-op gallery openings.

My new friends were mostly Amcrican-born Christians, natives. They loved to tell anecdotes about their hilarious Jewish neighbors. They loved to whoop over their discovery of halvah, sour pickles, pastrami, and other everyday food. People like my short stumpy mother, with her heavy accent and Russian-style exuberance, were "adorable." I was embarrassed in a way that I couldn't cope with and couldn't explain.

The nicest of the artists was William Chaiken, Bill, a Canadian G.I., very sweet and very talented and very interested in me, and he was even Jewish. I married him, and my mother and father liked him very much, and we had a nice Jewish wedding. We set up a studio just like Norma's on the top floor of an old building on Lewis Street around the corner from Stanton. But soon he joined two other artists in a spacious loft.

XXXVIII
The Wrecking Ball

In creating public works in New York City one had to paint over an already existing mural, a mural whose brush strokes were tiny and intricate and often, when one looked closely, quite wonderful, lending to the vast urban panorama subtle shadings and delicate tints and an endless variety, so that if it was crowded and confused and ugly it was also full of life and very human.

—Robert A. Caro, *The Power Broker: Robert Moses and the Fall of New York*

Slum clearance. It started down at the Italian end of Goerck Street, at the six-story tenement house right next to the parking lot where the blacksmith shop used to be, and at the next-door warehouse where the horses used to live, and where my sister Ruthie's boyfriend Milty used to sit in his car-park shack and my brother Sidney would listen to the Shadow program on his radio and go around saying "Who knows what evil lurks in the hearts of men? The Shadow knows."

Watching the six-story tenement go down was like watching an execution. A giant steel ball, tethered to its steel chain, swings from a crane attached to a truck. Swing, BOOM. Swing back. Swing, BOOM. Swing back. The brick wall collapses in slow motion, the dust rises, settles, rises, settles. A giant's dollhouse is exposed: six levels of square walls—pink, aqua, cream, lavender, all stamped with the reverse shadows of couches and bureaus and who knows what else. A zigzag staircase wavers, shivers, falls on its side in slow motion. The steel ball hangs on its chain and swings again. More bricks fall.

The truck leaves. It will be back. The crowd at the roped-off street corner shuffles away in silence.

I lingered with my neighbor Enela Fleigler. "Look!" she said. "There's the green parrot!" It was on the fire escape across the street from the parking lot, pressed against the old man's feet. The old man sat there on his milkbox staring at the ruin and stroking the green parrot's tucked-in head.

When the time came for the wrecking ball to smash the old man's building he refused to leave and they had to send the police to drag him out. I asked what happened to the parrot. Nobody knew.

XXXIX
Goodbye Lavanburg Homes

All the old Lavanburg tenants were moving. Who could withstand the sound of the wrecking ball crashing the buildings? Who could breathe with the mortar and mold filling their nostrils and settling in their lungs? Who could ignore the rats scuttling out onto the street in bolder and bolder packs? I went back to Lavanburg's to help my mother and father move to a project on Grand Street built by the garment workers union. We had all married and moved to our own homes. Ma was sitting in the living room among her bundles. No one had come to buy the piano, no one in our family had room for it. Ma said, "There will be grandchildren." But in the end she had to leave the beloved piano behind.

Even the once-immortal corner lamp-post, with its fluted trunk and wrought-iron leaves, was severed from its electric-cable roots and dragged away to a New Jersey dump along with all the faces of God, all the angels, all the fierce wrought-iron dragons guarding the front staircases.

BashaLeya

XL

The Gypsy Cave

When BashaLeya, MarthaLeah, was three years old she got ringworm. A rash of red circles spread across her chest. The Baby Clinic on East Broadway gave me a bottle of gentian violet and a box of large-size cotton swabs. They said to paint the gentian violet on her chest every night and keep her skin dry.

At that time I was a manuscript secretary for Jules Freund, an immunologist who was famous for Freund's Adjuvant, which boosted the power of vaccinations. His laboratory was at the Public Health Research Institute, behind the old Willard Parker quarantine hospital at the foot of East Fifteenth Street. People who came off the boat at Ellis Island with communicable diseases were shipped up the river and held there. It also had a lot of New York children sick with polio. I sometimes heard wailing in the courtyard outside the morgue.

Doctor Freund asked me about BashaLeya every morning. "How is your little girl?" he would say. He wanted real news, not polite answers, for he was very fond of children. Because of his reputation he even got the public schools opened at eight in the morning, a half hour before classes began, so that the children of working mothers could get inside the building and keep warm. When I told him BashaLeya had ringworm, he said, "That's good, she should be exposed to diseases while she's young. It builds up her immunity."

"But ringworm is caused by a fungus; you don't get immunity to that, do you?"

"It's all right," he said. "It shows she's mixing."

Our home on Lewis Street near Stanton, where BashaLeya was born, had gone under the wrecking ball when our neighborhood was turned into housing projects, and we were living on Henry Street behind the famous Garden Cafeteria, hangout of the East Broadway modern Jewish poets. BashaLeya went to an all-day nursery at a nearby church. At lunchtime I used to race a mile-and-a-half along the river from 14th Street to Grand Street and up East Broadway to see her, and raced there again after work to get her out of the crowded little TV room where the after-five-o'clock children waited for their mothers. Yes, she was mixing; the children who stayed late in that room got one cold after another and gave them to each other, all sniffles and runny noses.

On Friday evening my mother came to visit, carrying her usual shopping bag full of Saturday goodies. I was getting BashaLeya ready for bed and had just finished applying the gentian violet to her chest while she sat in her play chair. At the sight of BashaLeya's purple skin, my mother clapped a hand to her throat and shrieked.

"What's that? What happened? Who did that to her?"

"Please Ma, calm down. She just has a rash, and they gave me this at the Baby Clinic. It's only the juice of a flower."

BashaLeya, thrilled to be scaring her grandmother, stretched her mouth with her pinkies and pulled down her eyelids to make a monster face. But my mother couldn't take her eyes off the purple dye on her chest.

"After the baby is asleep," she said, "I'll tell you about when I was a girl in Russia, something I never told anybody in my life."

"No, no," Basha said. "Tell me too."

So BashaLeya brought over Twanalia, her doll, and Figaro, her hand puppet, and sat them down on the chair beside her. My mother took out her homemade bitter-almond cake. I made tea and set the table. When all was ready I lit the candles and shut the electric lights, the better to listen.

This is my mother's story as I remember it, and as Basha-Leya remembers it from the many times she made me repeat it to her afterwards.

"I was twelve years old," my mother began. She was born in Russia in 1894, so the year must have been 1906 or 1907. "I had a terrible itchy rash that would not go away no matter what they did for it. Epsom salts, zinc salve, you-should-excuse-me urine washes, nothing helped. I was ripping off my flesh. My father even took me to Kiev, to the biggest doctor, when it was not so safe at that time for Jewish people to travel on the train. The doctor gave me a brown salve, it smelled terrible, but still the rash did not go away. It spread out worse, down my whole front and inside my arms.

"One night after supper my mother told everybody she was going with me to visit her sick aunt EstaMalka. It was summer, and I still remember how when we came outside in the night the air smelled of hay and flowers. The streets were empty. Dogs barked at us from one yard to the next until we came to the end of the streets. I asked my mother, Why are we going this way? Aren't we going to Aunt EstaMalka's house? She said, Don't ask questions. I have to do something. Swear never to tell anybody where we are going, or you will get us both in the worst trouble. So I kept quiet but I began to feel a little afraid.

"We walked way out into the birch woods until we came to a road between the trees. It led to a big open field where there was still some light in the sky. On the other side of the field was a Gypsy camp. My mother led me through the field right up to the Gypsies, Tsigayna, we called them. The men were sitting around the fires near the edge of the field, smoking their pipes. My mother greeted a few of them by name as we passed. I could not see much of the camp wagons because of the darkness behind the fires.

"We came to the end of the field where the horses were tied up, and we climbed up among some rocks into the woods, towards a fire that was flickering through the trees. There on the hill, in front of a big rock, was a witch, just like in the fairy tales, sitting at the fire and tending a big pot on an iron stand. She greeted my mother like a friend and even asked how was everybody in the family. They talked in Romany, Gypsy language. I understood it better than I let my mother know. They were talking about my rash. She asked where it started, how it spread, if I ate any strange food lately, touched any strange plants, a million questions. Then she made me open my blouse and she took me so close to the fire that I thought I would burn up before she finished looking. Finally she said to my mother, Is she a good girl? Does she obey you? My mother swore that I could be trusted with anything. And it was true, I was a very responsible girl. So the witch said, I can help her, but you have to do everything I say, exactly as I tell you. She lowered her head and put out her hand. My mother gave her some coins. The Gypsy peeked at the money and put it in her skirt. She said, Listen. Someone close to you will soon die. You must get hold of that person's nightgown. Don't let anyone see. Bring it to me with your girl on the next moonless night.

"We rushed back to town and dropped in for a quick visit to Aunt EstaMalka so no one should catch on that we had gone to the Gypsies.

"Not long after that, Aunt EstaMalka died. My rash was worse than ever. I couldn't help tearing at it and I was full of sores. One night after the funeral, when you couldn't see the moon in the sky, my mother made another excuse and took me back to the Gypsies. The nightgown was folded up under her skirt. This time the road to the open field was pitch black and we had to follow the glowing mushrooms along the side of the roads to find our way.

"Everything in the Gypsy camp was the same as before, and at the far end of the field, on the hill, the witch was sitting at her fire behind her pot. My mother gave her the nightgown. She took me by the hand and brought me around the big rock to the other side and into a pitch-black cave. My heart beat in my ears so loud I couldn't hear nothing, so I was like blind and deaf combined. The witch made me take off all my clothes. Then I felt her stroking something on me, something cold and wet all over the front of my body and inside my arms. I was freezing till it got dry. Then she put on the nightgown and my clothes on top of it. She brought me back around the rock, and by the light of the fire she stitched up the bottom of the nightgown so it wouldn't peek out from my skirt. She said to my mother, You must take her straight home, cover her up in bed up to the chin, and do not let her get up until the next dark of the moon. She must keep the nightgown on all this time, and no one must come near her except you. Tell your girl that if she peeks under the nightgown, or if she talks about this, she will right away turn purple and die.

"Well, to make a long story short, I had to stay in bed in Aunt EstaMalka's nightgown. I felt like a ghost was inside me. I was numb all over. I stayed still, with the featherbed quilt covering me up to the chin. My mother let nobody come near me, and she took care of everything I needed. But after two days in the room with nothing to do, I couldn't help myself, I peeked under the nightgown. At that very minute, just a second, I turned purple. I pulled the featherbed over my head, faint with fright. I peeked again. It was true. My skin was purple. I lay like a board and waited to die from the witch's curse. But nothing happened, and when the time was up, I got up from my bed completely cured.

"I never told nobody till now, when I see the exact same purple all over BashaLeya's chest. So can you imagine? I can't

303

believe it. The witch in the Gypsy cave in Russia gave me the same medicine you got in America with the best doctors in the world!"

I looked at my wide-eyed daughter. "There aren't really any witches," I said. "The Gypsy woman was a wise old lady who knew how to use the healing powers of plants. But if she had been caught practicing medicine she could have been thrown in jail or worse. So all her hocus pocus had a reason. For instance, she said to come back at the dark of the moon. That gave her time to gather the gentian flowers and it also hid you from passersby on the road. All the other things she did—the dark cave, the dead person's nightgown—were to keep you from seeing the purple dye, and if you did see it, to make you afraid to tell anybody. She had to protect herself, and also your mother. The cave at the side of the rock might have been—probably was—a little hut, an herb and medicine shop set up against the rock and covered with brush. I remember seeing an illustration of such a shop in an old storybook."

"So how did she know my Aunt EstaMalka was going to die before the next moon?"

"She didn't have to know. In those days in Russia, families were large and there was always somebody dying."

"It could be like you say, I'm not saying no. I can only tell what I saw with mine own eyes. To mine eyes she was a witch."

XLI
My Dream of Mama

My mother died suddenly, of a heart attack, age 64. The family gathered in a torrential rain. I didn't remember which hospital. The nurse told us her last words. "I have four wonderful children, two couples, a boy and a girl, and another boy and a girl. Very smart children. My boys never raised a hand to me."

I dreamed I was walking up the metal stairs at my old school, P.S. 188, holding onto the banister as I climbed up to the fourth floor. I was on my way to something I dreaded but I knew I had to keep going. Then, in a shadowy corner of the top landing I saw something dark and scruffy, like a porcupine. It turned into my mother! She was dressed in spidery gray rags. She looked tired, spent.

"Ma, what are you doing here? You're supposed to be dead!"

"Who told you? Don't worry, I'm not dead yet. What I've been through. Don't worry, go ahead upstairs."

"Ma, you can't stay here in the corner of the stairs."

"You go ahead," she said. "Don't worry about me."

"But I can't leave you. I can't leave you. Mama I can't leave you." I was crying, talking and crying in my sleep.

"Okay," she said. "I'm going." She was now upright. Her corner brightened. Light came from the stairs above. Her dress was vaguely nice.

"I'm going, I'm going. Don't worry." And she disappeared in a glowing light, rose up and up, glowing, just like an angel.

Two grandchildren and four great-grandchildren bear her name, PessaHayntsa, so she will be remembered and her story will surely be told in our family history to the fourth generation.

XLII

The Torn Photograph, the Split Gravestone, The Death of Papa

After my mother's death my brother Maxie went to her home to get some of his things and found that Ma's half of the wedding photograph on the dresser had been torn away. That's how much Pa had hated her. And that's how little he understood that her children had loved her. And then, when the family met in Ruthie's house to go to the cemetery together on the anniversary of Ma's burial, as required by Jewish law, he didn't show up.

Ma had been buried in the Workmen's Circle cemetery on Long Island, at a plot reserved for members from her town of Kovel near Kiev in the Ukraine. There we found to our horror that Pa had erected, in the next row and one plot behind Mama's grave, a separate gravestone for himself and another woman! Under the year of death, left blank, his side of the stone said "beloved husband and father" and her side said "beloved wife and mother." A scandalous shame before all the friends and relatives of Kovel!

We went to the office. My mother had reserved the customary single stone with the plot next to hers reserved for the husband's stone. Pa had put it up for sale. Maxie bought it on the spot for himself. So now he would be taking his father's place in death as in life.

Poor Papa. Not long after his marriage his second wife got Alzheimer's and was shipped back to her family who, thank God, had insurance to cover her care.

So Pa was left alone. He wanted to reunite with the family and see his grandchildren, but we refused to see him. So he went to a psychiatrist, took his advice, split away the other woman's side of the double gravestone, sent Ruthie a picture with a humble apology, and begged us to take him back. For the sake of the grandchildren, who loved him after all, and to set for them an example of respecting our elders no matter what, we allowed him back in the family and at the head of the table at the Passover seders.

Papa spent his last years as a volunteer at the old-age homes. He composed comical poems in rhyming couplets and he organized dance nights with waltzes and foxtrots and Jewish circle dances and chain dances. I was with him when he was escorted to the large auditorium at the Educational Alliance and awarded a medal as the Volunteer of the Year.

Pa died of heart failure just a week before the bas mitzvah of his twelve-year-old grandchild Bari, the first female in our family to take her place in the synagogue as an adult, on the ground floor instead of upstairs behind a curtain. I was sitting beside Pa's hospital bed at the end when his heart gave out. It was to me that he whispered his last words: "Tell Bari to celebrate the holidays, to celebrate every day of the year." It was the dream of his father, the bard and keeper of the rituals at the Willett Street Synagogue.

Fay, circa 1965

Afterword

"Be as honest as you can; exclude anything that seems like vanity. Don't follow an assumed image that is not yours."

—Hanya Holm

Dance is still with me. I see it all around me. In a turn of the head, a lift of the heel, a slant of the eyes. In a dash though traffic, a children's game, a baseball game. Form. Space. Movement. Patterns. Fast against slow. Dark against light. This is my language. What I am.

Photo by Peg Tassey

Fay Webern was born on the Lower East Side in 1927 to Russian-Jewish immigrant parents and grew up living at the Lavanburg Homes, an experimental utopian housing community for low-income families. A talented child dancer, she studied from the age of seven with a member of Hanya Holm's dance company, but her professional ambitions were dashed by an accident she suffered at the age of fifteen. She later had a long career in publishing, rising to copy chief at Scientific American and then senior editor at Encyclopedia Britannica, Harper and Row, and Random House.

Upon retiring in the late 1990s, she studied non-fiction writing at the Gotham Writers Workshop with essayist Tyler C. Gore. With his encouragement, she soon became a regular reader at NYC venues such as The Knitting Factory and Arlene's Grocery until she moved to Vermont in 2002, where she still resides.